Treat

&

Remaking of the World
1919–2019

Treaty of Versailles
&
Remaking of the World
1919–2019

Aloka Moulik Chatterjee
Achala M Moulik

authors
UPFRONT

Copyright © Achala Moulik 2018
moulikachala@gmail.com

First published in India in 2018 by:
AuthorsUpFront Publishing Services Private Limited

info@authorsupfront.com

Achala Moulik asserts the moral right to be identified as the author of this work.

Typeset by K. Balasundaram
Cover design: Neena Gupta

All rights reserved. No part of this publication may be reproduced, stored in a retrieval system, or transmitted, in any form or by any means, without the prior written permission of the AUTHOR, or as expressly permitted by law, or under terms agreed with the appropriate reprographic rights organisations. Enquiries concerning reproduction outside the scope of the above should be sent to the AUTHOR.

To

Our parents, Leela and Moni Moulik
who gave us a memorable youth

and

Professor C.A.W Manning, Dr Georg Schwarzenberger,
Dr Miriam Bowley, Dr Susan Strange
and Dr A. James,
brilliant and eclectic professors who taught us
International History and International Relations
at the London School of Economics and
University College London

CONTENTS

PREFACE

My sister Aloka began writing this book in the summer of 2015. She had just completed an English translation of a famous Bengali classic for children, *Tales of Tuntuni: The Wise Bird* which was published in December 2017.

I was then writing my book on the Russian Revolution. Before embarking on a writing adventure I always consulted Aloka and asked for her views. She offered many suggestions on the upheaval. Hearing her insights on this era I asked her to write a book on international relations of this period.

She was a brilliant student of International Relations at London School of Economics (LSE) and wrote excellent papers on problems of international law, peace and security and relations between nations. Aloka's professors and tutors at LSE, who are now legendary names, praised her papers and her contribution at classes. The conservative Professor Manning, head of the Faculty of International Relations at LSE respected her intellectual honesty because she never offered consoling myths to curry favour. They advised her do a post-graduate degree on the subject. Fate decided otherwise.

She had an uncanny gift for predicting the outcome of events – such as the declaration of Emergency in India, the USA-led invasions of Afghanistan in 2001 and Iraq in 2003.

We decided to jointly write the book as we had both studied Political Science, International Relations & Law at London University. When Aloka visited me in Bangalore during 2015–2017 we gathered her and my notes and papers from the trunk in our study where family documents, photos and papers were stored. Over three years we structured and composed the narrative. When she visited me in Bangalore in early November 2017 we had put much of script together.

On the morning of 19 November 2017 Aloka and I had a long conversation about many things including our joint book. It was our last conversation in this world. An hour and half later she left all those who admired, loved and cherished her.

Cruel fate has given me the task of publishing the books of two loved ones after their departure. My husband had completed three brilliant books when he was called away. These were published and received critical acclaim. And now my sister left this book to be published.

In the midst of desolation I finalized the script. The task took me on a journey backwards in Time to our days at London University, where Aloka was a bright and beautiful student. I captured the security of our parents' home, the stimulation of learning and discussing with great teachers, the camaraderie of wonderful friends with whom we debated our ideas and shared our dreams.

In this healing journey I found the truth of Rabindranath Tagore's words – "Those whom you love are never lost. They live on the threshold of your thoughts."

PART I

TREATY OF VERSAILLES

1

AN ELUSIVE PEACE

Dig two graves when you go to seek vendetta.
—Corsican proverb

No peace treaty in history paved the way for war as did the Treaty of Versailles in 1919. Conceived in victory, drafted in a spirit of vengeance and half-heartedly implemented, this peace treaty was an interregnum between two terrible wars.

To offer a measure of justice to the signatories of the treaty – its genesis, as in most things in the universe, was in the past. The Treaty of Vienna in 1815 sought to suppress the two forces of nationalism and liberalism unleashed by the French Revolution. Britain, Austria, Prussia, and Russia formed the Concert of Europe to implement this policy. The ramshackle structure of the *ancien regimes* was hastily repaired; feudal and authoritative rulers were reinstated. Leaders of these governments did not realize that an idea whose time has come cannot be suppressed.

Bowing to popular French demands, the restored Bourbon French king agreed to the return of Napoleon's body from St Helena to Paris in 1821 when it was interred with veneration at the Hotel des Invalides. This revived the Napoleonic legend and inspired sporadic rebellions from 1821 to 1848, known as the Year of Revolutions in Europe.

Paradoxically, the idea of a nation state had its genesis in Napoleon's imperial campaigns. Though the Treaty of Vienna attempted to put the clock back, Time had inexorably moved forward because the idea of nationalism had been sown in the minds of subjugated Europeans. Napoleon's campaigns had humbled the pride and power of the imperial Hapsburgs, Hohenzollerns and Romanovs. The various races which lived in the lands ruled by these dynasties had glimpses of a more honourable scene when French armies briefly liberated them. Metternich's Concert of Europe sought to suppress the aspirations through force – but failed.

Nationalism and Liberalism challenged the Vienna settlement of 1815 and gained momentum throughout the 19th century. There was an awareness of cultural identity, pride in language, literature and material heritage that had received scant respect under imperial rulers. Nationalism was muted in independent sovereign states such as Britain and France and later Germany. Nationalist sentiments were more intense among people under foreign rule such as the Irish, Italians, Greeks, and Slav peoples of Southern and Eastern Europe. The idea of nationalism in Asia and Africa took much longer to gain strength.

2

THE LONG PRELUDE TO WAR

The first rebellion was in Greece in 1821 which sought to end Turkish-Ottoman rule. Though Tsar Alexander I was hostile to revolutions, his sympathy was with fellow Orthodox Christians who had affinities with Russo-Byzantine culture. Greek independence would also have the benefit of reducing Turkish power that was an irritant to Russia in the Black Sea. Though the Greek revolt was led by Prince Alexander Ypsilanti in 1825 and Ottoman rule ended in 1830, a German prince became king of Greece in 1832.

An astonishing revolt took place in St Petersburg in 1825. As in Greece the Decembrist Revolt was led by a group of aristocratic officers of the Imperial Army. Its leader was Prince Sergey Volkonsky, head of an imperial regiment and member of one of Russia's powerful families. The rebels were inspired by Russia's greatest poet Alexander Pushkin who had been exiled to the Caucasus for his poem *Ode to Liberty*. When the rebels were executed or exiled Pushkin saluted them in his moving poem *To Those in Siberian Mines*. The Decembrist Revolt was mercilessly crushed but the fire of rebellion had been ignited. It would fructify ninety years later in the Bolshevik Revolution of 1917.

Greek independence had a domino effect in Eastern Europe. Demand for freedom from Ottoman rule began in Serbia,

Bulgaria, Macedonia and Romania. Seeing the success of Greek rebels, Italians began agitating against Spanish and Austrian overlords. Secret societies such as the *Carbonari* sprang up in Italy, first agitating and then demanding freedom and unification. The *Risorgimento* or Resurgence, inspired by traditions of the Renaissance as well as Napoleon, saw the emergence of a national and cultural consciousness. A cluster of brilliant litterateurs such as Manzoni, Leopardi and Foscolo, political prophets such as Mazzini, composers like Verdi, ignited ideas of nationalism and liberalism in Italians. Under the leadership of Count Cavour of Piedmont, Italy achieved independence from Austria, Spain and the Papacy, and gained a constitutional system. The Papacy resisted Italian unity because loss of control over Papal States in Central Italy would weaken authority and reduce revenues of the Catholic Church.

Unlike Greece and Italy, unification of Germany was led by the conservative Prince Otto von Bismarck of Prussia. To achieve this, Prince von Bismarck waged a series of limited wars against Denmark (for control of Schleswig-Holstein), Austria (which ruled small German states) and France. By early 1870, all German kingdoms and principalities had been annexed by Prussia. Alarmed by the growing power of Prussia, and provoked by a minor incident, Emperor Napoleon III declared war. The Franco-Prussian War continued from July 1870 to May 1871. France was defeated. The culminating triumph of Prussia was when Kaiser Wilhelm I was proclaimed German Emperor at Versailles, the splendid palace of French kings. The harsh provisions of the Treaty of Frankfurt were implemented: Germany annexed Alsace and half of Lorraine and Metz. Furthermore, France had to pay an indemnity of 5 billion francs and cover the costs of the German occupation of France's northern provinces until the indemnity was paid.

Defeat of France ended its hegemony in Europe. Bismarck's Germany then became the most powerful European nation until its defeat in 1918. Having attained the limited goal of unifying German states under Prussia, Bismarck strove to maintain balance of power and avoid large wars which he said would pave the way for revolutions – which is what happened in 1918 when the Tsar, Kaiser and Austrian emperor were deposed.

The years 1871 to 1914 marked an uninterrupted forty-three years of European peace.

In the era of elusive peace Britain was interested in industrial development and political reforms at home. The Admiralty made its navy the largest in the world. This would facilitate acquisition and protection of British colonies overseas. Russia took advantage of the Franco-Prussian War to repudiate the Treaty of Paris of 1856 which had compelled it to demilitarize the Black Sea. To reach a compromise between British and Russian interests, the British government accepted Russian action to control the straits of Dardanelles. Nevertheless the stage was set for the rivalry between these states.

The sagacious German Chancellor made a mistake when he surrendered to popular demand for uniting the provinces of Alsace-Lorraine on the French border. Annexation of these provinces had infuriated the French people. France pursued an irredentist policy for recovering the two duchies. This became one of the main aims of French policy until this was achieved in 1918.

To isolate France, Bismarck adopted various strategies. He incited anxiety in monarchical governments about French republicanism. Tsarist Russia viewed with alarm Prussian-Austrian power in the Balkans. Apprehensive of wars between the three empires, the German Chancellor sought to unite the three empires through the *Dreikaiserbund* or Union of Three Emperors. But the union ignored the inherent conflict between them. The Pan-Slav movement and Slavophilism in Russia was a direct challenge to Austrian power in Central and Eastern Europe.

Despite his promise to establish peace in France, Napoleon III, like his great uncle, strove for *la gloire* not only at home but also overseas. France and Britain fought against Tsarist Russia in 1851. Victory in the Crimean War whetted their imperial appetites. Napoleon ordered the expansion of both the French army and navy. Under the reign of Napoleon III, France strengthened its grip on Algeria. When the Ottoman Turk's control over Algeria, Tunisia, Libya and Morocco weakened, France annexed these kingdoms. From North Africa the French army made forays further south to secure ports and bases. Napoleon III never forgot his uncle's Egyptian campaign. To establish a firm foothold in Egypt, he assisted a French company and Khedive Ismail to build the Suez Canal.

The British Empire in India was firmly established after the Uprising of 1857 when the rebellious Rajas and Nawabs were defeated. Rule of the East India Company ceased; Indian territories came under the direct control of the Crown. France had colonies on Indian soil – Pondicherry in the south and Chandannagar in the east. Here Indian rebels found both arms and sanctuary. But France also wanted Asian colonies and conquered the kingdoms of Cambodia, Vietnam and Laos which were lumped together as Indochina without considerations of their diverse ethnic and cultural heritage. When Britain began waging the Opium Wars against China, France also looked for bases there – which would fructify in the late 19th century.

Napoleon III's Mexican adventure (1861–1867) failed; it resulted in the execution of the Hapsburg Prince Maximilian, whom Napoleon III had championed in the hope that Mexico would become a colony of France in the New World.

The age of colonial empires had begun.

3

THE SCRAMBLE FOR AFRICA

It was necessarily accompanied by building of standing national armies. Germany resorted to universal conscription and Austria followed suit. While the peasants and workers provided cannon fodder, the upper classes were drafted into the officer corps for a year's training, and were required to do full reserve duty along with others. By 1914 the major European states had huge standing armies that took up five to ten per cent of the national budget of these economies. This was simultaneous with the arms race.

Most European states embarked on building empires in Asia and Africa. The Iberian nations had earlier established empires in Latin America. After the Meiji Restoration in 1867, Japan also embarked on imperial adventures in China and Korea which soon brought it in conflict with Tsarist Russia.

Acquisition of overseas territories was an important adjunct to the industrial revolution; its progress needed raw materials for factories. It was necessary to conquer the lands which contained these resources. The 'Scramble for Africa' began in the 1880's; it ensured competition for acquiring colonies. European governments expected overseas colonies to provide markets for their manufactured goods. This fructified to a large extent.

Britain's industrial revolution progressed exponentially by bringing raw materials from India and through taxes imposed on Indians. This wealth had a multiplier effect; more territories were added to the British Empire which extended from Gibraltar to Hong Kong – the largest empire in history. The Suez Canal became a joint British-French project in 1875. The Canal brought their colonies in closer proximity due to the shortening of distance. No longer was it necessary to take the circuitous route via the Cape of Good Hope. Eventually Britain took control of the administration and revenues from the Canal – which continued until 1956. British occupation of Egypt altered the balance of power. It provided Britain safe passage and security for their route to India and also gave them dominance in the Eastern Mediterranean and West Asia.

The Netherlands prospered in Indonesia; raw materials from this colony aided Dutch industrial development. Belgium made huge profits in the Congo from rubber, minerals and diamonds. Accompanying this was their infamous mistreatment of Congolese labour. Even in that insensitive age, other European nations condemned the atrocities. Long after other imperial powers had retreated, Belgium held on to the Congo through violence.

While insisting on application of the Monroe Doctrine in the Western hemisphere, the United States went across the seven seas to colonize the former Spanish colony of the Philippines after the Spanish-American War.

The world's colonial population at the time of World War I was approximately 560 million people, of whom 70.0 per cent were in British territories, 10.0 per cent in French, 8.6 per cent in Dutch, 3.9 per cent in Japanese, 2.2 per cent in German, 2.1 per cent in American, 1.6 per cent in Portuguese, 1.2 per cent in

Belgian and 0.5 per cent in Italian possessions. The domestic population of these states was some 370 million people.

Rivalry between Britain and France in Africa culminated in the Fashoda Incident. French troops claimed an area in the Southern Sudan, and British force acting in the interests of the Khedive of Egypt resisted them. Eventually the French withdrew; Britain and Egypt gained control over the area. Thus Egypt became a protectorate of Britain.

Zanzibar became a focal point of commercial interests to Britain, France and Germany who established consulates there. Trade in spices and ivory brought rich profits. Britain and Germany became competitors in East Africa when Germany established a protectorate over coastal territories of the Sultan of Zanzibar. Later Germany handed control of these territories to Britain in exchange for large tracts of land in Tanganyika. Britain established the East African Protectorate in late 19th century. British settlers established farms in the fertile lands. Roads and railways were built, commercial enterprises flourished under British and Indian entrepreneurs. Most of East Africa came under British rule.

Portugal, which built colonies in Latin American, Indian Goa and Chinese Macau in the 16th century, also joined the 'Scramble for Africa'. Earlier, after the conquest of the North African port of Ceuta, Portugal commenced the infamous slave trade of Africa. Notorious sugarcane plantations were established on the islands of Madeira, Cape Verde, and the Azores. Here African slaves worked and died rapidly. Portugal expanded its trading ports along the African coast, then Angola and Mozambique.

In the 'Scramble for Africa' of the 1880s, Italian politicians were keen to establish colonies in Africa. They harked back to

Roman times when much of North Africa was under the Roman Empire following the defeat of formidable Carthage. Italy first turned to Ottoman-held Tunis where many Italian farmers had settled. This led to tension with France, which wanted the same territories. Italy then turned to Ethiopia but was defeated by the local king in 1896 at the battle of Adowa. The humiliating defeat would be avenged by Mussolini in 1936. In 1911, Italy annexed the North African emirate of Libya. For once, other European nations dropped their rivalries and endorsed Italian annexation of Libya – something that would happen again in 2011 with disastrous consequences for the people of that nation.

Japan was the only Asian nation to evade colonial rule through an enlightened leadership. After the Meiji Restoration, Japan began a program of economic, social, industrial and military modernization. This power encouraged it to seek colonies in China, Korea and Manchuria. Japan successfully defeated China in 1894 and then imperial Russia in 1905. The growth of its power and wealth led it to challenge the formidable power of the United States in 1941.

4

MILITARISM AND IMPERIALISM

Though German militarism has been blamed for the new spirit of aggression, glorification of wars and battles is as old as mankind. Epics of ancient India, Persia, Greece, Rome, Scandinavian Sagas, the Lieds and Eddas glorified the warrior. The Fourth Estate contributed to this war culture by depicting military men as heroes. By encouraging militarism, the sober values of diplomacy, dialogue, negotiations were sometimes discarded. The words of the Prussian political theorist Carl von Clausewitz – "war is a continuation of policy by other means" – became acceptable though Prince Metternich, the imperial Austrian Chancellor, had deplored such a statement.

This philosophy promoted the importance of military power. It was aided by the aims of imperialism – to extend territories and acquire the natural wealth of foreign lands. For protection of these interests a large army and navy was an imperative. In between these forces were the nationalist demands of smaller states. Imperialism and militarism augmented each other. Sanctity was bestowed on this by linking militarism with national pride and patriotism.

Militarism played a determinant role in this changing scene. It has been defined by the German historian Alfred Vagts, as the "domination of the military man over the civilian, an undue preponderance of military demands, and emphasis on military considerations". As European nations gained in economic strength there was also a desire for military power. This brought into prominence military leaders in the years preceding World War I. This is what Prince Bismarck had feared and to which his former protégé the Kaiser fell prey. Bismarck and the French leader, Clemenceau felt that wars were too important to be left to generals. However military men began gaining importance. Their influence prevailed over sober statesmen. Military victories rather than peace and stability became a goal. The burgeoning arms lobby played a prominent role in this. Armament barons prodded generals and admirals to increase the defence budgets.

Thus began the arms race.

***

Glorification of modern militarism had its genesis in Prussia in the mid-19th century when Field Marshal Helmuth von Moltke implemented new strategies, rigorous training for soldiers and officers, and development of advanced weaponry. As the century progressed generals and admirals, rather than statesmen, decided foreign policy. In Britain militarism was regarded as essential for protecting the country's political, territorial and commercial interests in its Asian and African colonies. Other European nations also invested heavily in strengthening their military and navy. Expenditure in this sector increased exponentially. This set off a spiral effect as major powers competed for supremacy.

The following table lists estimated defence and military spending in seven major nations between 1908 and 1913 (figures shown in US dollars):

NATION	1908	1909	1910	1911	1912	1913
	(in million dollars)					
Great Britain	286.7	306.2	330.4	345.1	349.9	374.2
Germany	286.7	306.8	301.5	303.9	331.5	463.6
France	216	236.4	248	277.9	307.8	363.8
Russia	291.6	315.5	324	334.5	387	435
Italy	87.5	115.8	124.9	133.7	158.4	142.2
United States	189.5	199	197	197	227	244.6
Japan	93.7	95.7	100.2	110.7	107.7	104.6

The primary cause for World War I was triggered by the compulsions of the industrial revolution. Competition for raw materials, search for markets for products, expansion of territories and the military might to protect these produced fierce economic rivalries between the powers. The arms race and militarism was the result.

Added to this was the rivalry among the two camps within Europe. Germany and Austria sunk their differences and forged an alliance. It was a natural alliance of two Teutonic races which had affinities of language, music and culture. Tsarist Russia under Alexander III realized that he required allies against his two fellow emperors. So Tsarist Russia allied with Republican France and the constitutional monarchy of Britain to form the Triple Entente. Russia benefitted through French investment in industrial growth; the Trans-Siberian Railway was built by French capital loans under French supervision. Ballet companies from Russia went to Paris. Most dramatic of all, the *Marseillaise* which had been forbidden to be played or heard in Russia was heard and played when French statesmen visited St Petersburg. The autocratic Tsar Alexander III stood bareheaded while the French republican anthem was played.

Foreseeing the potentials of a European conflagration, German Chancellor Prince Bismarck strove to keep the three potential adversaries – Germany, Austria and Russia – bound in an alliance. "Revolutions," he declared, "are made not by revolutionaries but by politicians who make wars. Our endeavour is to prevent wars." The alliance was broken by the new German Kaiser, Wilhelm II who wanted war. The stage was now set for a European conflagration.

For seven centuries Hapsburg Austria had dominated Central Europe; by the 1890's Austria began to make inroads into Slav territory and annexed the Serbian province of Bosnia-Herzegovina in 1908. Russia objected to this annexation but could do nothing as Prussia, France and Britain supported Austria. They wanted to curtail Russia's burgeoning influence in Eastern Europe where Slav nationalism was gathering momentum. Austria dreaded the rise of pan-Slavism which threatened to dismantle the ramshackle multi-racial Hapsburg Empire. Striving to be the paramount power in Europe, Germany saw its real rival in Russia. It was a prelude to war; it needed an incident to ignite the tinderbox. The tinderbox was ignited on 28 June 1914 – in the Serbian town of Sarajevo.

On a visit to Sarajevo the heir to the Hapsburg Empire Archduke Franz Ferdinand was assassinated by a young Serbian rebel, Gavril Princip. The tragic irony lay in that fact that Franz Ferdinand went there to soothe the resentment of Slav nationalists who wanted freedom from Austria. A furious Austrian government issued an ultimatum to Serbia, which was blamed for inciting Slav nationalism. But their real target was Russia, the guiding spirit of pan-Slavism that could dismantle the two Germanic empires. Playing for time the Russian Foreign Minister Sazonov asked Germany to intervene. Germany refused and declared that Austria and Serbia must reach an agreement. Russia turned to Britain's Foreign Secretary Sir Edward Grey to intervene. Serbia was persuaded to accept all Austrian terms except the annihilation of its independence. But Austria did not want peace; it wanted to destroy Slav nationalism.

On 28 July 1914 Austria declared war on the little nation and began bombarding Belgrade. Tsar Nikolas II ordered the mobilization of troops along the Austrian border but hoped Kaiser Wilhelm would intervene. Telegrams flew thick and fast between the imperial cousins – Nicky and Willy – the former trying to calm hostilities and the latter eager to begin a war. When the Tsar refused to cancel mobilization of his troops, the Kaiser declared war on Russia on 2 August 1914. Britain and France joined Russia.

Thus began World War I.

5

THE MAIN COMBATANTS

In July 1914, Britain was at the zenith of power, prosperity and glory. It had an empire straddling several continents. The subcontinent of India was the jewel in its crown. Neither the empires of Rome, or Spain, or Genghiz Khan had such extensive territories. The achievements of Elizabethan and Victorian England in literature, painting, and theatre had reached an apogee. Its universities were destinations for young people across the world. British Parliamentary democracy was an example admired if not emulated by other European states. Though it was a society governed by the privileged, inroads into this had been made peacefully throughout the 19th century by a robust mercantile class. Its proletariat clamoured for reforms but it was not prepared to commence revolutions. Members of its educated elite went to serve the British government in far flung colonies thereby bringing British traditions to these shores. British citizens claimed with pride that they "had a passport for every land".

This grand edifice changed forever in the summer of 1914. On 4 August, the British government headed by Prime Minister Herbert Asquith entered the war. The ostensible reason was that Britain had to safeguard neutrality of Belgium as per a clause of the Treaty of London of 1839. German invasion of Belgium therefore became the *casus belli* though the deeper causes of this conflagration have been narrated earlier. Britain's relationship with members of the Triple Alliance, France and Russia, were crucial factors. The Foreign Secretary Sir Edward Grey felt that secret naval agreements with France obliged Britain to aid both France and Russia. It was fear of German dominance that made Britain enter the war. If Germany defeated France and Russia, Britain and its vast empire would eventually become the target of German aggression.

At the outbreak of war, the British royal family encountered an identity crisis because of its blood ties to German ruling families, Britain's prime adversary in the war. Before the war, the British royal family was titled House of Saxe-Coburg Gotha after the family name of Queen Victoria's Consort. To sever all dynastic connections with German royalty, King George V assumed a new dynastic name – House of Windsor – and abolished all German titles for himself and members of the British royal family.

As war began, the first Defence of the Realm Act (DORA) was passed on 8 August 1914. It accorded wide ranging powers to the government including requisition of buildings or land needed for the war effort. Curbs and restrictions were placed on private citizens; loitering in sensitive areas was forbidden, pubs were closed by 10 p.m., and the death penalty was introduced – presumably as a deterrent to traitors.

By 1914, France had become a powerful European nation with an extensive, multi-racial empire. After a period of humiliation caused by defeat in the Franco-Prussian War, France steadily gained importance as an industrial nation. Her colonies in North Africa and East Asia provided resources to fuel the economy. The aggressive 'global policy' of Kaiser Wilhelm II spurred France to look around for alliances and found an unlikely partner in Tsarist Russia. The Franco-Russian Alliance was concluded in 1894, followed by the Entente Cordiale with Britain in 1904. This group formed the Triple Entente (1907) to counter the Triple Alliance (1882) of Germany, Austria-Hungary and Italy.

To counter the growing threat of German militarism France introduced a mandatory, universal two-year military service and modernized its army. It became an army of citizen-soldiers with a simple procedure for swift mobilization. The general socio-political stability of the country and growing prosperity gave security to its citizens. Later, on reflection, it was felt that the late 19th century and early 20th century was a period of golden calm for France.

The serenity was broken in July 1914 when the two armed camps threatened each other. The French President, Raymond Poincare, promised Tsar Nikolas II unequivocal support if Germany declared war on Russia, though France had little interest in the Balkans. Austria declared war on Serbia on 28 July. Russia knew that Serbia's annihilation would weaken its influence in the Balkans and refused to accept German-Austrian terms. The Central Powers declared war on Russia on 2 August and France, its ally, followed suit by mobilizing some three and a half million soldiers for its army. Thus republican France and tsarist Russia joined to wage war on a common enemy.

Throughout its history the people of Russia always rallied behind their rulers in a crisis. Peasant and prince, worker and academic, rebel and poet cast aside their differences with the throne and threw themselves into the struggle. The year 1914 seemed no different. Nikolas II saw the outpouring of loyalty to him. Forgotten were his cruelties, oppressive policies and privileges of the aristocracy. The Tsar was forgiven all this because he promised to lead Mother Russia to victory over the Germans. There was not the slightest doubt that imperial Russia would prevail over the Germans "who know only how to make sausages".

Hatred of Prussia and Germany was widespread. France and Britain were hailed as friends. As officers and soldiers of the imperial army eagerly marched to the frontline through columns of summer dust, they joked on how they would reach Berlin by the end of summer and walk on the Unter den Linden as conquerors. This confidence sprang from the fact that the Russian imperial army was massive in number. Some 15 million men were in the army from 1914 to 1917. The Russian government did not realize that adequate training, equipment, arms, transport and communications are the sinews of warfare. These inadequacies in a land of great distances were severe handicaps. Germany, France, Austria, and Britain were far smaller in size and therefore easier to command. But the ordinary soldier, like the Russian peasant, had an uncanny sense of what lay ahead. They remembered an old Russian proverb: "It is a wide road that leads to war and only a narrow path that leads home again."

The gods of war had been preparing the European Armageddon for two decades. Both sides lost the flower of their youth in catastrophic battles. Somme, Verdun, Paschendale became synonymous with immense carnage.

6

THE BLAME GAME

This book is partly about the aftermath of World War I. It would require a modern Thucydides to record a history of this war from the view point of all the combatants as the Thracian-Greek historian did in the Peloponnesian War. The deaths, mutilations, maiming of soldiers, the ghastly existence in the trenches, and the grim conditions as prisoners of war, had no equal until then. But the massacres of World War II would exceed that of World War I in barbarism.

A catastrophe such as World War I provoked a blame game. Many books have been written about the 1914–18 conflict, seeking to apportion responsibility for the war. The illustrious German historian, Fritz Fischer created a stir in 1961 with his book *Griff nach der Weltmacht* where he held that Germany was mainly responsible for starting the war as it wanted to be the master of Europe. The historians, Margaret MacMillan, in *The War that Ended Peace: How Europe Abandoned Peace for the First World War* and Christopher Clark in *The Sleepwalkers: How Europe Went to War in 1914,* have presented different narratives. MacMillan states that Germany could have restrained Austria in its plan to dominate the Balkans and challenge Russia there. She misses the point that Germany did not want to restrain Austria because both nations had a common agenda – containment of

Russia, an idea which many Western European powers had from the 12th century, but without success. Christopher Clark's thesis that Germany entered into the war without its own volition also makes the same error. The Kaiser wanted war; he had been preparing for war from the time of his coronation. Since Prince Bismarck opposed the Kaiser, he resigned as Chancellor. The Franco-Prussian War was a prelude to the final showdown. Another historian, Niall Ferguson, states in his book, *The Pity of War* that Britain should not have become involved as the result was not worth the cost. Britain had no choice but to become involved because German victory would have destroyed British power and its vast empire.

7

THE RUSSIAN REVOLUTION AND TREATY OF BREST-LITOVSK

As World War I ran its bloody course, an epochal event occurred in Russia that would change the history of the 20th century.

Bismarck's prediction – that wars, and not revolutionaries, create revolutions – was about to be fulfilled. It came in March (February, according to the old Julian calendar) 1917. The February Revolution was a series of violent demonstrations and riots on the streets of St Petersburg. It succeeded in deposing Tsar Nikolas II when he was at army headquarters in Stavka with his haemophilic son Tsarevich Alexei – to teach him the art of war.

The revolution had been brewing for a century since Napoleon invaded Russia in 1812. Napoleon's army was defeated but not the ideas of liberty and equality that came with the French army. The dream of Russia's greatest poet Alexander Pushkin – of a revolution to sweep away tyranny and oppression – seemed to be at hand. The classic ingredients for a revolution were present; military defeat, mutiny of the army, shortage of food and fuel, and rage against those who had created the misery.

In the bone chilling winter of 1917 people of St Petersburg stood in endless queues in front of bakeries to buy their bread ration. The war had brought chaos to the railways; carriages carrying food to the war front and to the cities from the hinterland now ceased to function. Russia's General Winter inflicted ordeals on Russians as well. The punishing cold made boilers of train engines burst. Thousands of trains were stranded on the snowy wastes. Factories closed due to lack of fuel and metals; unemployed factory workers had no wages to buy bread. Workers, liberals, intellectuals, politicians marched through the snow covered streets shouting abuses and slogans that were high treason a year ago. Now they were appropriate and could not be suppressed.

On 8 March 1917 bread riots broke out in St Petersburg. Moscow and other cities followed suit. They were reminiscent of those of Paris in July 1789. Bakeries were looted; unemployed, hungry and shivering factory workers came out to protest. Soldiers from barracks ready to go to the front were called to quell the mob but they joined the crowd. Next, the dreaded Cossack troops were summoned to disperse rioters but they fraternized with the people. The imperial capital had the stillness before a storm. A general strike was called on 10 March. From the army headquarters at Stavka, the Tsar treated the incident as a minor irritation and rejected the Minister of Interior's plea for negotiations. Furious, he asked the commander of St Petersburg garrison General Khabalov to suppress the uprising. Untrained soldiers hastily collected from villages refused to fire on the crowd. The Tsar then ordered General Ivanov to send war-hardened troops to crush the uprising. What followed was a mutiny that Russia had never witnessed. Regiments that had been the pride and power of the autocracy – Semonovsky, Ismailovsky, Litovsky, and finally the formidable Preobrazhensky – all mutinied. The Tsar's fatal response was to suspend the Duma, thereby destroying the only bridge between himself and the people. All the Tsar's ministers wanted to resign. Defiant students, soldiers, politicians sang the *Marseillaise,* the French revolutionary anthem.

In a series of complicated and astonishing moves, the Mensheviks assumed power and established a Provisional Government headed by Alexander Kerensky. Accompanying this was the formation of the Petrograd Soviet, a local council representing workers and soldiers. Most of those who assumed power after the spring Revolution, in the Provisional Government and in the Petrograd Soviet wanted a democratic form of government.

Returning to St Petersburg, and seeing the revolution gathering momentum, Nikolas II, Tsar Autocrat of All the Russias, abdicated, first in favour of his son and then in favour of his younger brother, Grand Duke Mikhail Alexandrovich Romanov. This fulfilled the prophecy of a holy monk – "The Romanov dynasty began with a Mikhail and will end with a Mikhail." Mindful of this prophecy no Romanov heir was christened Mikhail. This Mikhail was not in the line of succession but he became Tsar for a few days to fulfil the prophecy. The Tsar and his family were imprisoned in the imperial palace at Tsarskoe Selo, awaiting rescue.

Alexander Kerensky, head of the Provisional Government, was anxious to send the Tsar and his family into exile – for their safety – because he sensed the groundswell of antagonism against them. The Provisional Government requested the British government to provide asylum to the Tsar and his family. King George V of Britain, first cousin of Nikolas II, tried to help. Their mothers were daughters of King Christian IX of Denmark.

The British Prime Minister Lloyd George knew that the imperial couple, perceived as pro-German, would not be welcome in Britain. He refused asylum with these chilling words, as recorded in his memoir:

> The Russian Empire is an un-seaworthy Ark. The timbers were rotten and the crew not much better. The captain was suited for a pleasure yacht in still waters, and his sailing master had been chosen by his wife, reclining in the cabin below.

Despite their acute disappointment neither the Tsar nor the Tsarina ever imagined the terrible fate awaiting them in a cellar at Ekaterinburg.

In the meantime Alexander Kerensky tried to bring in a semblance of order and stability. He wished to contain violence and avoid the civil war looming on the horizon. But Miliukov, the new Foreign Minister made no effort to stop the war against Germany.

Observing the Russian scene in April 1917, Vladimir Lenin felt that the revolution he and his comrades had planned and dreamt of was receding. Lenin believed that Kerensky's mild socialism was stealing the thunder from the communists. Cooperation with the Provisional Government could only strengthen Kerensky's hands. He therefore instructed his Bolshevik friends in St Petersburg not to cooperate with the Provisional Government nor conclude an understanding with any other party. Giving instructions was one thing; participation was another. He wanted to be in the eye of the storm, to direct events that now seemed ripe for a revolution. While he and his wife Nadezhda Krupskaya discussed how to leave Berne for Russia, a singular event shaped itself.

Lenin was summoned to hold secret discussions with German Embassy officials. The subject discussed was the end of war between Russia and Germany. After sustaining crushing reversals on its western front, Germany wanted peace with Russia in order to concentrate all efforts on that front. Unlike his fervent anti-German compatriots Lenin had no particular animosity towards Germans. He regarded German and Russian soldiers as hapless victims of imperial wars. At the outbreak of World War I he had declared: "The old robbers (Britain and France) are fighting the new robber (Germany) for colonial expansion and raw materials." In an extraordinary chain of events that reads like an Eric Ambler thriller, the German government put Lenin, his wife, and other notable Bolsheviks in a sealed train which sped across Switzerland, Germany, Sweden and Finland. Bolshevik party members and Russian citizens waited on the platform with red banners. Lenin and his party arrived at St Petersburg's Finland Station on 16 April 1917 – a date that changed the destiny of Russia – and the world.

When Lenin arrived at Petrograd railway station the guard of honour lining the platform cheered him wildly. For a moment Lenin thought they had come to arrest him! Then, recovering with joyous relief, he delivered a fiery speech, commencing with these words, "Hail to the Global Socialist Revolution!" The overthrow of Tsarist autocracy was declared the primary step for a new Socialist revolution. His plan of action was opposed by some of his supporters. His onetime ideological guru, Georgy Plekhanov, called his plans "crazy" and warned that it would pave the way for anarchy throughout Russia. Lenin ignored Plekhanov's admonition and the reservation of other colleagues because he had the staunch support of the Russian proletariat. His promise to bring peace, bread, and power to the people was an irresistible agenda. He met with overwhelming support.

But after a failed coup in July 1917 Lenin and his followers escaped to Finland. From there he sent letters to colleagues, advising armed revolt. He returned in October and persuaded his colleagues that the floundering Provisional Government had to be overthrown.

Lenin lost no time in denouncing the war against Germany as shameless slaughter of hapless men. There was general bewilderment at this; more confusion followed when Lenin advocated overthrow of the monarchy, its army and its bureaucracy – the weapons of Tsarist oppression. He was greeted with laughter and then jeers. Moderates within the Bolshevik party protested; Marx, they said, had declared that there has to be a transitional phase from autocracy to proletarian revolution. Unfazed, Lenin propounded his famous *April Theses* and then laid aside Marxist theories to declare "peace and land and all power to the Soviet". This is what the people wanted and won him instant and popular support.

But Lenin could do nothing to stop the war against Germany. Afraid of Russia's withdrawal, Britain, France and United States urged the Provisional Government to fight on in return for a loan of $325 million. War Minister Kerensky readily agreed. War weary soldiers began their march on the Galician frontier. Initial victories met with terrible reverses as the Austro-German cavalry decimated Russian ranks. Defeated, wounded, seeing the massacre of their comrades, Russian soldiers began a massive retreat from the front. Ill equipped and untrained, with no desire to fight for an oppressive monarchy, peasants and workers began deserting the battered imperial army.

"This journey home", wrote Boris Pasternak in his epic *Dr Zhivago*, "was of what every soldier dreamt. Nothing could halt the exodus from the battle front."

The war debacle of July 1917 provoked an uprising; millions took to the streets to protest against the war and demanded the overthrow of the Provisional Government. Workers in industrial areas of Russia were in revolt. A furious peasantry began seizing lands from landlords. The Tsarist General Kornilov tried to stage a coup in St Petersburg but failed. Kerensky wavered between Kornilov and the Bolsheviks. In the meantime the Bolsheviks organized workers into Red Guards.

By mid-1918 control of the Russian government was in the hands of the Bolshevik Party under Lenin. Bolsheviks controlled the crucial territory from St Petersburg to Moscow. Their writ did not run to the vast countryside. Landless peasants and workers in industrial regions welcomed the new government but affluent landlords were hostile to the communists regime. Vladimir Lenin was aware that these people and former members of the old imperial army under Kornilov and Denisov were planning to overthrow the Bolsheviks.

The war with Germany was draining Russian blood and money. Lenin realized that to establish Bolshevik authority over the country, the war had to end. This was the moment of triumph for a war-ravaged Germany. This is why they had sent Lenin to Russia in a sealed train. In return for peace the German Kaiser and his generals demanded all lands won by the wars of Peter the Great. This included Ukraine, the Crimean peninsula, Poland, Finland, Estonia, Lithuania, and Latvia. Sixty million people – more than one third of the population of the Tsarist Empire – lived here. The territory comprised 25 per cent of Russia's agricultural lands and contained 75 per cent of its iron ore and coal deposits. While these exorbitant demands were being discussed and when many Bolsheviks asked Lenin to reject these terms, news came that the German army was advancing towards St Petersburg. Hastily, the seat of government was transferred to the traditional capital Moscow. The workers and soldiers who had been the main support of the Bolsheviks demanded peace and bread – the slogan on which Lenin and his party had come to power. The fear of a coup by the remnants of the Tsarist regime could not be ruled out. Reluctantly and angrily, Bolshevik leaders agreed to German terms.

The brilliant Marxist theoretician Leon Trotsky, who like Lenin had spent many years in exile, was sent to negotiate terms of peace. On 3 March 1918 the two sides met at Brest-Litovsk, a town on the Polish border to sign the hateful treaty. The Bolshevik delegation felt humiliated by the insolent behaviour of the Germans and swore future vengeance. Russians did not have to wait long. In November 1918 Britain and France inflicted on defeated Germany the harshest terms of war reparations through the Treaty of Versailles. The lands ceded to Germany by the Treaty of Brest-Litovsk were returned to Russia. Freed from the war Lenin and his colleagues now concentrated on consolidating their position.

The German threat had not ended; a few of the Tsar's adherents such as Count Benckendorff and Trepov sent messages to Count Mirbach, German Ambassador in St Petersburg, for rescuing the Tsar and overthrowing the Bolsheviks. The Germans briefly considered this plan. They belatedly realized that by ending the war with Russia through the Treaty of Brest-Litovsk, they had established an enemy on their eastern border that might prove to be much more dangerous than the tottering Tsarist regime.

Raging against the Treaty of Brest-Litovsk, Leon Trotsky openly declared the need for permanent world revolutions, especially in Germany where the Social Democrats such as Karl Leibknecht and Rosa Luxemburg were gaining in prestige and influence. The Treaty of Brest-Litovsk gave Germany relief from waging war on two fronts. By concluding truce with Russia the German army could now concentrate on the Western front to deal with France and England.

But the victory that Germany hoped for and which might have actualized was thwarted by the entry of the United States into the war.

8

AMERICA ENTERS THE WAR

The United States had no intention of entering World War I. The spirit of Monroe Doctrine still prevailed – to maintain distance from the Old World. America was a land of escape from the inequality and injustices of European society. The poor migrants who went to America carried racial memories of oppression in Europe. The rivalries between the Central Powers and the Triple Entente in no way concerned them. America was home of the brave and the land of the free; so they looked askance at the imperial policies and territorial aggrandizements of European states. British interference during the American Civil War in 1864 had fortified the resolve to be free of European designs.

There were other practical considerations as well. During the war America replaced Britain as exporter of goods to Europe. Its financial institutions profited as well. The United States benefitted financially by keeping out of the war.

The idealistic American President, Woodrow Wilson, assured his fellow Americans during his election in 1916 that the United States would remain neutral in the war that had engulfed Europe. However the events in Europe overrode these reservations.

In May 1915, a German U-boat sank the British liner HMS *Lusitania,* in which many American citizens drowned. Similar attacks on ships caused anxiety in the United States. Hostility to

Germany was generated by these acts. Another provocation was the revelation of the 'Zimmermann Telegram' – a signal intercepted by British intelligence from the German Foreign Minister to the German ambassador in Mexico. The message stated that if Mexico joined Germany the territories seized by the United States would be restored to them. This changed American attitude to Germany. In April 1917, the US Congress voted to declare war on Germany, Austria and Italy.

President Woodrow Wilson reneged on his earlier pre-election assurance of maintaining neutrality and now assured Americans that US intervention would ensure this was "the war to end all wars". To add a touch of idealism he stated that "American intervention" would "make the world safe for democracy".

Troops did not arrive in large numbers until 1918 but US intervention was decisive. When he arrived in Paris in July 1917, General John Pershing of the US Army went to the tomb of Marquis de Lafayette in a symbolic gesture of fraternity as that French aristocrat had joined the American rebels during the American War of Independence in 1776. This visit sent a message that America stood on the side of freedom and democracy.

The devastation of war, felt so deeply in Europe, had insignificant impact in the United States. Its losses were much lower than those of European combatants. It was able to emerge from the conflict full of strength and optimism, convinced of the value of its institutions and way of life.

9

IMMEDIATE IMPACT OF WORLD WAR I

World War I inflicted terrible suffering on people. Some 16 million people, both combatants and non-combatants, were killed. An entire generation of young men was annihilated. Among them were brilliant writers, artists, teachers, inventors, scientists who did not live to contribute their gifts to their societies. The gender ratio became unbalanced. The necessities of war however produced innovations in medicine, warfare, science and social behaviour.

World War I changed the nature of warfare. Deployment of advanced weaponry, airplanes, submarines, and tanks required technology and new strategies. Mass production techniques developed during the war for manufacturing armaments revolutionized other industries in the post-war years. The first chemical weapons were also used when the German army used poisonous gas at Ypres in 1915. Conscription was introduced for manning huge armies. It is no small irony that while universal military service was introduced in Britain, there was not a corresponding universal adult male suffrage.

The debate on the rightness of the war necessitated winning popular support for war. For the first time propaganda became another weapon in the conduct of war. Both sides participated in the information warfare. Later, as the horrors of war in the battlefield and trenches were witnessed and revealed, there grew war literature and films condemning violence. The most famous novels on this theme were Erich Maria Remarque's *All Quiet on the Western Front* and *A Farewell to Arms* by Ernest Hemingway.

The need to deal with serious injuries and mutilations led to innovations in medicine and surgery. These experiments were made in military hospitals. Heavy casualties in battle led to the establishment of blood banks. For the first time it was recognized that horrors of battle produced trauma and shell-shock; psychiatrics treated these cases.

In a reversal tendency of previous wars, where the masses suffered more than the privileged, during World War I, people of the affluent strata suffered more. The devastation of war created changes in the socio-political systems of Europe. The Russian Revolution influenced these changes. The working classes demanded universal suffrage, labour rights, and improved conditions in their place of work. The shortage of manpower among the privileged economic and social classes compelled recruitment of officers from the unprivileged classes. Elitist mentality was per force effaced.

The depletion of the male population brought many women into the labour force. Tasks previously performed by men were now done by women. Employment in these sectors and earning power brought about a change in women's outlook. This expedited women's suffrage so long held back by patriarchal societies.

Begun with aggression and bravado, the horrors of war, mutilations, trauma and the loss of human lives generated a strong European peace movement. It received support from the non-violence movement in India where demand for independence gained momentum.

The war also expedited the European socialist and labour movements. The Russian Revolution strongly influenced the attitude of the working classes. The Bolshevik accusation that the proletariat were cannon fodder for waging imperialist wars fortified the demands of the proletariat for economic benefits. The Socialist movement thereby gained momentum after 1918.

The civil disruptions caused by war impacted the economy of European states as well as their overseas colonies. The dire situation in Germany compelled the government to assume control over banks, distribution of food and other commodities as well as foreign trade. Price control for essential commodities was first introduced. The inspiration for this came from Soviet Russia which began a planned economy and nationalized all private held enterprises of Tsarist times. The doctrine of *laissez-faire* took a back seat when it was realized that state intervention in economic life was necessary in times of crisis and high inflation. The financial crash of 1929 fortified this belief.

10

TREATY OF VERSAILLES

The Treaty of Versailles was signed on 28 June 1919 after months of protracted negotiations in the splendid Palace of Versailles, once the residence of the kings of France. The locale was intended to symbolize French victory while its size accommodated the numerous delegates to the conference. The heads of governments of Britain, France and the United States were present. Vanquished Germany did not participate in the negotiations as it was not invited for the deliberations.

In 1919, a defeated Germany was presented with peace terms by the victors of World War I along with an ultimatum – sign or be invaded. The German government signed the Treaty of Versailles reluctantly. Conservative parties considered it as betrayal. A few of the politicians involved in signing and accepting the treaty were called traitors and were killed. Germans found the terms of the treaty repugnant and an attack on their pride and progress. They were angered by the punitive terms and felt it was unjust to punish the people for what their militarist government had done to wage war in 1914.

This created deep resentment in Germany. Was that nation alone responsible for the war? Versailles was called 'the diktat', a harsh settlement dictated by the victors. Territories which were part of the German empire were redistributed to the victors or their allies. Huge reparations were imposed. The treaty benefitted the victors and punished the vanquished. It set the stage for a future conflagration.

The negotiations revealed a split between the French, who wanted to dismember Germany and the British and Americans, who did not want to create pretexts for a new war. The eventual treaty included fifteen parts and 440 articles.

The British Prime Minister Lloyd George was anxious not to antagonize Germany. With the establishment of the formidable Soviet Union and its communists ideology, he felt that a weak and defeated Germany was a lesser threat than challenge of communism posed by Russia. He was apprehensive that an embittered Germany might turn towards Russia for cooperation and forge an alliance against France and Britain. The French leader Clemenceau was determined to punish Germany for the damage caused to France in terms of human lives and infrastructure. He believed that the terms of the treaty should be harsh enough to deter future wars.

American President Woodrow Wilson was astonished by the large scale devastation caused during World War I. He had not wanted the United States to be drawn into a European conflagration but the 'Zimmermann Telegram' forced his hand. By 1918, the mood in the United States was opposed to further involvement in Europe. Wilson wavered between reconciliation with Germany and punishing it, wanted the establishment of the League of Nations but with minimum American participation. His vision of a new world – principles of national self-determination and disarmament – was laudable. He felt that the League of Nations could achieve this; he had not thought it through how weaker nations would contend with the ambitions of stronger ones, nor did he suggest how these high ideals would be enforced. The US Senate refused to ratify the treaty, and the government refused responsibility for most of its provisions.

The Treaty of Versailles comprised of sections defining territorial, financial and military agreements and terms.

Part I created the Covenant of the new League of Nations. Germany was not allowed to join until 1926. The other parts stipulated redistribution of lands conquered by Germany and redrawing its borders, war reparations, payment of damages caused to Allies and other financial obligations.

For five years the French and the Belgians sought to enforce the terms of treaty rigorously but failed. France wanted to occupy the industrial belt of Ruhr in 1922. Britain and the United States pressurized France to end the occupation to which France eventually agreed. Some modifications were made to the terms of the treaty.

It was not only Germany, which had to atone for the war. Germany's chief ally Austria was compelled to sign the Treaty of St Germain which distributed its previous imperial territories to new sovereign states. Austria became a diminutive state with a great capital at Vienna that remained the cultural centre of the Teutonic world.

Hungary signed the Treaty of Trianon whereby its territories were also truncated. Turkey signed the Treaty of Sevres which redistributed lands held by the Ottoman Empire to Arabs and Greeks and Balkan peoples. This treaty demolished the power and status of the dreaded Ottoman Sultan and paved the way for a revolution under Mustapha Kemal, soon to be known as Kemal Ataturk or Father of the Turks. He was soon to repudiate this humiliating agreement.

A massive conflagration as World War I was bound to influence foreign policies of combatant and non-combatant nations alike, especially those with overseas colonial possessions.

In West Asia the British and French promised various benefits to Arabs and Jews in return for their support against the Ottoman Empire. The notorious Sykes-Picot Pact created by the British and French governments arrogated to themselves spheres of influence and created the states of Iraq, Syria and Lebanon. The Jews were promised a homeland in Palestine under the unjust Balfour Declaration, prelude to the establishment of the state of Israel, which has created the most enduring and bitter conflict in West Asia. The Arab people had lived in this region from antiquity; the Jews had migrated to Europe to escape Roman rule and to seek wealth. They faced persecution in Europe due to commercial reasons; they were money lenders, pawnbrokers and bankers. Poor Europeans resented the economic power of the Jews.

To give the Jews a state by evicting Arabs from their homeland has been one of the great injustices of modern history, especially if one remembers that Arabs generously gave sanctuary to Jews fleeing pogroms and persecution; they offered land and loans. The Jews utilized these lands in Palestine as the nucleus of their future state.

Neutral political analysts have observed that state frontiers were created with total disregard of ethnic and sectarian considerations. Iraq was formed by merging three Ottoman provinces – dominated respectively by Shias, Sunnis and Kurds. By severing it from Kuwait, seeds of future tensions were sown. These stateless groups had regional autonomy as well as stability in Iraq while the fate of Syrian and Turkish Kurds is fraught with danger.

Redrawing of the European map was more dramatic. The vast Ottoman and Austro-Hungarian Empires were fragmented and reduced. National states were established; Poland, Czechoslovakia and Yugoslavia. Centuries of alien rule had left the economies of these nations impoverished. Minorities in each of these states clamoured for greater autonomy which created and laid the foundations for future tension between them.

Poland had been partitioned by three European powers – Russia, Prussia, Austria – in 1795 and thus it ceased to be a nation-state. Polish hostility to its powerful neighbours was the leitmotif of their existence in the 19th century and even after formation of the new state in 1923, old antagonism and suspicions continued and was subsequently justified.

If there was a beneficiary of World War I, it was the United States. The terrible battles had not been fought on its soil. Consequently US cities were not devastated, its people were not made homeless nor were they killed in large numbers. The loss of American manpower was negligible compared to Europeans and the subject nations that fought – Indians, Arabs, Africans, Australians, Canadians. Due to these reasons the United States emerged stronger than Britain or France. The war made the United States a leading financial and commercial power.

11

EFFECTS OF WORLD WAR I

A new era in world history began in 1498 when Vasco da Gama landed on the southwest coast of India. Thwarted by the Papal Bull which confined the Portuguese Empire in South America and accorded to Spain more freedom to expand, the king of Portugal looked towards Asia for expansion. The fabled wealth of India – cotton, calico, gold and spice – brought Portuguese galleons to the Malabar coast. The Portuguese were followed by merchant-soldiers from the Netherlands, France and then finally Britain. Denmark established a small colony, Bandel, on the banks of the river Ganges and Tranquebar on the Coromandel coast. The age of colonial empires lasted four and half centuries.

The slow dismantling of empires began imperceptibly in 1918 with the end of World War I. The immediate casualties were those of Austria and Germany. The Hapsburgs and Hohenzollerns were deposed and their former territories were drastically reduced. The aftermath of the war created numerous new nation states and galvanized independence movements in Europe's overseas colonies.

While the imperial Romanovs were deposed, the Tsar's empire continued in the Soviet Empire, but the entire social political, economic and ideological structure was transformed by Bolshevik victory. It may be debated whether the Bolshevik victory would have come with such astonishing ease had the Tsar's imperial army won victories instead of sustaining calamitous defeats.

As stated earlier the Peace of Versailles brought prominence to the United States and to its Utopia – seeking President Wilson. His idea of the League of Nations was doomed to failure from the start because the principles informing it ignored the temper of the times. But Europe ceased to dominate the world and the balance of power was altered irrevocably. This changed international relations between various important nations and would usher significant changes only after World War II.

Diplomatic alliances and promises made during World War I, especially in the Middle East, also came back to haunt Europeans a century later.

There have been unending debates about which nation caused World War I, with a tendency to lay the blame on Germany. The fact is that all the states were responsible in one way or other. Domination was the main impulse; both Russia and Austria wanted hegemony in the Balkans, Germany and France fought for domination of Europe, Britain for imperial supremacy. Such intense and opposing ambitions could only result in a wide conflagration. The poetic justice was that none of these ambitions fructified.

In his book *The Economic Consequences of the Peace,* John Maynard Keynes foresaw the troubles that lay ahead. The financial crash of 1929 brought poverty and chaos all over the world. As European and American economies collapsed their dependent nations encountered the ripple effect. Adolf Hitler took advantage of Germany's desperate economic condition to seize power by promising stability. The humiliation of Germany gave rise to Hitler and Nazism with grim consequences for the Western world and Russia. There again Hitler alone cannot be blamed for World War II when European states indirectly collaborated with him because of their own short sighted aims.

12

THE LEAGUE OF NATIONS

The League of Nations was the utopian dream of American President Woodrow Wilson who called for the formation of "a general association of nations...affording mutual guarantees of political independence and territorial integrity to great and small States alike". The Fourteen Points so enunciated were in due course accepted by all the Allies as a statement of their war aims as well. Thus a utopian hope was transmuted in a few months into the formal and official purpose of the soon-to-be victorious Allies.

The South African statesman Jan Smuts propounded his views in a document in December 1918 titled *The League of Nations: a Practical Suggestion*. Smuts declared that the League must be "a great organ of the ordinary peaceful life of civilisation... woven into the very texture of our political system, and that in the long run its power to prevent war would depend upon the extent of its action in peace".

The League of Nations was conceived in the aftermath of World War I to prevent further wars and its attendant horrors. Not since the Black Death of the 14th century had Europe experienced such a demographic disaster nor such a large-scale man-made destruction as was World War I. At the Peace Conference in 1919 there was a universal feeling that future wars must be stopped by drawing up a Covenant for the League of Nations. It was believed that war had to be outlawed by declaring aggression as a crime against humanity. To make this effective, this intention had to be made a basic tenet of international law rather than declaration of a moral imperative. All nations were enjoined to participate in the endeavour. Out of this commitment evolved the novel concept of collective security.

Throughout the 19th century attempts had been made by European states to promote international cooperation in commercial and scientific sectors. These had no political implications – except the Zollverein which gave rise to commercial unity among German states. Over many years lawyers had evolved plans and rules for the settlement of disputes between states by legal means or by arbitration. These had been subsumed as international law. At The Hague Conferences in 1899 and 1907 attempts had been made to adjudicate disputes through tenets of international law that had been first propounded by the jurist-philosopher Grotius. An attempt was made to establish an international court for hearing intra-national disputes. However nations were not willing to curtail their sovereignty and submit their case for such adjudication.

At the Paris Conference in 1919 it was recognized that the armaments race, secret diplomacy and opaque negotiations had precipitated war. Further, politicians and statesmen were accused of not taking into consideration the welfare or opinion of their people when important political or military decisions were taken and when these decisions profoundly affected their lives and welfare.

The devastation of war accelerated the establishment of such an international legal organization to preserve peace and security of nations.

From its very commencement the League was a divided house. Enthusiasm waned even at the drafting stage. However the urgency of purpose prompted its speedy adoption in April 1919. The Covenant of the League of Nations was a brief and concise document of 26 articles. The first seven articles established the constitutional basis of the new system. Article 1 defined the League's original members, which comprised of all the Allied signatories of the peace treaties and those thirteen countries which had been neutral in the war, if the latter chose to join without reservation. Others could be admitted by a two-thirds majority of the Assembly, and any member could withdraw after serving two years' notice.

Collective security is not a new concept. From ancient times, communities and tribes bonded together to protect themselves from common foes or waged wars for mutual benefit. One of history's example is the alliance of Greek states against Troy or Viking tribes against Mediterranean kingdoms.

For the first time, the concept of collective security for preventing wars and preserving peace was incorporated as part of international law. The Covenant intended to deal with the subject of collective security; arbitration and judicial settlement. Towards this purpose it intended to establish an international court, and to strengthen ties promote international cooperation in economic and social affairs. Disarmament and transparent diplomacy had high priority in the agenda.

This program was not approved by Pacifists who rejected the idea of collective security and use of force to attain this security. The ardent supporters of international cooperation on the other hand emphasized the need to have a military force under the control of the League in order to implement all its decisions by its political authority. The Covenant of the League of Nations partially realized the plans made during the war, and the creation of working institutions.

For the next two decades the Covenant continued to be a theoretical guide but not a practical authority for implementing the activities of the League. For the first time there emerged a sense of moral responsibility for determining the conduct of states in the international community. Resultantly its principal documents were studied and scrutinized by jurists, academics and political theorists. The concept of the Covenant of the League of Nations passed the theoretical test and provided guidelines for action in crises. But it was in implementation of the grand concept that the Covenant failed and its purpose defeated – not because of the flaws in the concept but because of the motives and ambitions of the signatories. The history of the League of Nations exposed the inherent contradiction between international law and sovereignty of nations. By the time the Covenant came into force in January 1920, opposition to it had gathered momentum across the Atlantic Ocean.

The US Senate and the Republican Party opposed President Wilson's views and policies of international cooperation. Since the United States had not experienced the horror of global war on its territory, the fate of Europe did not concern its political community. They preferred the policy of Isolationism which they believed would insulate them from the effect of other nations' warfare. To absolve themselves of the responsibility of sabotaging the efforts of the League and to simultaneously curb their President, the Senators raised objections to some of the provisions of the Covenant which Wilson could neither overlook nor accept. The majority did want to ratify the provisions of the Covenant with or without reservation, which President Wilson was likely to accept. Thus the votes fell short of the two-thirds majority required under the US Constitution. Both in November 1919 and in March 1920 the proposal to ratify with substantial reservations was defeated. Tragically, the United States, whose president was a votary of collective security and peace, did not become a member of the League of Nations. This had a negative effect on the success and longevity of the organization.

The principle of collective security enunciated in the Covenant was jeopardized. It was expected that imposition of economic sanctions would restrain a nation with aggression in mind and that it would consider negotiation of disputes rather than resort to force. However the absence of the United States from the League weakened the efficacy of economic sanctions as the United States, by then a great economic power, would pursue its own policies towards an aggressor and offending nation. The prospect of sanctions could no longer intimidate nor act as a deterrent to an aggressor.

Notwithstanding the US refusal to join the League of Nations there was general approval among the European people that the existence of the League of Nations was a safeguard to peace. Amidst this atmosphere of optimism the first meeting of the League Council was held soon after the Treaty of Versailles was ratified. Thus the League began a troubled journey through international crises that would end with the outbreak of World War II in 1939.

The League, like its successor, the United Nations, possessed a large and complex structure. The Assembly and the Council decided the nature, membership, and competence of the rest of the League's principal organs and institutions. It determined their activities and provided the funds for these. The Assembly consisted of delegates from member-states who represented their governments' views and policies. These nations also sent representatives to participate in various non-political activities.

The Assembly resolved to meet every year when discussions would be held on the activities performed and programs for the future. There were wide-ranging subjects which concerned the activities of the League. Committee meetings were held on specific subjects lasting several weeks. The decisions arrived at in these meetings were required to be adopted by the Plenary Assembly through unanimous voting. Generally vetoes were not exercised on routine matters. If delegates had reservations on the subjects their views were recorded and they abstained from voting at the Assembly.

As the Council was entrusted with the task of deliberating on political matters, the Assembly confined itself to other activities of the League, such as the admission of new members or the revision of obsolete treaties. The Assembly debated and discussed problems of disarmament where every member-state had a voice.

It is generally agreed that the Assembly of the League of Nations was a successful initiative. It provided a forum for all member-states to discuss and express their views on all aspects and problems of international relations. It was in fact constituted as a global parliament.

The League Council was originally intended to comprise of the Big Five – United States, Great Britain, France, Italy and Japan – as permanent members. They would be supplemented by four other nations elected by the Assembly for a specific period. It was expected that the Soviet Union and Germany would be given permanent membership. The Council met almost every month and then thrice or four times a year. In times of crisis, the Council held emergency meetings. To enhance the prestige and power of the Council, the European member-states sent their foreign ministers to these meetings by 1923. The Council's functions were primarily political; major territorial disputes, disarmament, violence against minorities, settlements and arbitration on administrative matters.

Sir Eric James Drummond, the first Secretary-General of the League of Nations, initiated a new tradition in international institutions. International civil servants who served the League were directed to serve the interests of the League and not promote the interests of their national governments. This was not always possible – if the official belonged to a powerful member-state – but it set the tenor and attitude of international civil servants for the future. The same principle of political neutrality that governed national civil servants was expected of those who served in international institutions. This promoted international cooperation to a substantial degree and enabled officials from different regions to work together for a common purpose. This was indeed a novel experiment.

The League of Nations suffered from the handicap of financial constraints. The richer member-states collaborated to reduce expenditure, perhaps as a bargaining point to implement their own political agendas. The average annual budget for the League, the International Labour Organization (ILO) and the Permanent Court of Justice combined was less than $550,000. This meagre allocation was considered sufficient for salaries and maintenance costs for its building, Palais des Nations. This edifice was the headquarters of the League of Nations and later became the office of the United Nations at Geneva. However opponents of the League lamented that the cost of maintaining the League was higher than its attending benefits.

The Assembly, Council, and Secretariat were the central organs of an extensive structure. There were other institutions which fell into two main categories – those of a legal or political character intended to assist the League in preventing tension and settling disputes such as the Permanent Court of International Justice, the Permanent Mandates Commission and commissions concerned with military affairs and with the problems of disarmament. There were organizations which were concerned with socio-economic problems such as the ILO, which was administratively a part of the League but which functioned autonomously, the Economic and Financial Organization, the Organization for Communications and Transit, the Health Organization, and the Intellectual Cooperation Organization. There were organizations that were involved with humanitarian problems; curtailing of the international drug trade, protection of women, child welfare, the abolition of slavery and refugee problems. These organizations maintained standing committees and numerous subcommittees for special subjects. They held regular meetings. These ancillary organizations looked into general agreements and treaties, of advice and assistance to particular countries or regions, or of consultation and exchange of ideas and methods.

These units functioned even during crises. They performed anonymously and were generally neutral in their discharge of duties. It was not an easy task especially when international tensions began mounting. This was the first time that the international community and international organizations collectively addressed themselves to human welfare.

The League of Nations was a political failure because it could not prevent wars. But it laid the foundations for the vast network of international organizations that prevail today for the good of humanity.

13

EPISODES OF DEFIANCE

Article 11 of the Covenant of the League of Nations declares: "Any war or threat of war is a matter of concern to the whole League and the League shall take action to safeguard peace."

Tensions were inherent because the division of territories did not pay sufficient attention to the complex ethnic and linguistic claims of the populace thus affected.

The first crisis began in Italy, which had been on the side of the Central Powers during World War I. Hardly had the ink dried on the treaty documents in 1919 when the first violation of the League Covenant took place. Italian nationalists resented that the three victor-nations had not kept their assurances to Italy. The Adriatic seaport of Fiume had been ceded to the newly created state of Yugoslavia. Led by their great poet Gabriele d'Annunzio, in an expedition resembling an opera buffa, the port was occupied by Italians and this self-styled *condottiero* ruled Fiume for a year. The League of Nations watched the extraordinary spectacle but did nothing. Finally the Italian government bombarded the port upon which d'Annunzio and his followers surrendered but not before the poet became a national hero.

This was the first mockery of the League of Nations and that too by a group of filibusters!

Another episode which challenged the Covenant of the League of Nations began in the mineral rich town of Teschen, on the frontiers of Czechoslovakia and Poland. Both states wanted this area as it would help their industrial growth. Polish and Czech soldiers fought to gain control of the town. The League ordered that the town should be under Poland while the suburbs containing the coal mines should be under Czechoslovakia. Poland resented this and tension continued over this League ruling until the outbreak of World War II.

A dispute began in 1923 over the Lithuanian capital of Vilna (now Vilnius) which had belonged to the kingdom of Lithuania in the middle ages. Russia had annexed Lithuania in the 19th century but the population of Vilna was dominated by Poles. When Lithuania became a sovereign state after the Russian Revolution, Vilna was declared capital of the new state. Poland refused to hand over the city to the new state. A nation like Poland with no military power could defy the League. The same year, when civil war was raging in Russia and the Army of Intervention was fighting to restore Tsarist rule, Poland invaded Russian territory. The League legitimized the annexation of Russian territory by Poland by refusing to act. This aggression was condoned because Bolshevik Russia had to be contained. Churchill was a strong advocate for destroying the Bolshevik regime.

More importantly the Army of Intervention was a flagrant violation of the Covenant. The League also ordered a blockade to prevent essential food and medicines to be sent to Russia during a famine and typhus epidemic there. As a result millions of Russians died. Soviet Russia which would have been a valuable supporter of the League turned against it for its cynical double standards.

The message that the League of Nations sent to the world was – violence perpetrated by the organizers of the League was acceptable. The aggression of the opponents was to be resisted and condemned.

The blatant double standards was to be demonstrated in 1922 when the Weimar Republic of Germany could not pay the instalment of the punitive reparations imposed by the Treaty of Versailles. The German economy was near collapse. Chancellor Gustav Stresemann pleaded with Britain and France to give him time. But a victorious France and Belgium invaded the industrial belt of the Ruhr in 1923 and seized its minerals and metal products.

Europeans, Asians and Africans watched how two members of the League of Nations violated the very Covenant they had composed and endorsed. From now on might, and not right, became the un-worded motto of the League.

A minor incident but a symbolic episode occurred when Italy bombarded the Greek island of Corfu because Greek activists had shot some Italian members of a League of Nations study team. When Greece appealed for the intervention of the League, its members did nothing. Emboldened, Italy asked Greece to pay a huge fine as well. A strong Italy under Benito Mussolini was more valuable as an ally to the League than a weak Greece. Mussolini then demanded the return of the Adriatic port town of Fiume. After witnessing the bombardment of Corfu the Yugoslavian government did not want the same fate for Fiume as it did not have the firepower to resist the growing power of Italy.

Within five years of the establishment of the League of Nations, its prestige began to diminish before the world. The cynicism of its members destroyed the ideals with which the League was conceived.

14

GERMAN RESENTMENT OF THE TREATY OF VERSAILLES

Many political analysts were critical of the terms of the Treaty of Versailles. The criticism came from thinkers of both victorious Britain and triumphant France – notably John Maynard Keynes – who voiced his reservations and prediction in his famous *Economic Consequences of Peace*.

The Treaty claimed to make provisions for preserving peace and banish wars which itself was an unrealistic idea given the inherent aggressive instincts of homo sapiens. Some analysts as well as practitioners of *realpolitik* observed that the Versailles Treaty delayed the advent of another war, while others like the present authors believe from the facts before them that the Treaty actually created conditions for another terrible war. When Hitler rose to power in the 1930's and expedited World War II, these predictions seemed prescient. After the atomic dust had settled over the world scene and Germany had once again to be mollified against the common foe – Soviet Union – apologists for the Versailles Treaty tried to disassociate the terms of the treaty with the rise of Nazism and even to find redeeming features in this otherwise disastrous settlement!

Chancellor Gustav Stresemann, the sagacious leader of the Weimar Republic, foresaw the danger of a different genre of *revanche* from Germans and sought to pre-empt this by asking Britain and France to modify the harshest clauses of the Treaty and pacify German pride.

But this is to anticipate future events.

When the German military leaders, Paul von Hindenburg and Erich Ludendorff, saw that defeat in the war was inevitable they expressed willingness to negotiate terms of peace. To deflect blame from their failure they arrogated the task of negotiating peace to the new socialist government. A defeated Germany agreed to an Armistice based on President Wilson's Fourteen Points. However the terms offered by the victors were quite different and seemed unjust and arbitrary to most Germans. But German leaders were in no position to refuse the offered terms. Hindenburg and Ludendorff claimed that though Germany had not been defeated the civilian leaders had betrayed the nation. Thus the military responsible for waging war escaped responsibility and the civilian leaders bore the guilt of signing the humiliating Treaty of Versailles. The people of Germany felt that it was not a peace treaty but a capitulation and called their representatives 'November Criminals'.

In a Germany of conflicting attitudes and emotions against the Treaty of Versailles, it is not difficult to understand the circumstances that led to the eroding of confidence in the Weimar Republic and the easy allure of Nazism. As the economic situation deteriorated in Germany, and Nazism as a political credo began to be formulated, the civilian Hitler astutely endorsed Ludendorff's blaming of the civilian government of Stresemann. Hitler decided that it was necessary to first discredit the German leaders who were signatories to the treaty before repudiating it. Members of the Weimar government and the intelligentsia, especially the socialists, did not accept this theory;

they sensed the danger of encouraging militarists who had brought Germany to war in the first place. Unfortunately the liberals and socialists did not possess the technique or the ideology to influence the masses as did Hitler's ruinous oratory. The creators of the Versailles Treaty did not realize or perhaps did not foresee the dangerous weapon for revenge they had embedded in the clauses of the treaty – of war guilt and punitive action – which would be used by Hitler and his Nazi acolytes to such apocalyptic effect. The fact that a prosperous Jewish community, many of whom were socialists, did not blame the treaty for Germany's woes only fortified Hitler's anti-Semitic and anti-Socialist agenda.

It has been speculated that Hitler would have remained a marginal and innocuous agitator had the German economy not collapsed. But the severe economic and commercial depression was not Germany's alone; it impacted the entire world as many countries and regions were connected to the economies of major powers such as the United States, Britain and France. But Hitler veered attention away from the general malaise and focussed on the fact that the German economy had already been afflicted, not so much by the global stagnation but by the punitive reparations. The German people found in him a redeemer – from debts, reparation and humiliation.

This was the principle flaw of the Treaty of Versailles – it heedlessly offered an instrument of revenge to Germany and the excuse for another war. The Treaty had another flaw – it also allowed the victors to salvage their acute economic problems through impoverishment of Germany.

It appears both unjust and unfair that Germany was called upon to pay for the cost of World War I which had been waged by major European powers. None could be exempted from blame for the 'Scramble for Africa', arms race and political rivalry in the Balkans which caused the war. The war had damaged European terrain – the agricultural and as well as the industrial infrastructure. Repairing these naturally required massive funds. Britain and France wanted Germany to bear the cost. The Versailles Treaty stipulated reparations payments to the tune of 132,000 million gold marks. This huge amount caused Germans immense unease as well as deep anxiety as to how the payment would be made. The Dawes Plan of 1924 formulated the strategy; Germany would pay their new debts to the Allies, who would pay the United States for their debts, and US investors would send money to Germany for the rebuilding of the nation, allowing more repayments. The formula for reparations was unviable. Germany became inextricably bound to the American economy which had disastrous effects when the Great Depression of 1929 came within a decade of the treaty. This damaged the German economy. Unable to cope with hyper-inflation and massive unemployment the people turned to anyone who could remedy the situation.

The other flaw of Versailles was an inequitable distribution of German people in other nation states. This provided an excuse for an aggressively irredentist policy to unite Germans – not by bringing them to Germany – but by annexing the nations and provinces where they lived as would happen in the Sudeten crisis.

The same logic was not applied when it came to the question of non-Germans living in Germany. The Nazi agenda went further; the conquest of East Europe, subjugation of the Slav population and deportation to Germany to serve as slave labour and the repopulation of these Slav lands with the alleged superior or *Übermensch* Teutonic race.

The Versailles Treaty allowed the continued existence of a residual elitist army comprising of Junkers from the pre-war days which was hostile to the democratic Weimar republic and were lured by Hitler's attractive militarism. Unemployed and demobilized German soldiers swelled these ranks.

The Treaty of Versailles inflicted deep wounds between the victors and the vanquished. Germans felt the clauses of the treaty were both harsh and unfair. Had the wounds been only political there would have been less antagonism. But the combination of political injustice with economic ruin prepared a fertile terrain for Hitler's rise to power.

15

GERMANY'S REPUDIATION OF THE TREATY OF VERSAILLES

In his book *American Reparations to Germany,* Professor Stephen Schuker has written that "large parts of Belgium and France were so destroyed by trench warfare that they looked desolate, like moonscapes, just huge areas of land where nothing remained". As German territory was not so badly affected the Allies felt Germany should bear the cost for repairing the physical damage.

The International Reparations Commission took several years to assess the damage. The amount varied and finally settled down to $33 billion. The amount was so excessive that John Maynard Keynes, who was part of the British delegation, angrily left the conference in 1919 and declared that the reparations would cripple the German economy with serious consequences. Other distinguished economists concurred with his views. As it happened, the first instalment payment of $500 million in 1921 was paper money. The already acute inflation was aggravated by heavy printing of paper money thus devaluing the currency. An oft told story is of how a wheelbarrow full of paper notes was required to purchase a loaf of bread.

In this situation Germany could not pay and began defaulting on payment of reparations. France retaliated by occupying the

Ruhr industrial belt to enforce payments. At the hastily summoned London Conference, Britain made it amply clear to France that it could not make unilateral military moves to uphold clauses of the Versailles Treaty as this provoked hostility in Britain. So the plan to make Germany pay from its industrial production failed. The Dawes Plan to resolve the situation was not any more successful. In fact American investors in Germany sustained losses.

The Germans were relieved when Adolf Hitler rose to power in 1933 and cancelled all reparations. It was the first breach of the Treaty of Versailles.

The second breach was in the Maginot Line which was built to fulfil several purposes, the chief being to prevent a surprise attack by Germany. The other reasons were to protect Alsace-Lorraine and their industrial basin from German incursion, and to facilitate the speedy mobilization of the French army in the event of war. The idea of such a fortification came from the Frenchman, Andre Maginot who had fought during World War I.

There was another fear psychosis as well. French and Belgian territory had been the locale for some of the bloodiest battles during World War I. Millions of young Frenchmen perished. Consequently there was an acute shortage of men which impeded large scale conscription in the French army. The French government relied on the older generation to fill the ranks which in turn would affect the employment of experienced men in the industrial sector. A strong defensive strategy had therefore to be formulated. It sprang from the concept of *la puissance du feu* or the fear of fire, in which the power of artillery was installed and protected by concrete and steel that could inflict devastating losses on invaders. The answer was the Maginot Line.

Maginot Line fortifications were manned by specialist units of fortress infantry, artillery and engineers. The infantry were in charge of the lighter weapons of the fortresses, and would have to operate outside these parameters if necessary. Artillery troops looked after the heavy guns while the engineers were responsible for maintaining and operating complex equipment and communications systems. These troops were considered the elite force of the French army. The Maginot Line was intended to halt the main German blow if it came in eastern France and to divert the attack through Belgium, where French forces would meet and halt German incursion.

France recognized the imperative not only to retaliate in case of German attack but the need to keep its channels open for the import of British goods such as coal, tin, rubber, jute, wool and manganese. France's defensive strategy meant that Britain could safely maintain benevolent neutrality towards France and in the case of unprovoked German attack come to the aid of France. These speculations came to nothing.

The Allied Control Commission, responsible for ensuring that Germany complied with Part V of the Treaty of Versailles, was abolished in 1927 as a measure of goodwill or pacification. At that time the commissioners of the Control Commission issued a report stating that Germany never intended to abide by Part V of the Treaty and had every intention of rearming itself. Though the Treaty of Versailles stipulated that France would occupy the Rhineland until 1935, French troops were removed from there in 1930. French occupation of the Rhineland was intended to discourage Germany from acts of aggression as well as rearmament. This state of armed truce continued into the early 1930's. Once French troops left the Rhineland, France no longer had a whip hand since the deterrent against German aggression was removed.

It is difficult to explain why France withdrew its troops from the Rhineland when it believed that Germany would not allow the Rhineland's demilitarized status to continue forever, and that at some future date Germany would rearm, reintroduce conscription and remilitarize the Rhineland. French apprehension was justified when it came to be known a few years later that Germany was surreptitiously rearming itself with Soviet aid – an act which the Soviet Union later regretted. It was in this scenario that France began erecting the Maginot Line. The decision was prompted by fears of the possible consequence of French withdrawal from the Rhineland in 1930. These fears were not unfounded.

Even after emerging from a devastating war, both the German economy and its population were larger than that of France. Since the battles had been fought mainly on Belgian and French soil, the physical damage for these nations was more acute. The damage to terrain, buildings, farms and factories had a fearful psychological effect on the people who had witnessed and bore the brunt of the devastation. The financial cost of rebuilding infrastructure as well as military power made the French policy makers uncertain of their future vis-à-vis Germany. As the 1920's progressed amidst economic depression, the smouldering resentment in Germany, the spectre of Bolshevism, gradual distancing of Britain and America from European problems and disputes, France recognized the stark fact that it had to go it alone if there was another war against Germany.

Further, the Treaty of Versailles did not stipulate military sanctions in the event of Germany remilitarizing the Rhineland or flouting Part V of the Treaty. The Treaty of Locarno of 1923 laid down that Britain and Italy would assist France in the event of "flagrant violation" of the Rhineland's demilitarized status but neither state ever defined what this meant. It was clear that neither Britain nor Mussolini's Italy were anxious to fight against Germany for the sake of France, especially as Italy had old irredentist scores to settle with France in Nice and Savoy.

In spring 1940, soon after the outbreak of World War II more than a million German troops and 1,500 tanks easily crossed the purported impenetrable forest using existing roads and forest tracks. They encountered little opposition as the French units in this area had almost no air support and could not halt the inexorable onslaught of German bombers. The French army was driven back and the German Army moved forward until they reached the outskirts of Dunkirk. By June 1940 the German army came to the Maginot Line and cut it from the rest of France. Many of the fortress troops surrendered after the armistice, but others held on until they were captured.

One of the clauses of the Treaty of Versailles was to demilitarize the Rhineland and thereby reduce a future military threat from Germany.

After the Locarno Conference, an agreement was signed confirming the international frontiers enunciated by the Treaty of Versailles. The Locarno Pact also approved Germany's membership of the League of Nations. By bringing Germany into the comity of nations, it was intended to obtain its cooperation. Assured of Germany's good conduct, Britain and France agreed to remove the last Allied troops in the demilitarized Rhineland in 1930.

Four years later Adolph Hitler came to power. In 1935 he repudiated the military clauses of the Versailles Treaty and in March 1936 began remilitarizing the Rhineland. German troops moved into the Rhineland on the specious argument that the treaty signed between France and Russia was a threat to German security. German officers were directed to retreat in case the French forces retaliated. Astonishingly France took no action. The League of Nations watched in silence.

In his book *Mein Kampf* (1925) Hitler had declared that he would abolish the Treaty of Versailles. The League of Nations Disarmament Conference was held in Geneva between 1932–1934. The conference was organized by League member-states, the United States for the reduction and limitation of armaments. After coming to power Hitler rejected the proposals and demanded equality of arms and military parity with Britain and France. When he realized that this was not acceptable to the Allies, Hitler abrogated terms of the Treaty by building up the German army. In defiance of the Allies he held a massive rearmament rally. Surprisingly the main powers were acquiescent. Perhaps they believed that it would be unwise to antagonize a resurgent Germany. Britain went further; it concluded a naval agreement with Germany whereby Germany could have a navy one third of the British one. This was a violation of the Versailles Treaty that permitted Germany only six battleships. Hitler reintroduced conscription in 1935 through the Military Service Law and enhanced investment in all the three defence forces of Germany. At the outbreak of World War II Germany possessed 95 warships, 8,250 fighter aircrafts and a standing army of one million men. These made a travesty of the Treaty which permitted Germany only a hundred thousand men and no aircrafts. Whatever wishful thinking the Allies entertained, it should have been obvious to even a neutral observer that Hitler planned war. The rehearsal for this was the Spanish Civil War.

The third breach of the Treaty of Versailles by Hitler occurred in 1938. The Treaty forbade Anschluss or union between Germany and Austria. An attempted Nazi putsch in Austria failed in 1934, but Hitler tried again in 1938. Austrian Nazis organized riots, while Hitler pressurized the Austrian Chancellor Schuschnigg to declare Anschluss. Schuschnigg asked both France and Britain for help; when this was refused, he suggested a plebiscite. To prevent the possibility of a 'no' vote, Hitler invaded Austria. German troops were greeted by a frenzied, stage-managed demonstration. Some 30,000 Austrian opponents were imprisoned. Next month, in a referendum, 99 per cent of Austrians voted for the Anschluss.

By the end of 1938, Hitler was doing the same thing in the Sudetenland, which the Treaty of Versailles had ceded to Czechoslovakia. Sudeten Nazis, led by Henlein, caused trouble, claiming that they were being oppressed by the Czechs. Hitler demanded union, and threatened war. This time, although the Czech leader Edvard Beneš was prepared to fight, it was Britain and France at Munich that broke the Treaty of Versailles and gave Sudetenland to Germany. This left Danzig and the Polish Corridor open for the next assault.

It can be argued that it was not Hitler alone who broke the Treaty of Versailles. It was a short-sighted Britain and France that followed a disastrous policy of pacification. The pacification of Germany may have been prompted by the fear of the Soviet Union and illusion that a mollified Germany would establish amity with Britain and France.

16

THE ROME-BERLIN-TOKYO AXIS

Italy's invasion of Ethiopia in 1935 irrevocably changed the existing European geopolitical framework.

Hitler's rise to power was facilitated by his promise to the German people that he would nullify the Versailles Treaty and end the Anglo-French encirclement that curtailed the sovereignty of their once powerful militarist state. As many European nations were signatories to the Treaty of Versailles, Germany was left without allies. The temporary truce with Soviet Russia, forged after the Treaty of Brest-Litovsk, began to wear thin as the world's two most formidable men – Stalin and Hitler – vied for power in a divided world.

Hitler reflected the views of his adopted German countrymen (he was Austrian by birth) when he decided to abrogate the Versailles Treaty. By 1934 he gauged the mood of Britain and France and proceeded with his agenda. But to do this he required allies. A ready ally was waiting for him across the Alps – Benito Mussolini.

No two men could have been more different but sometimes convergence of interests facilitates a marriage of convenience. This unlikely alliance requires thumbnail sketches of the two bridegrooms.

Benito Mussolini began his political career as a Socialist school teacher from Central Italy. After World War I he turned to Fascist philosophy and was elected prime minister in the monarchical Italy of 1922. His socialist agenda endeared him to his compatriots, who lived in poverty while a few were privileged. This popular support helped him to assume power in 1926. King Victor Emmanuel III feared Mussolini's neo-imperial ambitions; he therefore encouraged monarchist officers to curb Mussolini's dominance of the armed services. But these men admired Mussolini for his high intelligence, acute ability to judge men, and understanding the aspirations of his own people as well as the temper of his time. His earlier allegiance to socialism made him effect economic reforms to alleviate poverty in Italy, especially among the peasantry in South Italy. He introduced a system of rural credit for farmers, drained the Pontine marshes, initiated agricultural cooperative societies, and invested heavily in industrial growth in northern Italy. It was during his regime that Milan and Turin became industrial capitals. Turning to the lawless South Italy and Sicily, Mussolini evicted the notorious Mafia – who emigrated to the United States! He laid the foundations for a modern Italian state with emphasis on education and technology and curtailed the power of the oppressive Papacy. He carried out successful campaigns to conquer Libya and subdue Somalia and thereby extended Italian influence in the Mediterranean and Red Seas.

Mussolini bore close resemblance to a great Italian statesman, Ludovico Sforza, Regent of Milan, whose overarching thirst for power nullified his commercial and economic achievements, and shadowed his contribution to the Italian Renaissance. Like Mussolini, Duke Ludovico forged an alliance with a powerful foreign king which brought him to a tragic end.

Luigi Barzini, a famous Italian writer (and friend of the authors' father) observed that Mussolini resembled a hero of medieval

Italy – Cola de Rienzo – whose tragic fate was that of Mussolini. Both won the adulation of the masses and both were killed by a disillusioned populace. The great German composer Wagner composed an opera, *Rienzo*, on this fascinating man.

Seeing Mussolini's success and authority, Hitler made overtures to the Italian leader with the common purpose of checking British and French power. Soon after taking over Hitler went to Italy on a state visit in 1934. He met Mussolini in Venice. Hitler noted the adulation of the Italian people for their *Duce*. Hitler acted the role of the admiring junior partner until the day he could become master of Europe. But leaders of the Italian armed forces were wary of the German leader; they saw through the facade of humility. Mussolini's acute judgement of men failed him when he assured his military leaders that the Fuhrer was innocuous.

Germany and Italy signed a series of Protocols in late October 1936 which formed the Rome-Berlin Axis. After signing the Treaty of Versailles, Italy had been an informal ally of France and Britain. Having experienced a century of Austrian occupation in its northern provinces, Italy was uneasy about renewed Austrian designs on its northern frontiers. Italy's invasion of Abyssinia in 1936 encountered British disapproval; Hitler knew that Mussolini's repudiation of the clauses of the Versailles Treaty would isolate him even more. Further, by allying with Italy, Germany was assured of security on its southern frontier. After the Axis was formalized, Hitler exulted, "The Alps have disappeared!" He rejoiced that the Alpine mountain frontier that separated Austria from Italy had been removed.

The Rome-Berlin Axis was more to Hitler's benefit than Mussolini's. Italy was drawn into military campaigns that were both ill-conceived and with little benefit. But for Hitler the alliance was a boon; it emboldened him to commence repudiation of the Versailles Treaty step by step and year by year.

Germany acquired another ally in November 1936 when it signed the Anti-Comintern Pact with Japan. They believed they had a common adversary in Soviet Russia. Japan had fought and won a war against Russia in 1905. They had territorial disputes on the Pacific coast. Monarchical Japan abhorred Communist Russia. Hitler also shared Japan's dread of communism though his attitude to Russia varied, depending on the situation. Germany and Japan agreed to cooperate to check the spread of communism.

Hitler visited Rome in 1938 where the Italian king and Mussolini met him at the railway station. This was to announce the strength of the Rome-Berlin axis. The Rome-Berlin-Tokyo Axis signalized the alliance of the three totalitarian powers. They had a common ideology for world domination and for suppression of dissent at home though Mussolini's methods were far milder than that of Germany and Japan.

The alliance of these three powerful states with their authoritarian ideologies caused apprehension among other nations. President Roosevelt viewed the Anti-Comintern Pact with misgiving; Japan was offering a challenge to the United States in the Pacific and East Asia. Japan had declined to attend a Brussels Conference on the Sino-Japanese dispute in 1937. Premier Stalin recognized the danger of the Anti-Comintern Pact to the Soviet Union and its ideology. Ever taciturn, Stalin did not voice his anxiety but American Ambassador Joseph Grew read the warning signs and recorded his insightful views.

If the present triangular combination is analyzed it becomes immediately apparent that not only is the group not merely anti-communist, but that its policies and practices equally run counter to those of the so-called democratic powers. Thus it can be seen that the question resolves itself into the simple fact that it is a combination of those states which are bent upon upsetting the status quo as opposed to those states which wish to preserve the status quo, or, more simply, of the 'have nots' against the 'haves,' and that anti-communism is merely the banner under which the 'have-nots' are rallying. The threat to England is very real and immediately apparent upon reflection that with the addition of Japan to the Rome Berlin axis the life-line of the British Empire is threatened from the North Sea through the Mediterranean and beyond Singapore.

Japan confirmed these misgivings by attacking an American warship on the Yangtze River. American President Franklin Delano Roosevelt saw the imminent danger and persuaded the US Congress to approve a rearmament program. He followed up with disapproval of Japanese occupation of China and proclamation of its "new order". Like leaders of other states President Roosevelt was caught in a predicament; he condemned Japanese aggression but did not pursue this with armed action. Once again they pursued the mirage of peace.

At this crucial juncture Hitler performed a surprising volte face by cancelling the Anti-Comintern Pact. He had more pressing matters at hand than suppressing communism. He wanted to lull Soviet Russia into a sense of false security to pave the way for a future invasion of Russia. With reciprocal cunning, Stalin played out the charade.

As war clouds gathered, German Foreign Minister Joachim von Ribbentrop and Italian Foreign Minister Count Galeazzo Ciano signed the Pact of Friendship and Alliance in 1939. Then in 1940 when the Nazi army marched across most of Europe, the

Pact was formalized into the Tripartite Pact between Germany, Italy, and Japan that came to be known as the Axis powers.

Under the terms of this alliance, Japan recognized the leadership of Germany and Italy in Europe, and Germany and Italy correspondingly recognized the leadership of Japan in East Asia. According to Article 3 of the Treaty, the three parties agreed "to cooperate in their efforts on the aforesaid lines", and they further undertook "to assist one another with all political, economic, and military means when one of the three is attacked by a power at present not involved in the European war or in the Sino-Japanese Conflict". This clause was directed against the United States. Article 4 of the Treaty made the first formal provision for military, naval and economic collaboration. It declared: "With a view to implementing the present Pact, Joint Technical Commissions the members of which are to be appointed by the respective Governments of Japan, Germany, and Italy will meet without delay."

World War II brought these powers together for pursuing this formidable agenda.

17

DANGEROUS DEFIANCE

Manchurian Crisis – 1931

Apart from being an economic disaster, the Great Depression had political implications as well. While weaker nations struggled with poverty and hyper-inflation, the stronger ones seized the economic crisis for their own advantage.

Japan sought to find a remedy through territorial expansion. By the 1930s, Japan was determined to extend its empire. It had already annexed the Korean peninsula and controlled the Manchurian Railway. In September 1931, Japan claimed that Chinese soldiers had sabotaged the railway, and attacked the Chinese army which did not retaliate because it felt that Japan was deliberately provoking a war. Despite the Japanese government's order to withdraw, its army invaded Manchuria and named it Manchukuo. Meeting no opposition, the Japanese army marched into China and captured the important city of Shanghai in 1932 even though the Japanese government told its army to withdraw. Thousands of Chinese soldiers and civilians were killed by the Japanese army.

China appealed to the League of Nations. The League sent a delegation under Lord Lytton to Manchuria to investigate the matter. It took a year to report a blatant aggression; by that time

Japan was firmly ensconced in Manchuria and in parts of China. With this fait accompli in hand, the study team facetiously recommended that Japan should return Manchuria to China. Worse still, the League of Nations summoned a Special Assembly of the League a year and a half after the invasion by Japan. Most member-nations voted against Japan and recommended that Manchuria should be returned to China. Japan not only voted against the Resolution but observed that China was not a sovereign state and did not have a government as it was wracked by civil war. Instead of leaving Manchuria, Japan walked out of the League of Nations. To demonstrate its contempt for the League, Japan next invaded the Chinese province of Jehol adjacent to Manchuria.

The League of Nations did nothing except to suggest imposition of trade sanctions. The United States and Britain refused to agree because Japan was a valuable trading partner. Nor did the League place embargo on the sales of arms as required under its Covenant.

Britain and France were impressed by the efficiency of the Japanese army and had no wish to create a crisis with a rising Japan. Further Japan had pleased them in 1920 by sending its troops to join the Army of Intervention to Russia and had briefly occupied Vladivostok. Japan was the only Asian power to challenge Russia. This obsession to 'contain' Russia would have dire consequences later. In 1931 Japan was deemed a useful if not a reliable ally.

This inability to oppose a state which had blatantly violated an important Article of the League of Nations emboldened governments that were planning territorial expansion.

Abyssinian Invasion – 1936

The unification or *Risorgimento* of Italy in 1870 was imbued with the idealism of Mazzini and Gioberti, the stirring novels of

Manzoni, the poetry of Leopardi. Having experienced the harsh rules of Austria in the north and Spain in the south, the Italians wanted a modern liberal state. Nationalism gained ground only in the late 19th century. Italian politicians nostalgically remembered their Roman history and its imperial conquests. Italy therefore belatedly joined the 'Scramble for Africa'. However the strategic resource-rich areas had already been conquered. Somaliland and Eritrea were still available.

The crisis in Abyssinia (northern half of present-day Ethiopia) from 1935 to 1936 brought international tension nearer to Europe. It also brought Nazi Germany and Fascist Italy openly together for the first time. The affair once again highlighted the perilous weakness of the League of Nations.

Italian attempts to expand in East Africa and for capturing Abyssinia had met with failure in the 19th century. The dedicated Abyssinian army had defeated its Italian opponents at the Battle of Adowa. This humiliating defeat at the hands of an old fashioned army and loss of some six thousand soldiers injured nascent Italian pride. The desire for revenge grew as the Italians prepared another invasion of this ancient kingdom which had been the home of early Christianity. That Abyssinia was the oldest Christian kingdom had no spiritual impact in the land of the Popes.

Benito Mussolini fanned old imperial aspirations. He restored the Roman Forums, erected stone maps on ancient Roman walls indicating the expansion of the Roman Empire from its capital to the far reaches of Europe, Asia and Africa. Far-fetched dreams of rebuilding that empire obsessed Mussolini. Churchill may have called him "the sawdust Caesar" but Mussolini envisaged himself as another Roman Caesar.

With duplicity worthy of Machiavelli, Mussolini signed a treaty of friendship with Emperor Haile Selassie of Abyssinia while he planned invasion of that country. In December 1934, Mussolini falsely accused Abyssinians of aggression at an oasis called Walwal. He ordered Italian troops stationed in Somaliland and Eritrea to attack Abyssinia. In October 1935, the Italian army invaded Abyssinia. The old-fashioned and outmoded Abyssinian army could not resist the well-equipped modern military machinery of Italy. Apart from aerial bombardment, the Italian army and air force rained mustard gas on the hapless Abyssinians. Thousands died. The Abyssinian capital of Addis Ababa fell in May 1936. Emperor Haile Selassie was deposed. The Italian king Victor Emmanuel III ascended the ancient throne as Emperor.

Somaliland, Eritrea and Abyssinia were united under the name Italian East Africa.

Emperor Haile Selassie made a moving appeal in the Palais des Nations in Geneva, headquarters of the League of Nations. He warned member-states against blatant aggression and unprovoked aggression of a country by another which was a violation of the principal tenet of the Covenant.

"Today it is I. Tomorrow it will be you," he prophetically warned the member-states.

The League of Nations paid lip service to its Covenant by condemning the attack. All League members were ordered to impose economic sanctions on Italy. Deliberately and with the same duplicity employed by Mussolini, time was allowed to Italy to reorganize material. Sanction was not imposed on the all-important oil and fuel for conducting the war. The chief members used a specious argument that Italy would in any case get its oil from America – a non-League country.

Britain and France were also reluctant to provoke Italy in the Mediterranean Sea where Britain had two large naval bases – Gibraltar and Malta – though at that time the Italian navy did not have the capability to retaliate against Britain's powerful navy. Britain could have closed the Suez Canal to Italian ships and cut off its supply route to east Africa, but did not. The fate of an African nation did not seem important enough. It was more important to keep European allies happy.

In an effort to end the war, the British Foreign Secretary – Samuel Hoare – and the French Prime Minister – Pierre Laval – met in December 1935. The Hoare-Laval Pact was a cynical arrangement by which Italy would keep its conquests, and leave a strip of territory to Abyssinia. The plan naturally suited Italy but there was an outcry in Britain. The British public condemned the flagrant condoning of the aggression against a hapless Abyssinia.

Mussolini's army overran Abyssinia. It was open defiance of the Covenant of the League of Nations. The world witnessed the cynicism of the British and French governments that allowed its own rules torn to shreds. The sanctions against Italy were not implemented; member-states were prepared to negotiate with aggressor nations to the extent of effectively giving in to them. Once more, aggression against a weak nation was condoned.

Mussolini and Hitler took note of Britain's and France's non-commitment to the Covenant of the League.

The day of reckoning was drawing near.

Spanish Civil War – 1936

The year 1936 was portentous in another way. The Spanish Civil War began that year; the combatants were the liberal secular Republicans on one side, and the authoritarian Fascists headed by General Francisco Franco, on the other. The Soviet Union sent arms and men to fight for the Republicans while Hitler and Italy supported their fellow Fascists. One wonders if Stalin realized that the Spanish Civil War was a rehearsal for the grim battle that lay ahead between the Soviet Union and Nazi Germany. Revolutionary ideals inspired intellectuals of Europe to side with the Soviet Union and Republican Spain in the terrible civil war. George Orwell wrote *Homage to Catalonia,* Ernest Hemingway wrote his masterpiece *For Whom the Bell Tolls,* and Pablo Picasso depicted the atrocities of Franco's army in his immortal painting *Guernica.*

Anschluss – 1938

The concept of a united Germanic state was visualized by Austria and Germany in 1919 when both nations suffered a humiliating defeat at Allied hands. The idea had its inspiration in the Holy Roman Empire when the Hohenstaufen and the Hapsburg dynasties ruled much of Central and parts of Southern Europe. This was an aim to unite all German-speaking people in one nation. Foreseeing this and mindful of the havoc the alliance of these two states had caused prior to World War I, the Treaty of Versailles forbade such a union.

In July 1934 Austrian and German Nazis joined together to plan a coup which ended in failure. An authoritarian right-wing government then governed Austria. The Austrian liberals and socialists who apprehended danger were not permitted to voice their concern over the looming threat of an Anschluss. This prevented development of a robust resistance to Hitler's plans. Finding no opposition, Austrian Nazis continued consolidating their power.

By 1938, Hitler had concluded alliances with Italy and Japan. All three states had defied the Covenant of the League of Nations. Germany had militarized the Rhineland, Italy had invaded Abyssinia, Japan had invaded Manchuria. They had met with little opposition from the signatories of the Versailles Treaty. He therefore was emboldened to plan a union or Anschluss with Austria.

Hitler instructed the Nazi Party of Austria to stir agitations, strikes and even incendiary activities. The Austrian Nazis held parades and marches, set buildings on fire, exploded bombs, provoked and organized fighting between Nazis and others. When the Austrian government banned them, Hitler held a meeting with Austrian Chancellor Kurt Schuschnigg and threatened to invade Austria unless Schuschnigg gave all important government jobs to Nazis. Under such formidable pressure Schuschnigg compromised by appointing an Austrian Nazi, Arthur Seyss-Inquart, as Minister of the Interior.

Astonishingly, Britain and France remained passive spectators in what was a gross violation of Austrian sovereignty. Patriotic Austrians met leaders of these two nations and sought assistance but no help was promised or given. On 9 March 1938, Schuschnigg announced his intention to hold a plebiscite to enable Austrian citizens to decide whether they wanted union with Germany. An enraged Hitler mobilized German troops on the common frontier and ordered Chancellor Schuschnigg to cancel the plebiscite. Schuschnigg had no choice but to comply. After considerable harassment and intimidation by Austrian Nazis, Schuschnigg resigned. President Wilhelm Miklas of Austria refused to appoint the Nazi Seyss-Inquart as Chancellor. The German Nazi minister Hermann Göring commanded Seyss-Inquart to send a telegram requesting German military aid, but he refused. Göring ordered a German agent in Vienna to send this infamous telegram. Germany invaded Austria on 12 March 1938.

The legitimate Austrian leader was replaced by Hitler's protégé, Seyss-Inquart, the Minister of the Interior. Now, as leader of Austria, Seyss-Inquart immediately asked Hitler to send the German army to help "restore order in Austria" where there was no disorder except that created by the Nazis. Hitler declared he had been invited by the Austrian leader to enter Austria. This bloodless invasion by the Nazi army brought in their wake the Gestapo and the SS stormtroopers who were charged with eliminating all opposition to Nazi rule. The former Austrian Chancellor Schuschnigg was humiliated in every possible way and Jews were given menial tasks on the streets. The Nazi regime of terror thus commenced in Austria.

Invasion of Czechoslovakia – 1938

Having succeeded in gaining Austria, Hitler then used similar tactics to seize the bordering northern and western Bohemia and northern Moravia of Czechoslovakia that contained over three million ethnic Germans.

France had made an alliance with Belgium and with the states of Poland, Czechoslovakia, Romania and Yugoslavia. This was intended to be a cordon sanitaire to curb Hitler. Regardless of this Hitler announced his intention to acquire territories in Czechoslovakia inhabited by German-speaking people. This was an excuse. The real reason was because this region had enormous economic and strategic value for Czechoslovakia as its border defences and banking systems as well as the nation's heavy industries belt were located there.

A conference was held in Munich in September 1938 to discuss the annexation of lands inhabited by German-speaking people who had settled there since medieval times. A new territorial definition was coined – Sudetenland. Major European nations except Russia were invited to the Munich conference. And even more bizarre was that the fate of the nation whose territories were to be discussed – Czechoslovakia – was not invited. The slogan, "About us, without us!" summarized the outrage of the people of Czechoslovakia. The Czechoslovaks accused Britain and France for betraying them despite the alliance hastily signed by France and Czechoslovakia a few months earlier to prevent German aggression. They called the Munich Agreement the 'Munich Diktat' by Hitler.

As soon as the document was signed, German troops crossed into Sudetenland. This was the prelude to annexation of entire Czechoslovakia. He wasted no time in declaring that the Wehrmacht must be prepared at all times for the liquidation of the remainder of Czechoslovakia.

Hitler encouraged separatists in province of Slovakia because he felt, "A Czech state minus Slovakia is even more completely at our mercy." He wanted airbases in Slovakia for military operations. He sent a military delegation to Bratislava (the capital of Slovakia), which put the Slovak leader, Tiso, on a plane to Berlin. There he forced Tiso to declare Slovakia's independence from Prague.

Similar thuggish treatment was meted out to the Czechoslovakian President Emil Hacha who collapsed under the strain; in that condition he was forced to sign a document requesting Germany to "place the fate of the Czech people and country in the hands of the Fuhrer". Hitler's Panzer Division rolled into inoffensive Czechoslovakia on the pretext of protecting Sudeten Germans. Hitler and his friends expressed contempt for the Slav race.

Britain acquiesced; a supine Chamberlain called the humiliating submission at Munich in 1938 as obtaining "peace for our times". He was echoing Lord Palmerston who after returning victoriously from the Congress of Berlin in 1878 had uttered these words. The Munich Agreement stated that Britain, France and Germany would guarantee the sovereignty of Czechoslovakia. Hitler knew beyond all doubts that that neither Britain nor France would oppose his territorial ambitions.

"Czechoslovakia has ceased to exist!" Hitler announced to the German people later that day, just before departing for Prague. That evening, Hitler entered Prague at the head of a ten vehicle convoy. But there were no cheering crowds. The streets of Prague were deserted. Hitler spent the night in Prague's Hradcany Castle, residence of the medieval monarchs of Bohemia. The next day, Hitler issued a proclamation establishing the Protectorate of Bohemia and Moravia. "Czechoslovakia", Hitler declared, "showed its inherent inability to survive and has therefore now fallen victim to actual dissolution."

The world waited for the response of British Prime Minister Chamberlain to the flagrant violation of the Munich Agreement. He responded to Hitler's aggression by observing that the British government was not bound to protect Czechoslovakia since the country in effect no longer existed after Slovakia had voted for independence. Chamberlain astounded his countrymen by stating in Parliament that "His Majesty's Government has no desire to interfere unnecessarily in a matter with which other governments may be more directly concerned..."

In the rest of Britain, however, there was violent reaction against Germany. The British Parliament witnessed anger and condemnation of Chamberlain and German action. The British media strongly condemned the annexation of Czechoslovakia. Hitler had tested the waters and found little opposition to his bloodless conquests. The Allies were lulled into a false sense of security, unwilling or unable to realize that the next time German troops marched into foreign territory there would be an actual and brutal war, a war which would draw them into unparalleled bloodshed.

Soviet Commissar of Foreign Affairs, Maxim Litvinov now saw the writing on the wall and advised Stalin against collaboration with Germany. Stalin responded unwisely with a pro-German gesture by appointing the pro-German Vyacheslav Molotov in place of Litvinov in May 1939. The German press, now under Hitler's command wrote warmly of Stalin.

Uneasy about the growing amity between Stalin and Hitler, Britain and France invited the Soviet Union to form a defensive pact to protect Poland from Germany. Stalin made terms unacceptable to Poland. The proposed treaty fell through.

Invasion of Poland – 1939

Ironically, soon after coming to power, Hitler signed a non-aggression pact with Poland in January 1934. This move was not popular with many Germans who resented the fact that by the Treaty of Versailles Poland had received the former German provinces of West Prussia, Poznan, and Upper Silesia. Notwithstanding this Hitler signed the Pact in order to pre-empt a Franco-Polish alliance against Germany which seemed imminent in 1934 as both nations were apprehensive of German military resurgence under Hitler.

The policy of appeasement pursued by Britain and France has been narrated earlier. The mood of mollification sprang from various motives. Both nations were exhausted after World War I. The human cost was no less than the economic cost. Their immediate concern was to rebuild their economies and industrial infrastructures. This could be achieved only if there was peace in Europe. Neither state was prepared to wage war in their weakened condition. Many people in these two countries believed that the Treaty of Versailles had treated a defeated Germany unjustly and that limited territorial adjustments and modifications could be effected to reduce tension with a resurgent Germany.

Another factor accounted for Franco-British appeasement of Nazi Germany. This was an old factor – fear of Russia. Since the time of Peter the Great when Russia became a European power other European states pursued the famous 'containment of Russia'. Winston Churchill, an influential British politician had long and arduously advocated the elimination of Bolshevik Russia. Winston Churchill has been portrayed as the relentless enemy of Hitler and Nazi German. This image blurs his obsessive antagonism to the Bolshevik Revolution. Prime Minister at a time when Britain was locked in a mortal combat with Nazi Germany, witness to the devastation that ended a century of British military eminence, Churchill mesmerized his compatriots with robust war rhetoric. But after Hitler invaded Russia, he toned down the anti-Hitler diatribes because his true antagonism was, and had always been, for Communist Russia.

Churchill was not alone in this. Numerous British aristocrats (including King Edward VIII) nursed fond hopes that the anti-Semitic, anti-Bolshevik Hitler would put an end to 'international Jewry' and the threat of communism which had seduced intellectuals and young men and women at British universities. The British aristocracy saw in Bolshevism an existentialist threat; champions of the proletariat could demolish patrician privileges, could incite British workers to rebel against the ruling class, and would try to liberate the benighted Asians and Africans from the blessings of British rule. As a young politician in the British War Office, he had pressed for Intervention against the Bolshevik regime in 1919.

This is illustrated by what Churchill wrote in *The Aftermath:*

> To the east of Poland lay the huge mass of Russia – not a
> wounded Russia only, but a poisoned Russia, an infected
> Russia, a plague-bearing Russia, a Russia of armed hordes not
> only smiting with bayonet and with cannon, but accompanied
> and preceded by swarms of typhus-bearing vermin which slew
> the bodies of men, and political doctrines which destroyed the
> health and even the souls of souls.

The Socialist British Prime Minister, David Lloyd George
called Churchill's hatred against Bolshevism as "madness in the
brain". Indeed Churchill's imagery and racist theories sound as
morbid as Hitler's infatuation with the Herrenvolk theory.

That Churchill's hatred of Russia was more than his hatred of
Germany is borne out by these words:

> Of all the tyrannies in history, the Bolshevist tyranny is the
> worst, the most destructive, and the most degrading. It is
> sheer humbug to pretend that it is not far worse than German
> militarism. Its atrocities are incomparably more hideous, on a
> larger scale, and more numerous than any for which the Kaiser
> is responsible.

And in a more informal chat with a fellow aristocrat Churchill
advised, "Kill the Bolshie, Kiss the Hun. Feed Germany; starve
Bolshevism; make Germany fight Bolshevism." This may have
been hyperbolic political rhetoric but there was an unexpressed
apprehension about that vast and enigmatic country which
influenced the policies of Britain and France. Since Hitler had
expressed his hatred of communism in *Mein Kampf,* other

European nations felt that it was wiser to appease Hitler who was an enemy of Bolshevik Russia than weaken him.

The authors feel this fear of communists ideology and the growing power of Russia was a determinant factor in appeasing Nazi Germany throughout the 1930's until it was late. The real enemy – Nazi Germany, and not Soviet Russia – was already at their gates. (This would not be the last time the fear of Russia led the West to ally with the real enemy. In 1979 the United States made a categorical mistake in arming the so-called mujahideen against the Soviet Union – an alliance whose fallout would make jihadists a global terror.)

The above reasons were responsible for Franco-British acquiescence to German rearmament (1935–1937), remilitarization of the Rhineland (1936), and annexation of Austria (March 1938). In September 1938, after signing away the Czech border regions – known as the Sudetenland – to Germany at the Munich conference, British and French leaders pressured France's ally, Czechoslovakia, to yield to Germany's demand for the incorporation of those regions. Despite Anglo-French guarantees of the integrity of Czechoslovakia, the Germans dismembered the Czechoslovak state in March 1939 in flagrant violation of the Munich Agreement.

Chamberlain did nothing to prepare for the defence of Poland. It was suggested that an alliance of Britain and Soviet Russia would halt Hitler's designs of invading Poland but the alliance failed to materialize. In 1939 Stalin, as devious as Hitler, hoped to deceive Hitler with declarations of friendship. Stalin, even more than Chamberlain, did not wish to be drawn into a war against Nazi Germany. British opinion was against collaboration with the Soviet Union. Even in the last days of August 1939, during the Danzig Crisis, Chamberlain was still trying to negotiate with Hitler through the British Ambassador and a Swedish intermediary Birger Dahlerus.

On 26 August 1939 Hitler demanded Danzig, but offered Britain a Non-Aggression Pact and a promise that Germany would defend the British Empire; Dahlerus was sent back with a message that "England was willing in principle to come to an agreement with Germany". Britain and France responded by guaranteeing the integrity of the Polish state.

On 1 September 1939, Germany invaded Poland. The Polish army was defeated within weeks of the invasion. From East Prussia and Germany in the north and Silesia and Slovakia in the south, German units, with more than 2,000 tanks and over 1,000 planes, broke through Polish defences along the border and advanced on Warsaw in a massive encirclement attack. After heavy shelling and bombing, Warsaw surrendered to the Germans on 27 September 1939. Britain and France realized they were the next targets. Using their guarantee of Poland's sovereignty as an excuse they declared war on Germany on 3 September 1939. The Soviet Union invaded eastern Poland on 17 September 1939. The demarcation line for the partition of German- and Soviet-occupied Poland was along the Bug River.

In October 1939, Germany annexed those former Polish territories along Germany's eastern border: West Prussia, Poznan, Upper Silesia, and the former Free City of Danzig. The remainder of German-occupied Poland (including the cities of Warsaw, Krakow, Radom, and Lublin) was organized under a civilian governor-general, the Nazi party lawyer Hans Frank. Nazi Germany occupied the remainder of Poland when it invaded the Soviet Union in June 1941.

PART II

WORLD WAR II

18

OUTBREAK OF WORLD WAR II

Germany and Soviet Union signed the Molotov-Ribbentrop Pact in August 1939.

This caused immense anxiety in Western Europe. Hitler had long planned an invasion of Poland, a nation to which Great Britain and France had guaranteed military support in the event of an attack by Germany. Hitler's pact with Stalin was designed to keep the Soviet Union neutral in the event of war against Britain and France. As early as 1939, German generals had warned Hitler against a war on two fronts. Hitler wanted a free hand to deal with the occupation of Poland. Further Stalin had agreed to the partition of Poland as Russia, Prussia and Austria had done in the 18th century.

On 1 September 1939 Hitler invaded Poland from the west; two days later, France and Britain declared war on Germany.

Thus began World War II.

On 17 September Soviet troops invaded Poland from the east. Poland could not resist attack from both sides. In early 1940 Germany and the Soviet Union divided control over the nation according to a secret protocol which was part of the Non-Aggression Pact. Soviet forces next occupied the Baltic States of Estonia, Latvia and Lithuania. When Finland offered passage to the Nazi army, the Soviet Union attacked Finland and defeated it in a brief war. During the six months following the invasion of Poland, Germany made no further moves against any other states on European territory. This interlude was called the 'Phoney War'. However there were battles on the sea between the British and German navies. German U-boat submarines attacked merchant shipping bound for Britain; more than a hundred ships were sunk up to March 1940.

Hitler's quest for the conquest of Europe began in April 1940. The German army invaded and occupied Norway and Denmark. On 10 May, German forces swept through Belgium and the Netherlands in what became known as a blitzkrieg, or lightning war. Three days later, Hitler's troops crossed the Meuse River and struck French forces at Sedan, which was at the northern end of the Maginot Line, the elaborate system of fortifications France had erected after World War I in the hope it would be an impregnable defensive barrier. But the German tanks tore through the Line and their planes attacked the rear. The defence strategy fell apart. The British Expeditionary Force was evacuated from Dunkirk in May 1940. The French mounted an offensive in Southern France which was swiftly crushed.

Seeing the collapse of France, Mussolini of Italy made the Rome Berlin Axis effective by declaring war on France and Britain in June 1940.

German forces entered Paris on 14 June; a new government formed by Marshal Philippe Pétain, a hero of World War I, immediately sued for armistice. Germany divided France into two zones, one under German military occupation and the other under Pétain's rule which was called Vichy France. With most of Europe under Germany it turned its eye on Britain whose protection against invasions in centuries past had been the

Channel that separated it from mainland Europe. Germany's planned invasion by sea was termed 'Operation Sea Lion'. As a prelude to this the Luftwaffe carried out wide spread bombing of Britain throughout the summer of 1940. The nocturnal air raids were particularly destructive. London stoically bore the brunt of the fury as well as the major industrial towns of Birmingham, Coventry and Manchester. Due to the density of population the civilian casualties here were enormous. The intense blitzkrieg was met by the courageous Royal Air Force which pushed back the Luftwaffe at the famous Battle of Britain on 14 September 1940. Encountering this unexpected resistance Hitler postponed 'Operation Sea Lion'. After exhorting his compatriots to fight Nazi Germany from hill sides and beaches, Prime Minister Winston Churchill sought and received necessary assistance from the United States in early 1941.

After Hungary, Romania and Bulgaria joined the Axis powers in early 1941, German troops overran Yugoslavia and Greece in April. Germany continued the pre-World War I Austro-German ambition to conquer the Balkans. This region had been a buffer between Western Europe and Russia from Byzantine and Ottoman times. The Versailles Treaty had created independent nation states in the Balkans which were militarily weak. They were ready prey for Hitler's army. He intended to use Eastern Europe as the bridgehead for invasion of Russia.

Hitler's decision to postpone the invasion of Great Britain was accompanied by negotiation by the Axis Powers of a tripartite alliance with Japan. Signed in September 1940, this Pact declared that a military attack on any member of the new Axis Powers by any nation would invoke the political, economic, and military assistance of the other two. It was aimed both at the United States as well as the Soviet Union. Germany and Italy lauded

Japanese aggression in the western Pacific. They also tried to ensure that Japan would attack the United States if the latter attacked German or Italian forces in the eastern Atlantic. This strategy was intended to keep the United States neutral in the war until Germany could overrun mainland Europe.

Germany made strenuous efforts to encourage Japan to enter the war against the British Empire. Foreign Minister Joachim von Ribbentrop tried to persuade the Japanese Ambassador to Germany, General Hiroshi Oshima, the benefit of this as Britain would collapse before German onslaught, leaving Japan to advance to South-East Asia, particularly the British colony of Singapore. The prospect of waging war against the United States was not universally approved in Japan. Japanese defence experts believed that such a war against an industrial giant would be a protracted one with no guarantee of victory.

It is astonishing that the Axis Powers did not form a joint military and naval policy. Japan retained its deep distrust of European nations after the war against Russia in 1905. To scrutinize military capabilities of its German partner, Japan sent emissaries to inspect it's defence establishments in early 1941. Somewhat satisfied Japan entered into military alliance with Germany. It was a cynical arrangement wherein both nations sought to gain advantage for itself rather than assist a loyal partner. Neither side envisaged a combined war against a common adversary. Germany planned to use Japan's military might against that of Britain in Asia which would render the British ineffective in the European theatre of war. Japan would thereby gain access to essential raw materials from conquered British colonies. By provoking the United States, Japan would engage it in the Pacific Ocean area. As Germany had no interests in East Asia so Japan had no territorial ambitions in faraway Europe.

The Pact was not so much for a common purpose but to gain benefit from an ally's war against another power. Similarly Japan sought to buy Soviet neutrality if it waged war against Britain in East Asia. By early summer of 1941 the Japanese government had prepared an 'Outline of National Policies in View of the Changing Situation'. As neither the governments of Germany or Italy participated in the decision making they could not coordinate their strategy. By contrast the Allied Powers frequently met and conferred during the war in Casablanca, Teheran, and Yalta. The defeat of both Germany and Japan may be partly due to the fact that they pursued their own agendas without a common purpose.

An embattled Britain could not deal effectively with Japan in East Asia. It was therefore the United States which felt the full blast of Japanese military might in the region. Large parts of China and European colonies were under Japan.

Even after witnessing the Japanese unstoppable advance in the Pacific, the United States was unprepared for the devastating attack on Pearl Harbour on 7 December 1941. This attack on Pearl Harbour gave President Roosevelt the resolve to enter World War II and obtain approval of the US Congress. When the United States declared war on Japan, Germany, Italy and the other Axis Powers immediately declared war on the United States. Japan continued with its victorious advance against the naval power of the United States until it was defeated in the Battle of Midway in June 1942. The tide turned against Japan from early 1943. In mid-1943, Allied naval forces attacked Japan strongholds in Pacific islands. This 'island-hopping' strategy soon brought costly victory. The Allied forces then planned the invasion of Japan.

19

STALIN AND HITLER

The mortal combat between two mighty dictators – Stalin and Hitler – was a phenomenon the world had not seen before. There had been other combats between nations led by their leaders but the battle between Stalin and Hitler was between two men who held absolute power over their nations. Both tyrants were of humble birth and were of nationalities different from the countries they ruled. Stalin was Georgian, Hitler was Austrian.

Germany had not been part of the Army of Intervention that tried to defeat the new Soviet state. The Soviet Union was not a signatory to the Treaty of Versailles of 1918 whereby Britain and France had imposed punitive war reparations on Germany. Consequently there was no cause for animosity between Russia and Germany in 1918. The terms of the Versailles Treaty were economically ruinous for Germany. The Great Depression and a runaway inflation added to Germany's woes. German morale was particularly low; its frontiers had shrunk and industrial belt in the Ruhr was shattered. The vindictive terms of the Versailles Treaty guaranteed a German *guerre de revanche* against Britain and France. By contrast, the Social Democratic Party in Germany looked to the fledgling Soviet Union for support; Germans felt no antipathy towards Russians. Both peoples were struggling against poverty. They had been united in the previous century by mutual admiration for their great literary and musical traditions which they considered to be superior to the rest of Europe.

The liberal Weimar Republic of Germany collapsed in 1929. The pristine ideals of communism also lay in tatters by 1929 when Stalin assumed total power. While Britain and France clung to their empires, Germany struggled for survival. Emergence of the Nationalist Socialist Party with Adolph Hitler at its head in 1933 promised the resurgence of Germany and changed the mood and temper of the country. As Hitler began repudiating terms of the Versailles Treaty the spectre of another war was seen but ignored by the world.

Stalin watched the rise of Germany with mixed feelings. There was satisfaction that Hitler had defied France and Britain by scrapping terms of the Versailles Treaty. Until 1936 Stalin had no conflict of interest with Hitler's policy. Both hated Jews. There was that small matter of burning the Reichstag when communists were blamed. But by 1937, Stalin had torn to shreds the ideals of Marxism and Hitler had displayed his contempt for European liberalism. Both looked upon Britain and France as adversaries.

The Soviet Union was in a transitional stage between an agrarian to an industrial economy. Its natural resources of manpower, minerals, gold and fuel were immense. But the capital goods industry was yet to stabilize. Heavy industrial machinery was purchased from the United States. Germany survived economically by exporting manufactured goods and industrial equipment to the Soviet Union in exchange for raw materials. It seemed as if cooperation between Germany and the Soviet Union would be mutually beneficial.

Maxim Litvinov, Soviet Commissar of Foreign Affairs, disagreed. As a member of the former Tsarist diplomatic service, he advocated signing of a Russo-French alliance. Litvinov condemned Germany for grabbing Russian territory under the terms of the Brest-Litovsk Treaty. He hastened to conclude a defensive treaty with France and Czechoslovakia.

Hitler's Panzer Division rolled into inoffensive Czechoslovakia on the pretext of protecting Sudeten Germans. Hitler and his friends expressed contempt for the Slav race. Britain acquiesced. Litvinov now saw the writing on the wall and advised Stalin against collaboration with Germany. He was replaced by the pro-German Vyacheslav Molotov.

Uneasy about the growing amity between Stalin and Hitler, Britain and France invited Soviet Union to form a defensive pact to protect Poland from Germany. Stalin made terms unacceptable to Poland. The proposed treaty fell through.

In a *danse macabre* France and Britain relished the thought of Nazi Germany and Communist Soviet Union engaged in a war to the finish. "Let the two devils (Stalin and Hitler) bleed each other to death," Churchill had earlier remarked wistfully to his king, Edward VIII. Stalin relished the idea of Germany embarking on a war of revenge against France and Britain. A long-drawn struggle between imperialist nations would weaken both sides while a neutral Soviet Union would concentrate on building its heavy industries and armaments. To do this, Stalin needed time. German invasion of Czechoslovakia left Stalin no illusions about any enduring friendship with Hitler. The day of reckoning was a matter of time.

As early as 1931, Rabindranath Tagore – aristocrat, educationist and metaphysical poet – wrote in *Letters from Russia*, "Russian people must build their strength swiftly. They have many adversaries."

In August 1939 the German Foreign Minister, Joachim von Ribbentrop arrived in Moscow. On 23 August he and Vyacheslav

Molotov signed the German-Soviet non-aggression pact. It is a matter of conjecture whether Stalin – taciturn, devious, ruthless, or Hitler – voluble, full of *sturm* and *drang,* ruthless, tried to outwit the other.

The terms of the Pact would enable Soviet Union to retrieve eastern Poland, which had been part of Tsarist Russia since 1776. Germany agreed to support the Soviet Union's claim on Bessarabia and accept Soviet "sphere of interest" in the Baltic and Balkan states. In return Stalin would allow Hitler to invade Poland which would provoke Britain to declare war on Germany. France would join Britain. Italy, an ally after the Rome-Berlin Axis would join Germany. Europe would once more experience Armageddon. And this time, Germany intended to inflict a crushing defeat on Britain and France for the humiliation of the Versailles Treaty.

While preparing for a denouement, the Soviet Union gambled with Nazi Germany to buy time. Earlier, Mikhail Tukhachevsky, commander of the Red Army who helped win the civil war for the Bolsheviks and evicted the Army of Intervention in 1922, advised Stalin to make massive investment in the armaments sector. He indicated the urgent need for 40,000 aircraft and 50,000 tanks. Defence expenditure increased from 12 to 18 per cent.

There were predicaments in the Red Army. During Stalin's Great Purge in the late 1930s, the officer corps of the Red Army was decimated and their replacements, appointed by Stalin for political reasons, lacked military competence and experience in warfare. Of the five Marshals of the Soviet Union appointed in 1935, only two survived Stalin's purge. Fifteen out of sixteen army commanders, fifty out of the fifty-seven corps commanders, one hundred and fifty-four out of the hundred and eighty-six divisional commanders and four hundred and one out of four hundred and fifty-six colonels were executed, and many other officers were dismissed. Some thirty-thousand Army personnel are estimated to have been executed. This was a devastating blow to the Red Army.

Stalin further demoralized army personnel by emphasizing the role of political commissars at the divisional level and below. This was to ensure the political loyalty of the Army to the regime. But in spite of efforts to ensure the political subservience of the armed forces, in the wake of the Red Army's poor performance in Poland and in the Winter War against Finland, about half the officers dismissed during the Great Purge were reinstated by 1941. Between January 1939 and May 1941, 161 new divisions were activated. Some 75 per cent of all the officers had been in their position for less than one year when the German invasion commenced in June 1941. This was due to the rapid increase in creation of military units before the outbreak of war.

That Stalin feared a Nazi invasion is indicated by the frenetic increase in production of armaments. By 1938 it was 40 per cent compared to 14 per cent increase in civil industry. Production of artillery, aircrafts and armoured vehicles received top priority. When Germany invaded Poland, the Soviet Defence Committee ordered construction of nine aircraft production plants, and seven plants for manufacture of aircraft engines. Consumer goods factories began producing war materials. While war waged in Europe in 1940, the Soviet Union increased production of combat airplanes over 70 per cent from the previous year. There was augmentation of weaponry for the Red Army with 7,000 new tanks and 82,000 artillery guns. Massive conscription of men and increased motorized rifle divisions and tank divisions enhanced the strength of the Red Army. The Soviet workday was increased from seven to eight hours and then to every day of the week. Discipline was on wartime footing.

The Red Army declared, "Should war be forced on Soviet Russia, we will conduct the war offensively and carry it onto enemy territory."

The conscripts were mainly peasants and workers who had little training in either combat or use of weapons. But as always, in time of national peril, Russian soldiers brushed aside all thoughts of danger to defend their motherland.

Stalin had expected Britain and France to fight for months. But France was saved from much damage by Marshal Pétain's deal with Hitler. After heroic resistance by the Royal Air Force against the Luftwaffe, Britain did not send ground troops to Europe. Taking advantage of British and French preoccupation with the war, Stalin sent troops to occupy parts of Eastern Europe to act as a buffer against German encroachment. In September and October 1939, the Soviet government held negotiations with Lithuania, Latvia and Estonia to establish military bases on Baltic ports. The Baltic nations were declared Soviet republics. When Moscow prepared to reoccupy Bessarabia, the former Russian eastern province of Romania, Ribbentrop assured the Soviet Union of German support. He demanded that Romania's remaining territory should be left free as Germany had commercial interests there.

There has been criticism of Soviet occupation of these territories during 1939. The Soviet Union defended the occupation on the ground that by extending the Soviet frontier into Eastern Europe it would have time to repel Nazi forces and prevent them from overrunning Russia. However at that time only four German infantry divisions and six militia divisions guarded the German-Soviet frontier. Foreign Minister Vyacheslav Molotov protested against the presence of German troops in Finland. All this deepened antagonism between Germany and the Soviet Union. Though Hitler was intent on 'Operation Sea Lion' – the invasion of England by which he could subjugate Britain and enable Germany to sequester the resources of the British Empire – he postponed it because it was more important for Germany to occupy Eastern Europe in order to grab that region's timber, fuel and food grains. Hitler felt that once Russia was defeated, he would be invincible and be master of Europe.

The prelude to war was assessed by the Soviet Union's excellent espionage system. They learned in December 1940 that Hitler had ordered his generals to defeat Soviet Russia in a swift and surprise invasion. All preparations for this massive attack were to be finalized by May 1941. In early 1941, Soviet and American Intelligence repeatedly warned Stalin of an impending German invasion. Russian double agent Victor Sorge informed Stalin of the date of the attack. Stalin knew that such an attack was imminent but decided not to escalate the tension between the two nations in order to buy time to strengthen the Red Army.

Germany concluded alliances with Hungary, Romania, and Bulgaria to provide easy access to Russia's western borders. Yugoslavia was a more difficult proposition. Though its government was pro-German, there was stiff resistance from the Yugoslav Communist Party headed by Josip Broz Tito who received financial and arms support from the Soviet Union. When the pro-German government was overthrown in March 1941, Hitler gave orders for the invasion of Yugoslavia and Greece. Germany's ally Italy became valuable in this Adriatic Sea campaign. Ships sailed for invasion of Yugoslavia from the ancient Roman port of Brindisi.

The Soviet Union now prepared in right earnest for a German invasion. By June 1941 Soviet armed forces deployed 2.7 million soldiers comprising 177 divisions near its western frontier. A total of 14 million reserves were activated. The army had 10,394 tanks, nearly 44,000 field guns and mortars. Over 7,139 combat aircraft occupied air force bases at the frontier. Some Western military districts established command posts close to the militarized frontier. Army staff and frontline administrative personnel were transferred there in mid-June.

General Georgy Zhukhov, Chief of Army Staff, instructed his officers:

> Wars are no longer declared; the aggressor strives far more to insure all the advantages of a surprise attack...The strategy of warfare is above all anchored in the correct thesis that the aggressor can only be beaten through offensive operations.

In May 1941, Stalin and Soviet dignitaries at the Frunze Military Academy commended the Red Army for its modernization and readiness for war. He announced:

> For us, the war plans are ready...There is a peace treaty with Germany, but that's just an illusion, a curtain behind which we can work.

He advised the Red Army:

> The present international situation, which is filled with unforeseeable possibilities, demands revolutionary decisiveness and constant readiness to launch a crushing advance upon the enemy... The soldiers are to be schooled in the spirit of an active hatred of the enemy and to aspire to take up the struggle against him, to be ready to defend our fatherland on the territory of the enemy and deal him a mortal blow.

Confrontation was imminent; German and Soviet armies massed along the frontier. German reconnaissance aircraft flew frequent sorties to monitor the Red Army. Stalin issued standing orders forbidding Soviet troops to fire on German aircraft in order to mislead the pilots about Soviet military strength. The Soviet government received information on the frenetic deployment of German troops and tanks that swarmed on Russia's western borders.

The people of Russia were soon to pay for Stalin's brutal and mindless purge of the Red Army hierarchy in 1937. The courageous and brilliant commanders who had won the Civil War and who had evicted the Army of Intervention in 1922 would have known how to meet the formidable challenge of the Wehrmacht. But they were buried under unmarked graves. The loss in terms of manpower and experience was incalculable. It is estimated that the casualties in 'Operation Barbarossa' were 4,973,820. The politically correct officers who had escaped the Great Purge of the Red Army proved their incompetence in the brief war against Finland and Poland. In panic, Stalin reinstated those he had dismissed. The charismatic General Konstantin Rokossovsky, who had been imprisoned on false charges was suddenly released and asked to take command.

The Purge left a relatively inexperienced leadership compared to that of their highly trained German counterparts. Hitler and his generals were fully aware of the depleted strength of the Red Army. This information gave Hitler the recklessness to invade a nation that no alien army had ever conquered. He had also entirely misjudged the temper of the Russian people.

They would fight not for Bolshevism; they would fight for their motherland.

20

OPERATION BARBAROSSA

'Operation Barbarossa' or *Unternehmen Barbarossa* was the code name for Nazi Germany's invasion of the Soviet Union. It began on 22 June 1941. The operation was named after the 12th century Emperor Frederick Barbarossa of the Holy Roman Empire who led the Third Crusade against Islam. Hitler's knowledge of the Crusades was shaky; he did not know that Emperor Barbarossa was drowned in a pool of mud near Jerusalem.

The ideological origins of the invasion can be found in Hitler's autobiography, *Mein Kampf* or *My Struggle*. As early as 1925 Hitler expressed a desire to conquer the newly established Soviet Union because Germans needed *Lebensraum* or living space. Hitler's contempt became hatred because Russia was ruled by "Jewish Bolshevik conspirators". Though Germany's historic destiny was *drang nach osten* (drive to the east), it had already suffered several defeats over the centuries, Hitler was determined to conquer Slav lands, and re-populate the conquered states with the Teutonic race.

German generals had warned Hitler that occupying Western Russia would create "more of a drain than a relief for Germany's economic situation". Hitler disagreed; he planned to dragoon Russian prisoners of war to serve in German industries. Further, occupation of Ukraine would supply Germany with agricultural produce while Russia's Caucasian oilfields would provide Germany the much needed fuel. Witnessing Soviet ineptitude in Finland in 1940, Hitler expected 'Operation Barbarossa' to be over swiftly; no one anticipated a protracted campaign continuing into the terrifying Russian winter. Clothes for the Russian winter had not been supplied to German troops; arrangements for vehicles and lubricants to function in the Russian winter were not made. Hitler ordered his generals to seize western Russia and Ukraine. Seizure of Moscow could wait. Generals Heinz Guderian, Gerhard Engel, and Ludwig Beck disagreed, stating that a captured Moscow would crush Soviet morale. But Hitler believed that after his victory over the Soviet Union, Britain would become a submissive ally. Western, central, southern and northern Europe, except Sweden, was already in his grip.

Hitler and his advisers underestimated the industrial and military might that Stalin had quietly built in ten years, albeit at horrific human cost. They underestimated Russia's three insurmountable assets – a boundless terrain that sucked in invaders while the defenders retreated and then pursued the invaders; crippling winters; fierce resistance of the Russian people. He had obviously not read Napoleon's ill-starred invasion of Russia.

About four million soldiers of Germany and its allies attacked the Soviet Union along a 2,900-kilometre frontier. Never in history had one nation deployed such a massive force against another nation. This formidable force was augmented by 600,000 armed vehicles and some 700,000 horses. These troops had been indoctrinated with anti-Slavism and anti-Semitism with plans for subjugation of the about-to-be conquered people.

At midday on 22 June 1941, the grim news of the invasion was broadcast to the Soviet people by Soviet foreign minister Vyacheslav Molotov with these words:

...Without a declaration of war, German forces fell on our country, attacked our frontiers in many places... The Red Army and the whole nation will wage a victorious Patriotic War for our beloved country, for honour, for liberty ... Our cause is just. The enemy will be beaten. Victory will be ours!

In this terrible hour of peril Stalin called upon Soviet citizens to fight – not for communism but for their motherland. Millions of Russians who had endured horrific cruelties, prepared as in 1914, to sacrifice everything for Mother Russia.

The siege of Leningrad was one of the aims of 'Operation Barbarossa'. The first heavy artillery shelling began in September 1941. All roads to the city were blocked so that fuel and food supplies could not reach the people. The German Luftwaffe dropped leaflets warning citizens of impending starvation. Germany expected Leningrad to "drop like a leaf".

Rarely in history had such onslaught met such resistance. Food supplies stopped. Germans bombed power stations so there was no electricity and heating. Dwindling food stocks could not be replenished. Rationing was unsuccessful. People brewed broth of leaves and seaweed, ate grease from machinery and then cats and dogs. Millions of seeds at the Plant Research Institute could have staved off deaths for a while. But scientists stubbornly guarded them for future agronomical research. Starving and exhausted, people died on the roads. Three thousand people were estimated to have died daily. Snow covered corpses littered the streets; there was nobody to bury them.

The Red Army fought on the outskirts of Leningrad and recaptured lost positions. Expecting that the siege of Leningrad would be swiftly over and citizens would surrender, German soldiers had not been provided with appropriate winter clothing. Many died in freezing temperatures. When the German forces retreated Russian engineers came to repair railway lines; trucks with food ploughed over frozen Lake Lagoda. But the supplies that reached Leningrad were inadequate. In the winter of 1941 some 52,000 people died. Though the exact number is not known it is estimated that about a million people died of starvation in one year.

Never in modern history did an enemy lay siege to a city to starve its citizens and quell them into submission. Such tactics, one likes to think, belong to medieval warfare. It was revived by Hitler's generals. Those who lived through those 900 odd days could never banish the horrific images of starvation and death. Stalin also showed incredible callousness by not trying to lift the siege because he wanted the full power of the Red Army to concentrate on Stalingrad the city bore his name. It is a tribute to the people of Leningrad that they were prepared to endure such devastation rather than surrender to the enemy. The Seige of Leningrad ended on 27 January 1944.

Leningradians offered another unforgettable spectacle of heroic dignity. In the midst of the siege Dmitry Shostakovich composed his famous 7th or Leningrad Symphony. To still German guns the Russian general defending Leningrad bombed Germany artillery and then broadcast the symphony over the city on loudspeakers. Resistance of the people stiffened.

The dilemma facing Soviet leadership was whether to free Leningrad by sending the Red Army there or concentrate on Stalingrad. The dilemma was resolved by the Germans who retreated from Russia's western front to concentrate on the newly opened front in Stalingrad.

Failure of 'Operation Barbarossa' was a turning point during World War II. For Germany it was a rude awakening. For the United States, Britain and France, Russian victory over the Wehrmacht made them realize that the Soviet Union was now a formidable force to contend with. The sagacious statesman, President Franklin Delano Roosevelt of the United States realized the imperative of alliance with Russia. He offered Stalin generous assistance in the war effort.

Russia would need every assistance for the bloodiest battle in history that was about to commence in a once-quiet town on the banks of the mighty Volga.

21

STALINGRAD

The Battle of Stalingrad was the turning point during World War II. It was the most brutal battle of World War II and one of the bloodiest battles in the history of warfare. Russian victory against a mighty adversary made it a superpower and changed the course of the war and history of the 20th century.

The Battle of Stalingrad began on 23 August 1942. It continued through the terrible winter of 1942 to 2 February 1943. It can be argued that victory of the Communist Red Army saved Europe from Nazi domination.

The Sixth Army of Germany under the command of General Friedrich Von Paulus advanced on Stalingrad and led the assault. At the rear came the Fourth Panzer Army. Germany's allies – Italy, Romania, Hungary and Croatia – joined the German forces at Stalingrad. General Paulus was tasked with occupying the oilfields in the Caucasus and Baku, centre of rich oilfields and the centre of communications in Southern Russia. The Reich's army desperately needed fuel in the third year of the war. Stalingrad stood on the path of Baku. Therefore Stalingrad had to be destroyed. Hitler told his generals that conquest of the city bearing Stalin's name would humiliate Stalin and shatter the morale of the Soviet Union. Hitler had no doubts about the outcome of the battle for Stalingrad. Russia had been severely wounded by 'Operation Barbarossa'. Russians were dying from war and hunger at a rate never seen in modern history. Hitler did not realize that Russians were grimly determined not to lose Stalingrad and the Caucasian oilfields. General Zhukov was given command of the defence of Stalingrad. Stalin instructed his chief commander, Georgy Zhukov, "Remember, not a step backwards."

Most of General Paulus' Sixth Army comprising some 300,000 men was inside the city where they wreaked unimaginable havoc in two months. Not only were soldiers killed; combatants died as well. The relentless artillery fire reduced the once prosperous town to a heap of rubble. There was hand-to-hand fighting in the streets between the two sides. Germans occupied large portions of the city but Russian forces often reoccupied areas within a few days.

After sustaining heavy losses of men and weapons, the Russians launched a fierce counter-offensive in November 1942. Marshal Zhukov surrounded the city with six million men. The regiment under Generals Prokofy Romanenko and Mikhailovich Chistyakov attacked from the north. Joining them was General Vasily Chuikov. The 52nd, 57th, 64th and 65th armies attacked from the south.

Then General Zhukov planned the counter-attack that defeated the German assault. He ordered his million soldiers to surround the city on all sides. The formidable German Sixth Army was trapped in snow-bound Stalingrad. General Paulus pleaded with Hitler to retreat and save thousands of German lives. On 24 January 1943 Hitler telegrammed Paulus:

> Surrender is forbidden. Sixth Army will hold their positions to the last man and the last round and by their heroic endurance will make an unforgettable contribution towards a defensive front and salvation of the Western world.

Trapped inside the city, soldiers froze in the cold. Food and fuel were scarce but most important of all ammunition was running out. It was the siege of Leningrad in reverse; the Germans were now the besieged. Acknowledging the possibility of defeat, Hitler made Paulus a Field Marshal, warning him that "no German Field Marshal has ever surrendered". But General Paulus defied tradition. On 31 January 1943 he surrendered the southern sector of Stalingrad. General Scherek surrendered the northern part. The battle of Stalingrad was the beginning of the end of the Third Reich caused by the huge loss of manpower and weaponry. Whatever was left of the famous Sixth Army of General Paulus began the retreat from Germany's eastern front in February 1943. Anticipating *Götterdämmerung*, Hitler, like a Wagnerian hero, stated grimly, "The god of war has gone over to the other side."

General Georgy Zhukhov contributed significantly to Russian victory in Stalingrad; he masterminded the assault on Germany and was soon to become the most decorated officer of the Soviet Army. Amidst jubilation in the Moscow Kremlin, Stalin observed, "Fascist Germany is facing disaster."

The losses sustained by both nations can never be known. The approximate estimate is loss of 750,000 men killed, missing or wounded from the German side while the Soviet army is estimated to have lost 478,741 men – killed or missing, while some 650,878 were wounded. Civilian losses were tragic. Despite the fact that thousands of Stalingrad inhabitants fled from the city by road or crossed the Volga on makeshift boats, some 40,000 people are estimated to have been killed – and not always by crossfire. Civilian Russians who helped their army compatriots were shot. Russians took some 91,000 German soldiers and officers as prisoners of war. General Paulus was taken a prisoner of war. He criticized the Nazi regime and went to live in East Germany after the war.

The intensity of the fighting can be gauged by a comparison. During World War II the American army lost 416,800 men from 1941 to 1945.

But the war was not over. Soon after, the victorious Soviet army began its advance towards Berlin. By August 1944 the Soviet army was inside Poland and parts of Romania. While the three powers met at Yalta, General Zhukov's army was readying to take Berlin, and US forces were preparing to invade Japan. Soviet victory over Germany impelled President Roosevelt to engage Stalin into a post war agreement on Europe. There had been a conference at Tehran in 1943 to discuss war strategy and now the Big Three – the United States, Soviet Union and Britain – met at Yalta on the Crimean coast to discuss a new world order.

The League of Nations had ended in shame by its failure to curb Italian-German aggression.

Now, the United States initiated establishment of the United Nations at Flushing Meadows to make another attempt to bring peace and security to a war-ravaged world. The American President knew that without Soviet participation, the United Nations would meet the same fate as its predecessor, the League of Nations.

Roosevelt, Stalin and Churchill wanted to establish a peaceful settlement between the victors. A triumphant Stalin prepared to state his terms for collaboration with the United States – acceptance of Soviet sphere of political influence in Eastern and Central Europe and expansion into Eastern Europe which Stalin stated was imperative for the security of Soviet Union; recognition of Mongolian independence from China; Soviet interest in Manchuria and Sakhalin islands. As President Roosevelt wanted Soviet support in the war against Japan and Soviet membership of the United Nations and independence of the Korean Peninsula, he was ready to cooperate. The Soviet Union became a founding member of the United Nations, a member of the Security Council with power to veto any decision detrimental to its interests. After the Yalta Conference the Allies established four occupation zones in Germany – French, British, American, and Russian. They divided the capital, Berlin, located in the Soviet sector, into four parts. The Russians promised free access from the western zones to Berlin.

Despite its apparent success, undercurrents of tension at the Yalta Conference presaged future conflicts on the horizon. That it succeeded at all was due to President Roosevelt's eagerness to end the war and usher in peace.

Soon after Stalin ordered General Zhukov to occupy Berlin. American forces had recently crossed the River Rhine, evoking fears that American troops would take Berlin. General Zhukov gathered two and a half million troops; 6,000 tanks and 40,000 artillery weapons were deployed for the final battle against Nazi Germany.

Though Germany was near collapse, its weak army offered a desperate resistance to the formidable Red Army. Germans were afraid of vendetta because their army had perpetrated atrocities during the war which had massacred millions of Russians. On 15 April 1945, Soviet forces launched a powerful artillery attack on German forces west of the River Oder which forced Germans to retreat from their positions. Zhukov then decided to send a huge force against them. German resistance was fierce but it was over in three days. The advancing Red Army suffered heavier losses than the retreating Germans. **Victory was dearly bought with the loss of 70,000 Russian lives.**

The battle for Berlin ended on 2 May 1945 when the hammer and sickle red flag was hoisted on the roof of the German Reichstag.

22

ALLIED VICTORY AND END OF WORLD WAR II

By 1943 British and American forces defeated the Italians and Germans in North Africa. The inscrutable and brilliant General Erwin Rommel retreated from his stronghold. Allied forces invaded Sicily and then the mainland of Italy. One of the bloodiest battles of World War II was fought on the hill of Monte Cassino. Mussolini's government fell in July 1943. As he fled from Rome he and his mistress were captured and killed; their bodies were then hung in the Piazzale Loreto in Milan. German forces began their retreat but they continued the war against the Allied armies. The liberation of Rome on 5 June 1944 was symbolic of Allied victory in Italy.

A massive invasion of German-held Europe commenced in June 1944. Allied forces landed on the beaches of Normandy in northern France. Nazi Germany began a losing battle in Western Europe. After the victory of the Red Army at Stalingrad Soviet troops began their advance to Poland, Czechoslovakia, Hungary and Romania. Germany offered futile resistance in the Battle of the Bulge in December 1944. The Allied land invasion of Germany was preceded by a relentless aerial bombardment in February 1945 culminating in the formal surrender of Germany on 8 May 1945.

Seeing the end of his dream of world domination Hitler committed suicide in his Berlin bunker.

At the Potsdam Conference in July–August 1945, American President Harry S Truman, British Prime Minister Winston Churchill and Soviet leader Josef Stalin discussed the ongoing war with Japan as well as terms of peace with Germany. It was decided to divide Germany into four occupation zones; each to be administered by the Soviet Union, Britain, United States and France. Stalin demanded a free hand in Eastern Europe. Considering the decisive role the Soviet Army had played in defeat of Nazi Germany, Churchill and Truman agreed to the Soviet Union's sphere of influence in Eastern Europe. Soviet cooperation and neutrality was now required in the defeat of Japan.

US forces sustained severe casualties in the two campaigns at Iwo Jima (February–March 1945) and Okinawa (April–June 1945). Though Japan was near defeat and the population unarmed, the United States began a new and terrible chapter in warfare by ordering the atomic bombing of Nagasaki and Hiroshima in the first week of August 1945. After this terrible catastrophe imperial Japan accepted the terms of surrender on 10 August 1945.

Thus ended the most devastating and destructive war in human history. The war was not confined to Europe. It affected the Middle East, Africa and Asia. Though never accurately calculated, the loss of human lives was estimated at around sixty million people, of which the Soviet Union alone paid with twenty seven million people dead. The warfare in four continents claimed approximately twenty seven million Russians, four million Germans, two million Chinese and one million Japanese lives. The Soviet Union, Britain and France lost millions of civilians.

Millions more were injured, and still more lost their homes and property.

Simultaneously with carnage and chaos World War II ushered in a new age in science, technology and medicine. Vaccinations against various maladies lowered mortality rates and enhanced population growth. Progress in electronics and computers (first developed by the British scientist Alan Turing at Benchley Park) transformed communication systems in the post-war world.

The use of atom bombs in Japan changed not only the nature of warfare but altered the very idea of humanism. It also facilitated the use of nuclear energy for peaceful purposes in industry.

Soviet victory over Nazi Germany enabled the spread of Soviet ideology and communism in Eastern Europe and China. The war ended with victory for two superpowers – the Soviet Union and United States. Neither had planned vendetta against Germany after World War I. Those who had drafted the Treaty of Versailles – Britain and France – paid a heavy price for trying to contain Germany.

A new age began with the two superpowers – the Soviet Union and United States – that would draw the world into another war, less destructive but more decisive, the Cold War.

PART III

THE COLD WAR AND NEW WORLD ORDER

23

THE COLD WAR – 1946–1991

It was the longest war in modern history. It was a unique war because neither side made a formal declaration of war. In the Cold War, the two formidable antagonists did not fight on battlefields. They declared that they fought for ideologies. These ideologies provided a camouflage for the quest for power and influence. There were no victors or vanquished in the interminable chess game between the Soviet Union and United States.

There was a third party in this war – the so-called Third World – which had lived under colonial rule. They watched the chess game with secret relish and flaunted their political virginity before those who sought to claim both their soil and their souls. Sometimes Third World nations were beneficiaries of the Cold War – such as Pakistan – that were morally and politically neutral but wrested what advantages they could. Sometimes those countries tried to play a dangerous game between the two Cold War combatants. These chess-board pawns – comprising millions of people in Asia, Africa, and Latin America – engaged in wars staged by the superpowers who waited and checkmated each other when they could. When blood was spilt it was that of the pawns' while the kings brooded over the next move on the chess-board of continents.

The Cold War was accompanied by an elusive peace because neither side dared to declare an armed conflict that could destroy both. The nuclear deterrent was regarded as the antidote to the certainty of mutual destruction, a myth which Japan rejected after the incinerating holocaust of Hiroshima and Nagasaki. But Europe enjoyed an enduring peace never before experienced in the history of the last millennium.

Britain, France, Germany and other Central European nations were exhausted after two world wars. Many of their cities were in rubble. These nations were the real beneficiaries of the Cold War because the United States aided their reconstruction to ensure that they did not turn to the communist ideology of the Soviet Union. But the people of Yugoslavia, who paid with their lives and who had fought Nazism did not claim benefits from the Cold War. Those who had collaborated with the Nazis were killed by their compatriots. The eight million Yugoslav people put into slave labour by Nazi Germany returned home.

The West began 'de-Nazification' at the Nuremberg and Tokyo War trials. While some prominent Nazis were sent to prison, others escaped to South America. The US rehabilitated and employed many German scientists and espionage agents to work for them. More astonishing was that some Nazi military men were employed by Israel in 1948 to wage war on Palestinian Arabs. The more notorious of these was Otto Skorzeny, a Austrian born SS Obersturmbannfuhrer who collected former SS Wehrmacht officers for the Mossad. Another former Nazi officer was Ulrich Schnafft. The Holocaust was forgotten in the land-grabbing that followed.

By the end of 1945 the mounting tension between the Soviet Union and United States impeded a peace settlement. United States held the advantage in nuclear weapons and world trade.

The Soviet Union strove hard to establish military parity and political eminence in the non-Western world where the Cold War conflict was fierce.

At the Potsdam Conference in the summer of 1945 a council of ministers drafted peace treaties. Protracted negotiations resulted in treaties with Italy, Romania, Bulgaria, Hungary and Finland. In 1951, the Treaty of San Francisco was signed between the West and Japan – a treaty that left Japanese sovereignty diminished.

Before the chill of the Cold War set in, there was US-Soviet cooperation at an international level.

The United States and Soviet Union were unanimous in their support for establishing an international organization that would maintain peace throughout the world. The failure of the League of Nations was not due to its organizational ineptitude but because it's founding members – Britain and France – continued to pacify Hitler when he began violating terms of the Versailles Treaty. During World War II, the United States, Soviet Union and Britain proposed a new organization. The draft Charter of the United Nations was composed in June 1945.

Apart from maintenance of peace and security, other organizations were established with specific tasks: Food and Agricultural Organization, International Labour Organization, World Health Organization and United Nations Educational, Scientific, and Cultural Organization.

These affiliated agencies proved more effective since the battle for power was not acute. But the United Nations suffered from the same impediment as the League of Nations; the conflict between international law and national sovereignty. The United Nations proved effective in maintaining peace only when both the United States and Soviet Union supported the same cause as in the Suez crisis of 1956.

The United States also helped establish other multilateral organizations such as the International Monetary Fund, the World Bank and GATT, the forerunner of the World Trade Organization. While the organizations were intended to offer economic assistance to developing nations, the long arm of the United States sought to influence economic policies of these nations.

The fundamental principles of any nation's foreign policy – capitalist, communist or non-aligned – spring from the need to maintain national security. For this internal stability is as necessary as maintenance of adequate defence force.

Soviet foreign policy makers emphasized the imperative to support national liberation struggles. Dismantling of colonial empires made the newly liberated sovereign states turn to the Soviet Union, an avowed opponent of colonialism that wanted to nurture friendly relations with Third World nations as this would help spread Soviet influence. Until 1991 the other tenet of Soviet foreign policy was safeguarding the power and influence of the Communist Party of the Soviet Union and preserving its presence and influence in Eastern Europe as guaranteed under the terms of the Warsaw Pact.

The United States, Western Europe and monarchies of the Middle East considered the Soviet Union's communist ideology to be a threat. Notwithstanding its vast size and ignoring its formidable potential, diplomatic recognition had been withheld by some states. But the Soviet Union's emergence as a superpower made her a founding member of the United Nations and one of the five permanent members of the Security Council. Recognition was accorded by all nations to this new superpower.

In 1955 Soviet leaders considered modifying Stalin's hostile anti-Western policy which they felt would provide them respite and energy to rebuild the Soviet economy and consolidate Soviet power. They stated that a nuclear war would destroy human civilization. So in 1955 Premier Nikita Khrushchev informed US President Dwight Eisenhower of Soviet commitment to "peaceful coexistence" with capitalist nations. Khrushchev advocated friendship with governments of non-aligned nations instead of collaboration with communist parties of those nations – a strategy Trotsky had advocated. This cemented friendship with non-Western, non-aligned nations.

Taking advantage of Khrushchev's 'Thaw', and misreading Soviet intentions, Eastern European nations sought to remove Soviet authority. There were uprisings in Poland in 1955, Hungary in 1956 and Czechoslovakia in 1968. The Soviet Army put down these uprisings. This earned severe criticism on the world stage but the Soviet Union successfully sent a message to the United States and its allies that Russia would not allow dismemberment of the Warsaw Pact.

Soviet relations with the United States fluctuated. When the Soviet Union shot down a United States U-2 reconnaissance aircraft over Soviet territory, Khrushchev stormed at the United States for violating Soviet airspace and cancelled a summit meeting with Eisenhower in 1960. When the United States refused Khrushchev's desire to turn over the western sector of Berlin to East Germany, the Berlin Wall was erected in 1961. After the Cuban Missile Crisis of 1962, Khrushchev's Russia advocated a policy of peaceful relations with John F Kennedy's United States.

These episodes were symptoms rather than causes of US-Soviet discord. The rivalry was about supremacy. Both the United States and Soviet Union sped ahead in missile technology and space achievements. While Soviet diplomacy triumphed in the non-Western world, the United States made the mistake of supporting oppressive regimes in West Asia and Latin America. Uneasy at the nascent power of the Soviet Union after the war, the United States began arming Germany. Yet both states feared a nuclear holocaust. To minimize the threat, Kennedy and Khrushchev established the 'hotline' between Washington and Moscow in 1963. To reduce the likelihood of accidental nuclear war, both states signed the Limited Test Ban Treaty. It was only in 1975, through the signing of the Helsinki Accords that the redrawn map of Europe was recognized by both sides.

Rival ideals of the Cold War cast its long shadow on most international events between 1946 and 1991. The West insisted that this war was about fundamental differences in perception – in economic and social development, private enterprise, individual freedom, etc. Russia challenged the West from a high moral ground. What about the socio-economic conditions of the impoverished non-Western world which had been colonized and plundered for several centuries to build the capitalist systems of Europe? Asians had not experienced either political freedom or equality during colonial rule. African slave labour had been the basis of the US economy until President Abraham Lincoln abolished slavery. In their own continent Africans were debarred from entering places visited by white settlers. The pernicious doctrine of Apartheid found many champions in the West which normally protested when human rights were violated by other nations. Adventurers from Spain and Portugal had decimated indigenous populations in Latin America and then built their colonies. The American United Fruit Company controlled the trade of Latin America. Western nations did not raise righteous voices against these demographic and ecological disasters until

Fidel Castro and Che Guevara opposed them in the late 20th century.

As for religious freedom, the Christian Church, allied with the State and exuding political power, upheld the cause of the poor and the oppressed through saints and mystics like Francis of Assisi. The Church had punished dissent from dogma by the stigma of heresy. The Italian astronomer Giordano Bruno was burnt at the stake for declaring that the earth revolves around the sun – a theory endorsed by Galileo a century later who managed, through Venetian diplomacy, to escape the wrath of the Inquisition. Thousands of free thinkers, agnostics and atheists were burnt at the stake for heresy. Conquered 'heathens' and 'pagans' of Asia who declined conversion to Christianity were treated with scorn until European Orientalists discovered the legacy of ancient 'pagan' civilizations.

It was not an easy ride for the Soviet Union. It had first to consolidate its position on its vulnerable frontier in Eastern Europe. From 1945 to 1948 the long arm of the Soviet Union extended to Eastern Europe where there were friendly coalition governments. Communist Party members occupied powerful positions in the coalition governments; opposition parties gained largely symbolic posts. The initial popularity of communists among people of Hungary, Romania and Bulgaria was because their upper classes had been oppressive and had allied with Nazis. Communists were integral to Partisan movements – the main resistance groups against Nazi rule. Eastern European governments headed by Communist Party members came under Soviet influence and were called Soviet satellites. Stalin kept these governments under strict control and viewed with suspicion communists who were also fierce nationalists. Tragically the scenario of the 1930's in Russia was now repeated in Eastern

Europe. Dedicated communists like the Hungarian Imre Nagy, whose first loyalty was to their nation rather than to the Soviet Union, were eliminated. In the end the removal of the nationalist communists adversely affected the Soviet Union.

President Harry S Truman responded to Soviet policy by announcing that the United States would support any country threatened by communist aggression. Soon after proclamation of the Truman Doctrine in 1947, the United States sent economic and military aid to prospective allies. The Truman Doctrine sprang from the theory of 'containment' of the Soviet Union propounded by George Frost Kennan, an American career diplomat and analyst whose advice fuelled anti-Soviet paranoia. He advised "a long-term, but firm and vigilant containment of Russian expansive tendencies". Later Kennan amplified this in his famous book, *Russia and the West*. He stated that cooperation with the Soviet Union was not possible because of that country's "neurotic view of world affairs and the traditional and instinctive Russian sense of insecurity…". These confrontational views were supported by the formidable arms lobby in Washington that wanted another big war.

President Truman did not wish to precipitate hostilities with the Soviet Union. He considered withdrawing troops from Europe to reassure the Soviet Union of America's peaceful intentions. The celebrated journalist and international affairs analyst Walter Lippmann advised that diplomacy and not militarism would bring stability in US-Soviet relations. He proposed withdrawal of US forces from Europe, a Germany unified but demilitarized. He believed that creation of dubious satellite states to support American policy would be unwise.

The struggle against Nazi Germany had brought the United States and Soviet Union together. Now the United States feared

Russia's declared intention to support international communism. After attaining the status of a superpower, secure in its nuclear position, its territory untouched by battles – unlike war-ravaged Russia – the United States expected a peaceful dominance of the world which a former ally was now challenging in the Balkans, China, and the United Nations Security Council. The United States was also uneasy with the Soviet Union's covert support of communist parties in France, Italy, Greece and Spain where war and poverty had made fertile terrain for communism.

To reduce the attraction for communist economics, Secretary of State George C Marshall advocated massive economic assistance through the Marshall Plan to impoverished Western European nations which helped their economies to recover. The European Recovery Program helped these European states to substantially increase industrial production which in turn offered employment. This brought a measure of prosperity higher than pre-World War II levels. Economic stability brought political stability to Europe.

The US marshalled Western Europe into a system of containment aimed at limiting and ultimately diminishing Soviet power.

The North Atlantic Treaty Organization (NATO) was formed by the United States in 1949. It was to provide the United States with allies in the forthcoming ideological, political and economic warfare against the Soviet Union. Canada, Britain, France, Norway, Denmark, Iceland, Italy, Belgium, Netherlands and Luxembourg became members of NATO. Greece, Turkey and West Germany joined later. This alliance 'contained' Soviet Union on its western frontier.

The southern frontiers of the Soviet Union were encircled by Iran, Iraq, Syria, Turkey, and Pakistan in 1955 through the

Baghdad Pact. By giving economic and military aid to these states, the United States expected these regimes to outlaw communism that was gaining ground among the disaffected Arab intelligentsia.

The Soviet Union responded by forming the Warsaw Pact in 1955 whereby the nations of Eastern and Central Europe became its military allies.

Stalin died in March 1953, bringing to close a tumultuous era in Russian history. There had been cruelty, oppression, sacrifice, progress and triumph. If greatness in politicians and statesmen is to be measured by achievements, then Stalin qualified for the adjective. He transformed the Soviet Union from a semi-feudal economy to a mighty industrial and military power. It is a matter of debate if a more humane leader would have been able to drag Russia from near defeat and disaster in 1941 to the victory of May 1945 when the triumphant Soviet Army captured a Berlin in rubble, the city where Russia's destruction was planned by Hitler. It was all at a tragic and terrible cost. Russia has always paid dearly for its triumphs.

After Khrushchev's denunciation of Stalin's rule, members of the Warsaw Pact demanded greater autonomy. The Hungarian Uprising in 1956 was followed by the Prague Uprising in the spring of 1968 led by liberal members of the Communist Party of Czechoslovakia which began to loosen censorship and opened relations with the West. Brezhnev responded by sending Soviet and Warsaw Pact troops to Czechoslovakia where the rebel Anton Dubcek was deposed and a pro-Soviet group was established. The Soviet Union announced the Brezhnev Doctrine (echoing the Monroe Doctrine 150 years back) which declared that the Soviet Union would maintain its hegemony in Eastern Europe. Soviet opposition to the reform movement intimidated similar attempts of Romania and the Polish Solidarity trade union movement of Lech Walesa. The Warsaw Pact countries devised an astute move by resorting to Euro-Communism which enabled them to establish commercial and economic ties with other European nations under the facade of communism.

It is only Yugoslavia that Stalin and his successors failed to dominate. The communist Partisan leader Marshal Josip Broz Tito who had fought against the German Army, now defied Stalin and set his own communist agenda. But even the liberal, non-aligned Tito could be intolerant of dissent. He imprisoned his friend and comrade Milovan Djilas for writing against the corruption of communism in his celebrated book *The New Class*. Marshal Tito performed a remarkable jugglery; as a communist he upheld basic tenets of Marxism, as a nationalist he defied Stalin and without joining NATO he received financial support from the United States.

The Soviet Union and its allies challenged the West in Greece, Turkey, and Iran and encouraged socialist/communist parties there.

The contest between the two nations continued with mutual fear, anger and bitterness but neither dared to declare actual war. After the Soviet Union exploded an atom bomb in 1949, the United States became cautious. The United States knew that an atom bomb could not be dropped on Moscow – as on Nagasaki and Hiroshima – without cataclysmic consequences to itself. The two armed camps ominously resembled the situation before the two world wars.

Speaking at the National Defence University, Washington, DC, General Fred Weyand, US Army Chief of Staff from 1974 to 1976 reflected the Cold War mood when he stated that the United States had to fight the Soviet Union on the political, psychological, economic and defence front. The soldier did not beat about the bush when he said, "This is what power is all about – to determine whether the US will be dominant or dependent in relation to the other nations in the world."

The setback to US prestige in the Vietnam War deepened its hostility to the Soviet Union which had supported the communist Ho Chi Minh with arms and funds.

Relations between the two superpower camps fluctuated between guarded amity to suspicious hostility. They decided to negotiate a viable nuclear and armaments policy. After signing the Treaty on Non-Proliferation of Nuclear Weapons or the NPT in July 1968, the two nations commenced discussions on Strategic Arms Limitation Talks (SALT) in 1969. Brezhnev and Nixon signed the Anti-Ballistic Missile Treaty and the Interim Agreement on the limitation of strategic offensive arms at the Moscow Summit of May 1972. Both agreements called a halt to deployment of strategic defensive and offensive weapons. There followed a détente between the two superpowers; they decided to limit the number of offensive weapons on both sides. The negotiations culminated in the Helsinki Accords in 1975, which ratified the post-war status quo in Europe. They also agreed to respect basic principles of human rights.

However, the Soviet Union continued to increase deployment of weapons, enabling it to attain superiority in strength compared with the United States. Although SALT II had been signed earlier by Presidents Leonid Brezhnev and Jimmy Carter in 1979, this was cancelled after Soviet intervention in Afghanistan later that year. The United States imposed a grain embargo on the Soviet Union and boycotted the Moscow Summer Olympics in 1980. The Cold War was now renewed with deeper antagonism.

Now, both possessed advanced nuclear weaponry. Ironically it was this fear of Armageddon that kept the two superpowers in check but through 'controlled conflicts'. The world became bi-polarized in hostility, in ideologies, in the arms race. Paradoxically it also became safer. It was in the proxy wars of pawns that lay the danger on the chess-board.

24

THE NON-ALIGNED MOVEMENT

The Non-Aligned Movement (NAM) was a dream doomed to failure because it was inspired by ideals that have no place in international power politics. Nations that had been under colonial rule were witness to the depredations of imperialism, the impoverishment by foreign powers that diverted resources from colonies to their lands, and finally the humiliation of foreign rule. Countries which gained independence from imperial powers decided that they wanted to shape their own political and economic destinies. They refused to be drawn into wars between European/Western states and become cannon fodder for fulfilling the hegemonic agenda of powerful nations.

That they could take this bold stand, ironically, was because of the Cold War. The Soviet Union was satisfied that former colonies of Western powers wanted to break free from the influence of former rulers. This drastically reduced the influence as well as power of the imperial/colonial nations.

Soviet foreign policy makers drew their guidelines from Lenin's Decree where he had upheld the right of self-determination of all subjugated nations. They recognized the need to vigorously support national liberation struggles. Dismantling of colonial empires made the liberated and new sovereign states turn to the Soviet Union, an avowed opponent of colonialism, which wanted to nurture friendly relations with Third World nations as this would strengthen Soviet influence. The other aims and certainly more serious goals were disarmament by nations which would eliminate the threat of war. This required peaceful coexistence with capitalist countries.

Prime Minister Jawaharlal Nehru of India and his cabinet colleagues were the driving force behind NAM. President Gamal Abdel Nasser of Egypt, President Sukarno of Indonesia, President Kwame Nkrumah of Ghana, and President Tito of Yugoslavia enthusiastically joined this group. Those nations struggling for independence lent their support.

As the world began to be divided into two armed groups, the first Afro-Asian Conference was organized at Bandung, Indonesia in the summer of 1955. The agenda was to formulate the purpose and strategy for non-alignment.

Representatives of twenty-nine nations met there to announce their agenda. These were national self-determination, mutual respect for sovereignty, non-aggression, non-interference in internal affairs of other nations and equality between all nations. The delegates adopted the Five Principles of Peaceful Coexistence, or *Panchsheel* as Nehru called it, designed to promote solidarity among nations emerging from colonial rule. A communiqué was signed and issued that announced NAM's objectives – promotion of economic and cultural cooperation, protection of human rights and the principle of self-determination, end to racial discrimination and a reiteration of the importance of peaceful coexistence. The leaders hoped to focus on the potential for collaboration among the nations of the Third World, promoting efforts to reduce their reliance on Europe and North America. The leaders unequivocally announced their intention not be involved in superpower rivalries and condemned the Cold War. The non-aligned nations declared they had battles of their own to fight – poverty, illiteracy, disease, malnutrition.

The Soviet Union under Nikita Khrushchev played an astute role at the Afro-Asian Conference. Soviet delegates came unobtrusively, carrying messages of goodwill and professed support to nations struggling for self-determination. They also announced their support for the policy of non-alignment to reduce tension in the world.

By contrast US Secretary of State John Foster Dulles sent neither benevolent greetings nor delegates. The State Department made a tactical error by observing that these newly freed nations were displaying disturbing socialist leanings. American foreign policy makers made no attempts to allay the fears of the non-aligned nations about their intentions.

Delegates at the Conference observed that while the United States professed to support national self-determination and freedom of Afro-Asian nations, their military and economic alliances were with the very powers that had a colonial past. Further, they observed that the racial discrimination so rampant in the United States and the ancillary segregation policies against Black Americans was a violation of equality and human dignity for which NAM strove. These declarations at the Bandung Conference stirred American hostility to NAM.

Khrushchev immediately advocated friendship with governments of non-aligned nations instead of collaboration with communist parties of those nations – a strategy Trotsky had advocated. This cemented friendship with non-Western, non-aligned nations. Simultaneously Premier Khrushchev informed US President Dwight Eisenhower of Soviet commitment to "peaceful coexistence" with capitalist nations. This reassured non-aligned nations as they did not want to be caught in superpower conflicts.

Within a year, the non-aligned world was dismayed to find that the principles of peaceful co-existence was flouted when the United States concluded two military alliances in the Third World – the Baghdad Pact that drew oppressive governments of West Asia and Iran, and the SEATO of South-East Asian nations, to counter Soviet influence in South and East Asia.

This produced a backlash. Resentment of American alliance with these states made the non-aligned states lean towards the Soviet Union. America's open support of Pakistan against India made the latter reluctant to condemn Soviet suppression of the Hungarian Uprising in 1956. The Soviet Union's unwavering support to India at the United Nations again made India silent during the Prague Uprising. Other non-aligned nations followed India. Soviet support, they declared, had no strings attached whereas American support meant curtailing of sovereignty through military alliances.

Sadly, the first real violator of the Bandung spirit was neither the United States nor the Soviet Union. It was a leading participant of the Bandung Conference. After exchange of visits with India, and reiteration of the Five Principles of Peaceful Coexistence or *Panchsheel* signed in Delhi, and effusive professions of 'Hindi-Chini Bhai Bhai' (Indo-Chinese Brotherhood) China began intrusions in Tibet whose guarantee of sovereignty and autonomy had been part of a treaty between the two nations.

Discontent with inadequate Soviet aid, annoyed by Soviet neutrality in the Indo-Chinese dispute, of peaceful coexistence with the United States, China grew increasingly hostile to the Soviet Union. Chafing in the role of a junior partner in the communist world, China began creating its own spheres of influence. It decided to become a nuclear power. Moderate communists of the Soviet Union opposed this confrontational attitude. China plucked allies from the Soviet sphere such as little Albania. The communist world was divided between Russia and China. Within a decade China would abandon its fierce commitment to Marxian ideology and plunge into an anti-Soviet, anti-Indian alliance with the United States!

In 1960, the General Assembly of the United Nations voted the Declaration on the Granting of Independence to Colonial Countries and Peoples. In 1961 NAM was officially declared in Belgrade. It was followed by the creation of United Nations Conference on Trade and Development which was intended to assist creation of a New International Economic Order.

As NAM was a byproduct of the Cold War, so it lost both its relevance as well as its urgency after dissolution of the Soviet Union. The question of neutrality did not matter if there were no superpowers fighting for dominance. The nations which had looked to the Soviet Union for military, scientific and technological aid had to look westward for support. Finally the lure of globalization and its attendant profits made informal alliances necessary.

Nevertheless NAM will remain as an experiment in international relations whereby nations sought to remove conflicts and wars by creating a new alignment of the non-aligned.

25

TWILIGHT OF EMPIRES

The dismantling of former European empires in Asia and Africa brought a paradigm change in geopolitical alignments. Imperial policies did not change; they came in a different garb. Emergence of the United States and Soviet Union provided a different scenario. The post-war rivalry and even present-day rivalry is not over annexation of territories but over spheres of influence, trade and information war. The global stage has another dimension not present in colonial times; the nation-states liberated from colonial rule or veiled protectorates have a voice in political developments, especially if in their territories they possess valuable fuel or mineral resources. Some of them, like Iran, have emerged from the status of pawns to knights and bishops on the chess-board of continents.

India

The overture to the Symphony of End of European Empires had commenced, paradoxically, in the high noon of imperialism. Its first stirrings were felt in 18th-century India when great British Indologists discovered what Indians had forgotten for a millennium under Muslim rule. Sir William Jones led the movement; he was the first Indian historiographer; he dated Indian history through corroborative evidence from Greek chronicles, translated Sanskrit classics, and brought the grandeur of Indian civilization to the attention of Britain and the West – and to Indians who had been barred learning from Brahmanical texts. Warren Hastings, the first Governor-General of India and an imperialist par excellence gathered scholars of the East India Company to study and translate Sanskrit works. He commissioned Charles Wilkins to translate into English the *Bhagavad Gita* – which contains the core doctrine of Hinduism. While annexing Indian territories, the East India Company also financed these cultural projects. Together with Sir William Jones, this enigmatic and brilliant man established the Asiatic Society – for furthering knowledge of Indian civilization. A gifted epigraphist, James Prinsep deciphered the Ashokan script and enabled historians and scholars to study the massive amount of chronicles and literary works belonging to the first and second millennia before Christ. Sir Alexander Cunningham established the Archaeological Survey of India to study, classify, restore and preserve the monumental physical heritage of India.

Another fervent imperialist, Lord George Curzon, fortified this movement by passing the Ancient Monuments Preservation Act, 1904 which laid down laws for preservation of Indian monuments and antiquities. A brilliant cluster of British Indologists followed. Their efforts were enriched by gifted Indologists from Russia and Germany. This was the prelude to the Bengali and later Indian Renaissance. It was also the starting point for the freedom struggle in India.

1905 was a momentous year of revolts. In Russia it was the prelude to the Bolshevik Revolution. In India it saw the growth of armed revolutionaries or terrorists as the British Raj termed them. The Indian National Congress was formed (again paradoxically) by a British civil servant, Sir Alan Octavian Hume.

This became the nucleus for the independence movement. When Indian leaders assured the British Raj of their loyalty during World War I hopes were raised that Britain might consider either self-rule, home rule or autonomy for Indians. When this did not fructify, murmurs of discontent were heard. These murmurs became roars of rage after the massacre of innocent civilians at Jallianwala Bagh in Punjab on 13 April 1919 which happened to be the Punjabi New Years's Day. The non-cooperation and civil disobedience movement began in 1921 under the leadership of Mohandas Karamchand Gandhi. The famous Salt March of 1931 expressed Indian defiance for the iniquitous salt laws. Wearying of promises and what he felt to be degrading passive conduct, Subhash Chandra Bose left the Congress Party and formed the Forward Bloc in 1939. His agenda was simple – eviction of British Raj by armed rebellion. He raised the Indian National Army towards this aim. But he died in mysterious circumstances in an air crash after taking off from Taiwan. Many Indians believed it was an assassination – to remove a charismatic rival to Gandhi and Nehru.

A nation which inspired India was the United States of America. The Hindu philosopher Swami Vivekananda attended the Conference of Religions in 1896 in Chicago. This austere sage in saffron robes with his vision of brotherhood of man inspired Americans. They helped generously in establishing Ramakrishna Mission centres in the United States, with headquarters in Los Angeles and New York. Donations for the centres were given by American magnates. Eminent Americans such as Henry Luce and Louis Fisher supported the Indian freedom movement.

World War II brought India to the notice of the United States. In the noble tradition of the founding fathers of America,

President Roosevelt offered moral and political support to the freedom movement in India. In their mid-Atlantic meeting the US President told Churchill that the days of empires were over. He was critical of British imperialism and said that the phenomenon belonged to 18th-century colonial exploitation. "How can we condemn Fascist slavery when we allow Asian and African nations to remain under colonial slavery?" he asked Churchill bluntly. Roosevelt and his Secretary of State, Cordell Hull, declared that the war effort in Asia would be greatly enhanced if India could participate as an equal member of the Commonwealth. They urged Britain to give India Dominion status urgently in 1941. Churchill refused. But President Roosevelt ensured that Article 3 of the Atlantic Charter stated that nations must be free to select the government they wish and that freedom must be restored to those nations from whom it "has been forcibly taken".

As World War II raged, Gandhi launched the Quit India movement, Subhash Bose and the Indian National Army carried out guerrilla wars. The war ended with millions killed and cities in rubble. An exhausted Britain agreed to Indian independence. President Truman welcomed India to the comity of nations on 14 August 1947.

The authors (then little girls) remember the heart-warming welcome accorded to Prime Minister Nehru when he arrived in Washington in October 1949. President Truman broke all protocol when he, as Head of State, received Prime Minister Nehru at the airport. With soul-storming power, a US Marine band played the Indian national anthem. New Yorkers rapturously greeted Nehru with ticker tape. Americans still cherished memories of their rebellion of 1776 and were willing to help a newly independent nation.

After independence, India became a member of the British Commonwealth. It was also anxious to befriend the United States. Divergences began when, in 1949, the United States asked India not to recognize communist China and warned of the danger of Chinese expansionism. Nehru, who had envisioned himself as the head of a new world order, sought to blaze his own path. By 1949 the chill of the Cold War was settling over the world.

It has long been debated in India as to what brought India its independence. Many have said that non-cooperation and civil disobedience would have been crushed if India had been under German or French rule.

The authors believe that the devastation that World War II brought to Britain in terms of serious depletion of manpower, damage to its industrial infrastructure, and financial losses due to the war, paved the way to their eventual departure from India. Britain could no longer maintain garrisons in its far-flung domains, from Gibraltar to Hong Kong. Desertion from the British-Indian Army to the Indian National Army and the Naval Revolt in Bombay demonstrated that Britain could no longer rely on Indians to maintain British rule. So after one hundred and ninety years of British rule, India became a sovereign nation.

Indonesia

Land of an ancient civilization with roots in both Hinduism and Buddhism, the three main islands of Java, Sumatra and Bali comprising Indonesia were ruled by many powerful dynasties. The islands were famed for their spices and minerals. Their merchants traded with Indian kingdoms and those on the coast of the Arabian Sea. As in the case of all Asian kingdoms, their wealth was their doom. In their eastward expansion the

Portuguese explorer, arrived in Java and Sumatra in the 16th century. A decade earlier the Portuguese Vasco da Gama had landed on the south-west coast of India and garnered the spice trade. Thereafter they established a colony in Goa. Portuguese galleons moved eastward and seized the Moluccas, the centre of spice trade on the Indian Ocean.

When Portugal-Spain was defeated by the Netherlands in the early 17th century, the Dutch East India Company was formed to control trade with Indonesia and in the course of that century extended their power over Java and the Moluccas. In the 19th century, the Dutch government took over the governance of Indonesia. To serve interest of Dutch trade, Indonesians were compelled to grow spices, tea and coffee that reduced the production of their staple food, rice. Plantations were established where the owners made huge profits. A century of ruthless exploitation followed.

As in many Asian countries, World War II brought salvation. Japanese forces occupied Indonesia, forcing the Dutch officials and settlers to flee to safer harbours. After Japan surrendered in 1945, Indonesians, under the leadership of Sukarno demanded freedom from the Netherlands. In August 1945 he declared independence for Indonesia with himself as president. It took two years before the various disputes could be settled, including the suggestion that the Republic of Indonesia would join a federal union with the Netherlands. Even after eviction from Indonesia, the Dutch tried to recapture the country in 1947–48. Both the United States and Soviet Union supported Indonesia which finally became a sovereign republic in 1949.

Independent Indonesia encountered teething troubles between chaotic democracy and authoritarian order. The communist party added another dimension by offering more equitable distribution of wealth and social justice. President Sukarno held sway over Indonesia for several decades until he handed power to Suharto who guided his country's destiny to stability and economic progress.

Vietnam

The Soviet Union was the nursery for socialist movements. Communists of Vietnam, Laos and Cambodia were trained there and developed friendships with Soviet ideologues. The French called the cluster of these different nations Indo-China; their ancient and diverse civilizational identities were submerged by simplistic colonial nomenclatures. Chafing under French rule, Vietnamese communists turned to the Comintern for guidance and support. Indeed it played a significant role in training Vietnamese communists.

Historians have suggested that Stalin was not enthusiastic about the establishment of the Communist Party of Vietnam in 1930. When Russia was in political-economic convulsions over collectivization, the founding of the Communist Party in faraway Vietnam did not seem portentous. Stalin did not support Vietnam's resistance against the French during 1930–1945. This was due to Soviet reluctance to jeopardize its French alliance in the anticipated combat against Nazi Germany.

Vietnam wrested its freedom from France in 1954 in the battle of Dien Bien Phu under the leadership of the valiant General Giap. The partition of Vietnam was decided at the Geneva Conference in 1954. The Soviet Union had not supported Vietnam against France but when Russia's relations with China deteriorated in the 1950's, Soviet Union came to the aid of Vietnam. The Soviets feared that Vietnam, having religious and cultural ties with China, could align with it. Aid was a dire necessity when Vietnam plunged into civil war against its southern province in South Vietnam, then an ally of the United States. The Soviet Union began providing substantial military assistance to North Vietnam in the terrible struggle that devastated both North and South Vietnam. The war lowered US prestige for employing methods that violated rules of warfare established by the Geneva Convention.

On 30 April 1975, the victorious army of General Giap entered Saigon. Never in the history of colonialism had an Asian nation humbled two major western powers – France in 1954 and the United States in 1975. Saigon was renamed Ho Chi Minh City after the great leader of the Vietnamese liberation movement.

The Soviet Union underwrote Vietnam's first Five-Year Plan. In 1978, Vietnam joined Comecon which was the Soviet Union's response to the EU. This group sought to promote economic integration of the Soviet Union, Eastern European members of the Warsaw Pact, Cuba, and Mongolia. China had slowed down economic assistance to other East Asian states when its trade relations warmed up with the United States. After Vietnam joined Comecon, China ceased to assist Vietnam, and in spite of growing animosity between them, Vietnam did not enter into a military alliance with the Soviet Union for fear of deepening hostility with China.

Vietnam's relations with neighbouring Cambodia deteriorated in the 1970's. On Christmas Day 1978, Vietnam invaded Cambodia. This occupation lasted ten years but Vietnam made incursions in Cambodian territory upto 1991. The war was unique; apart from Sino-Soviet skirmishes on the Usuri River this was the first and only war between two communist regimes. It led to a brief war between China and Vietnam.

Cambodia

The ancient kingdom of Cambodia was influenced by both Hindu and Buddhist culture. The great temples of Angkor Wat were built in the heydays of Khmer glory. Despite periodic invasion by neighbouring Thailand, which sacked Angkor Wat in the 14th century, Cambodia flourished in trade. When the Cambodian King Chan sought protection from Vietnam after invasion by a Thai army in the early 19th century, Vietnam established rule over Cambodia. Thereafter Vietnamese people began to settle in the kingdom of Cambodia. The Khmer people hated Vietnamese authority and revolted in 1840–1841. There were other uprisings upto 1845. Taking advantage of this, the Thai army again invaded Cambodia. Buffeted by both the Thais and Vietnamese the Cambodian king appealed to France for help as French missionaries acting as the advance army were already in Phnom Penh. France readily agreed and made Cambodia its protectorate in 1863. That same year the French botanist Henri Mouhot, while exploring the forests of this country, discovered the ruins of Angkor Wat.

French rule protected Cambodia from external aggression but not from the depredations of its new rulers. The French built railways, roads, and rubber plantations for their own prosperity and imposed heavy taxes on the Khmer people. By the 1930's the stirrings of nationalism were felt all over Asia; French rule created resentment in Cambodia. When Japanese forces occupied Cambodia, they arrested French officials and declared Cambodia free from French rule. Japan's defeat brought back the French but not for long. The Cambodian leader King Sihanouk dismissed the French government in 1954 and headed the government. He governed Cambodia from 1955 on behalf of his father and afterwards as King upto 1970. By 1968 the Communist Party had made inroads into Cambodian politics. Taking advantage of his absence, the National Assembly voted to remove him as head of state and the old kingdom became the Khmer Republic.

Cambodia's progress was halted by the horrific regime of Pol Pot, whose atrocities would put Attila the Hun and Genghiz Khan to shame. That it was perpetrated on his own people made it even more terrible. The Cambodians began to say that colonial rule was better than oppression of a native ruler. So when the Vietnamese army invaded Cambodia, the Khmer people looked upon the invading army as a saviour. They offered no resistance to the Vietnamese army.

As Vietnam was close to the Soviet Union, China feared that Vietnam would be the Soviet Union's cat's paw in South-East Asia. Vietnam condemned the genocide by the Pol Pot regime. Stung, Pol Pot demanded the return of Khmer lands seized by Vietnam in an earlier century. War began between the two nations. The army which had defeated the United States now swept along the Mekong River basin and stormed Phnom Penh. Eventually, after both the war and a civil war, a free government was formed under the communist leader Hun Sen. Cambodia is bravely forging ahead after a stormy past.

North Africa – Algeria

The history of North Africa can be painted in dramatic colours. It was the home of the intrepid Phoenicians who sailed over the Mediterranean, settled in the Levant, did brisk trade with the coastal kingdoms. After them came the Greeks, then the Romans and then the Arabs from Baghdad and Damascus and Cairo. The native people were Berbers, descendants of Phoenicians, who were ethnically different from the Arabs. Several Muslim dynasties followed – Abbasids, Almoravids, Fatimids. When the

Ottoman Turks rose to power and conquered the Byzantine Empire, they captured West Asia and North Africa.

As the impetus for overseas territorial expansion gained momentum, France, not to be left out of this imperial progress invaded and conquered Algeria in the 19th century. French rule was not popular; there were intermittent uprisings led by Berber tribesmen against oppressive foreign rule. As French military power increased, these uprisings were put down forcefully. The French needed *Lebensraum* and settled in the fertile areas of the country where they grew olives, fruits, and grapes for producing wine. These products brought them rich dividends and gave the settlers a stake in the land. Cheap Algerian labour enhanced profits.

When Ottoman rule ended after World War I, there were stirrings of revolt in West Asia and Algeria but a victorious France was in no hurry to lose its colonies. The scenario changed during World War II. Allied to Nazi Germany and under their instructions, the French Vichy government imposed higher taxes on Algerians. This and racial discrimination sowed seeds of an organized uprising. The Algerians hoped that the United States would come to their aid against French collaborators but the old regime continued. Not only that, the French settlers embarked on a land grabbing spree. Dispossessed Algerians became landless labourers in farms and estates owned by French colonists.

However the fires for an upheaval had been lit. It came ironically on Victory Day 1945 when amidst Allied celebrations Algerian-Berbers organized a procession in which the banner of Abd el-Kader, a revered Berber rebel leader of 1840, had inspired a discontented people. The police clashed with the marchers resulting in many deaths of the protesters. Europeans were killed in retaliation. The revolt spread to other regions of the country.

The colonial government arrested and summarily executed some 45,000 Algerians. The land of *liberté, égalité* and *fraternité* spilled the blood of their subject people.

And so began the Algerian War of Independence in 1954. It gathered force among peasants in the region of the Atlas Mountains followed by uprisings in urban areas. The isolated revolts proved ineffective. Algerian revolutionaries formed the Conseil National de la Révolution Algérienne in August 1956.

Although the French granted independence to Morocco and Tunisia in 1956, they refused to consider Algerian independence, stating that the country was part of Metropolitan France but the real reason was that there was huge economic benefit in retaining the colony. French settlers were fierce opponents of Algerian freedom. Successive French governments sent huge military forces to crush any further uprisings. The army there sealed off ports and frontiers to prevent shipment of arms from sympathetic comrades in Morocco and Tunisia. Martial law was imposed. Two groups of rebels were formed; the Armée de Libération Nationale in Algeria and the Front de Libération Nationale (FLN) in Tunisia and even Egypt. This divided both the strength and the cohesion of the rebel groups.

At a time when old imperial powers such as Britain and Netherlands had peacefully relinquished their colonies a decade earlier, France held a vice-like grip on theirs. While French brutality in Algerian drew the world's condemnation, there was fierce support for holding on to Algeria in France among the army and commercial classes. The renowned French writer Jean-Paul Sartre led liberal French opinion in support of Algerian freedom. Two famous Algerian revolutionaries – Ahmed ben Bella and Benyoucef ben Khedda – organized resistance against France. An undeclared civil war began in France between those who wanted to give Algeria freedom and others who vehemently opposed it. Meanwhile unabated violence, summary executions and bombings of rebel strongholds continued in Algeria.

Government after government fell between 1955 and 1958 in France. Then General Charles de Gaulle emerged from retirement to unify France and bring peace to Algeria. The Fifth Republic was established in May 1958 whereby the French Constitution gave executive powers to the President. His stature as war hero enabled him to act decisively. President de Gaulle purged the army of disloyal commanders and offered a peace plan to the Algerians based on the 1956 legislation which provided for the creation of local governments within the French Empire.

The FLN refused to accept the peace plan, and instead formed a provisional government-in-exile in Cairo in late 1958. They also launched a terror campaign in France and began to target Muslim moderates in Algeria. The French general Maurice Challe led an offensive that bombed rebel mountain retreats; civilians were dispersed from their home. When these tactics also failed President de Gaulle decreed that a referendum would decide the destiny of Algeria. The result, he knew, would be an overwhelming vote for self-determination.

The French settlers opposed the plan violently. The Organisation Armée Secrète (OAS, or Secret Armed Organization) perpetrated terrorist acts. The President warned the French colonists that they were starting a Hundred Years War. Violence broke out in French cities. In a near mutiny scenario, French soldiers were asked to disregard military orders. Responding to this, a dozen French African colonies declared their independence. This was to announce that the days of French imperialism were over.

A referendum on the future relationship between France and Algeria was held in January 1961 and immediate independence won by an overwhelming vote. The OAS's activities continued vitiating the relations between the two peoples. Finally France withdrew from Algeria in June 1962.

North Africa – Morocco

After conquering Algeria, France had looked for other colonies. In 1912 Morocco became a French protectorate. As in other countries under colonial rule, the demand for self-determination grew stronger during World War II. As President Roosevelt pointed out to Prime Minister Churchill when drafting the Atlantic Charter, "How can we say we are fighting Nazi tyranny when European nations have their colonies?" President Roosevelt encouraged the Sultan of Morocco, Mohammed ben Youssef, to demand independence. Mohammed ben Youssef began championing the Arab League and supporting Istiqlal, the Independence Party.

When France appointed General Alphonse Juin, Chief of Staff of National Defence, and General Augustin Guillaume, Resident General in Morocco as official representatives of the French government it was clear that France would oppose relinquishing its North African colonies. General Juin, supported by conservative French colonists, threatened to depose the Sultan if he supported the freedom party. Fearing for his throne, Mohammed ben Youssef agreed to abandon the nationalist cause. This did not prevent Istiqlal from forming the Moroccan National Front. The agitation for independence was accompanied by repression and bloodshed. Sovereign Arab nations sought intervention of the United Nations. The Pasha of Marrakech succeeded in deposing and banishing Mohammed ben Youssef and placing his protégé as the Sultan. The nationalists responded by increasing their agitation. Violence was perpetrated by both sides.

It was the season for Arab nationalism spearheaded by President Nasser of Egypt. Both the United States and Soviet Union urged the French government to reinstate ben Youssef as Sultan. In 1956 Morocco gained independence and Mohammed ben Youssef reclaimed his throne. French Morocco and Spanish Morocco joined to form a united sovereign Morocco.

North Africa – Tunisia

Tunisia had been a part of the Roman Empire several centuries before Christ. Here the imperial ambitions of Rome came into collision with Carthage which was ruled by a valiant dynasty. Hadrusbal, Hamilcar and finally Hannibal fought Rome in several Punic Wars. Then, as now, control of the Eastern Mediterranean trade route was important for the maritime states. Hannibal crossed the Alps on elephants and was at the city walls of Rome when he mysteriously decided to retreat. Legend records that it was on the request of a Roman goddess who later accompanied him to Carthage. Finally Scipio Africanus attacked Carthage and razed it to the ground. On its ruins, Tunisia was built. It became part of the Ottoman Empire and then came under French rule in the 19th century.

Drama is not unknown to Tunisia. During World War II it became the battleground between the Allies and Axis powers. For a while it seemed as if the irresistible Panzer Division of Field Marshal Erwin Rommel would sweep across deserts and ancient cities. Thereafter Allied forces pushed back the combined German and Italian armies under General Pietro Badoglio. The allies deposed the Tunisian Sultan Muhammad VII al-Munsif on the ground that he had collaborated with Nazi Germany and was replaced by another Muhammad.

The winds of anti-colonial agitation that swept over the Arab world also affected Tunisia. Neo Destour party headed the movement for independence and demanded reforms. The leader of the party, Habib Bourguiba, supported by the Arab League and the Bey, as the country's monarch was called, urged for the formation of a democratic government. France tried to delay this by suggesting joint sovereignty whereby Tunisia would remain with the French Republic. Rejecting such bizarre plans, Habib Bourguiba intensified his demands for independence of Tunisia. It helped that he was vigorously supported by the Tunisian General Labour Union. As in Algeria, so here, France responded by repressive measures. Political leaders including Bourguiba were arrested and tortured. Freedom fighters of Tunisia responded by activities that were called terrorism. The French government granted Tunisia internal autonomy. Tunisia gained full independence in 1956. In the country's first parliamentary elections, Bourguiba, leader of the Neo Destour party became President of the Tunisian Republic. A few months later Tunisia became a member of the United Nations.

African Continent

Sagres was a town on the south-west coast of Portugal where Prince Henry, venerated by his compatriots as 'the Navigator', established a maritime and cartographic research centre to explore the west coast of Africa. It is here that Europe's colonial dream began. The maritime station of Sagres ushered colonialism to Africa.

In 1400 CE Portugal under King Duarte was a rising nation, perpetually engaged in battles against Spain. He felt that conquest of alien lands would bring glory to Portugal. Seven centuries earlier Arabs from Damascus, Baghdad and later Morocco had conquered the Iberian Peninsula. Iberian kings made sporadic attempts at *reconquista* or reconquest of Moorish-held lands. But the Moorish Emirs had invested in the Iberian Peninsula; they were not to be dislodged. Portugal abandoned *reconquista* and conquered important ports of North Africa. They eyed Ceuta, a fortress town of Morocco facing Jabal al-Tariq – or Gibraltar.

Ceuta had strategic importance; this garrison town under Emir Saladin ibn Saladin was the gateway to Senegal and Timbaktu. Arabs did brisk trade in slaves, gold and ivory with African people. Moorish travellers and mariners in the service of Prince Henry told him about the riches of Africa. Portuguese men were sent as settlers to the recently discovered Azores and Madeira. Prince Henry wanted to explore a water route across Africa to connect the Atlantic Ocean to the Red Sea and Asia. He and his cartographers, astronomers and mariners planned the expedition to the west coast of Africa. Finally in 1415 CE, Ceuta was conquered by Dom Pedro de Menezes.

Africa's tragedy commenced with its discovery by Europe. Its gold and ivory were grabbed, its sturdy youth were captured and sold as slaves. In the 19th century, Britain, Belgium, Netherlands, France, and Germany vied with each other in the 'Scramble for Africa'. The enslavement of Africa began on a greater scale than envisaged by Henry the Navigator at Sagres.

In 1945, Africa had four independent countries – Egypt, Ethiopia, Liberia, and South Africa. Britain's colonies were extensive. Of these, Sudan was the first to gain independence in 1956, followed by Ghana in 1957, and then Nigeria. Both Ghana and Nigeria had competent leadership. They joined the British Commonwealth after gaining independence. The other colonies gained independence by 1965. Rhodesia declared independence that year but this was not recognized by either Britain or other states. The black majorities in Rhodesia and South Africa were disenfranchised until 1980. After gaining independence Rhodesia was named Zimbabwe. Namibia, Africa's last UN Trust Territory, became independent of South Africa in 1990.

In 1975, Spain ceded administration of Western Sahara to Mauritania and Morocco. Mauritania later withdrew, and Morocco's claim to the territory is not internationally recognized.

European colonial rule in mainland Africa ended by 1977. Most of Africa's island countries also became independent. Most independent African countries are defined by boundaries from colonial times. British Somaliland and Italian Somaliland merged into Somalia. Eritrea merged with Ethiopia in 1952, but became an independent country in 1993. After independence most former African colonies became republics except Morocco, Lesotho and Swaziland which retain their monarchs.

South Africa

One country remained to astonish the world – South Africa. The British and Dutch governments had fought here, each to establish its hegemony. Both people established farms and industries. Both participated in governance of this resource rich country. South Africa had been the scene of Gandhi's agitation for freedom and equality in the 1890's. Little had changed in the lives of native Africans until the African National Congress launched the freedom movement. It is difficult to understand how, after all the bloodshed of wars against tyranny and oppression, a regime like that of white South Africa could exist. The pernicious doctrine of Apartheid prevailed. The white population enjoyed privileges denied to the original inhabitants of the land. No condemnation by the United Nations, human rights group, economic sanction and boycotts could deflect the anachronistic government from its course. Finally, after many years of violence, oppression, and struggle, South Africa, under the extraordinary personality of Nelson Mandela brought in a black majority government.

The twilight of empires was assisted by the Soviet Union's policy of assisting liberation movements. It gave vigorous support by way of financial assistance to Ghana, Nigeria, South Africa, and Angola. In East Asia, Soviet Union played a major role in the liberation movements of Laos, Cambodia and Vietnam. Nations of Latin America, particularly Fidel Castro's Cuba and Salvador Allende's Chile, long subjected to the neo-imperialist policy of the United States and Latin America's corrupt military juntas, looked to the Soviet Union for support in their struggles. The Soviet Union was thereby able to extend its influence in the developing world during this period. New communist governments which had cordial relations with the Soviet Union rose to power in Vietnam, Ethiopia, and Nicaragua.

26

THE NEW MUSLIM WORLD

The Arab spring did not blossom in 2011. It came fourteen centuries earlier when their invincible armies swept from the Arabian peninsula to North Africa and West Asia towards Iran, Central Asia, China, Spain, Portugal and finally to the gates of Paris.

The Arab world had memories of their golden age spanning eight centuries, when dynasties from Damascus, Baghdad, Cairo, Cordoba, and Granada had ruled large swathes of the continents of Asia, Europe and North Africa. They had made immense contribution to art, architecture, mathematics, science, philosophy and literature. It was not easy for them to bow before the conquerors who captured their lands, cities and treasures. First came the Ottomans, and then Europeans, and later Americans from across the Atlantic.

Iran

While Iran is an important member of the Muslim world it is not part of the Arab world. Long before Islam made its appearance in the Arabian peninsula, Persia (Iran) was a great civilization and had a great empire that extended to the Mediterranean. Persian rulers Darius and Cyrus, both given the honorific 'the Great', marched to Greece and subjugated the

Hellenic world. To humble Hellenic pride, the Persian army destroyed part of the Athenian Acropolis. Alexander the Great retaliated a century later by setting fire to the grandeur of Persepolis. Later, he sued for peace and married Rukshana, a Persian princess from Central Asia, in the hope of uniting the two empires. That dream died with Alexander's untimely death. The Achaemenid and Sassanid empires dominated the region. Ancient Persia and ancient India had affinities in common divinities as well as a common root language. Their cultural frontiers met in Afghanistan.

Cosmopolitan Persians say that disaster struck them in 651 AD when the army of the Umayyad Empire conquered their country and enforced Islam on the Zoroastrian believers. The great writers, philosophers, mathematicians of Persia never ceased to lament their lost glory. Omar Khayyam of Naishapur expressed his nostalgia in his *Rubáiyát* and Firdausi lamented the lost grandeur of ancient Persia in the *Shahnama*. There was a second flowering under the Safavid dynasty of which the greatest, Shah Abbas I, built the splendid city of Isfahan, diverse strains of Persia's cultural past meeting in its edifices. The Safavid empire stretched from Iran to the Caucasus, Turkey and Afghanistan.

In the late 1930's Germany tried to woo Iran. Turkey was already an ally of the Axis powers. Though Iran declared its neutrality at the outbreak of war, both Britain and the Soviet Union made an undeclared invasion. The Soviet Union feared for its Caucasian territories and encouraged separatist movements in Gilan and Khorassan and sought to establish communist republics there. When the war ended and relations between the United States and Soviet Union began to chill as prelude to the Cold War, the United States stepped in to neutralize Soviet influence in 1946.

American and British prestige suffered irrevocably in 1953 when both nations arranged a coup against the popular and democratically elected government of Prime Minister Mohammed Mossadeq. He wanted friendship with the West but not at the expense of the Iranian people who had suffered the depredations of the Anglo-American Oil Company. Assisting and supporting him was the Muslim ulema (religious leaders) of Iran, the chief opponent of the Shah's partnership with the West. When Mossadeq began curtailing powers of the two countries and their company, the CIA overthrew him and installed a puppet regime under Reza Khan, son of a previous ruler who had been a major in the Iranian army. The puppet was anointed as Emperor of Iran who became an ally of the United States through the Baghdad Pact. This was a turning point in Iran's 20th-century political history.

Sensing a groundswell of opposition to his regime, Shah Reza Khan ushered in Enqelāb-e Sefid or the White Revolution in 1963. Reforms were introduced to modernize both the Iranian economy and Iranian society. These were opposed by the Muslim ulema who felt that the Shah was undermining the basic tenets of Islam. By mid-1978, the situation in Iran became turbulent. Defying the military and the secret police and the Savak, the populace protested in the streets. The military and police mowed them down. Leaders of the protest movement were killed. The United States toyed with the idea of a military coup to strengthen the hated Shah. Demonstrations intensified; police firing became a daily routine. All sections of the population were united in their opposition to the Shah. There was a general strike in October when mammoth protest rallies were held in major Iranian cities that crippled the country's economy. Mosques and madrasas became centres of opposition and strategy formulation. The

Savak had no idea of what was happening. Never in the history of Iran had millions taken to the street in protest against the Shah, regardless of the fact that they could be mowed down by a ruthless militia. The new prime minister Jafar Sharif-Emami tried to introduce reforms but Iran moved inexorably towards a revolution. Neither the French Revolution of 1789 nor the Russian Revolution of 1917 had such support of the masses.

In the security of the Neauphle-le-Château in France, the religious leader Ayatollah Khomeini watched the events in Iran which he had left in 1963 because he was a vehement opponent of the Shah's regime. The Ayatollah rejected patriotism as "paganism based on geographical concepts. Only Allah and Islam deserve reverence". He gave nodding approval to Marxism since it agreed with the Koran's directive to free the oppressed masses or *mostazafin*. He called the United States "the great Satan" against whom a jihad must be fought and whereby the former glory and power of Islam would be restored.

The revolt in Iran spread. Even the dreaded Iranian military extended covert help to the revolt. Sensing the nationwide opposition to the Shah, his staunchest ally, US President Jimmy Carter told him that he must go. William Sullivan, the American ambassador, asked the military to stage a coup which they refused to do. Iranians would not tolerate another CIA coup such as the one that overthrew their venerated Mossadeq.

Desperate, dying of cancer, the Shah and his family left Iran in January 1979.

Tehran burst into a festive mood. People marched through the streets, carrying banners that announced the end of a dark era.

Ayatollah Khomeini arrived in Tehran on a chartered Air France flight on 1 February 1979. To demonstrate his disdain for power and glory Khomeini declined all posts but his regime swiftly dismantled every feature of the Shah's regime. Finally, Ayatollah Khomeini issued a stern warning to Iranians that there would now be a government based on the shariah. "Opposing this government means opposing the shariah of Islam. Revolt against God's government is a revolt against God. Revolt against God is blasphemy."

The last remnant of the Shah's regime was destroyed in early February. The military alliance with the United States ended. Raising the banner of Islam, the Iranian ulema incited Afghans to overthrow their pro-Soviet government led by President Mohammed Taraki. This attrition continued throughout the 1980's. Then abruptly the two adversaries altered their course. Soviet policy underwent a subtle change in 1987 when Soviet President Mikhail Gorbachev changed his stance from supporting Iraq at the commencement of Iran-Iraq War to offering the olive branch to Iran, which eagerly seized it. Iranian President Rafsanjani visited Moscow, sought Soviet assistance to replenish its weaponry. Iran concluded major arms deal with the Soviet government in 1989.

Even after the dissolution of the Soviet Union the amity with Iran continued as the Russian Federation needed Iran's mediation with the Central Asian Republics and in Transcaucasia which had been under Soviet rule for seven decades. Chafing against sanctions imposed by the United States and its allies for Iran's nuclear program, Iran depended on Russian political support, military weapons and nuclear reactors. The Russian Foreign Minister Yevgeny Primakov advocated robust Russo-Iranian cooperation and approved sale of nuclear reactors and a gas centrifuge system that would enable Iran to produce nuclear weapons. Iran repaid Russian assistance by not supporting Muslim Chechens and Muslim Bosnians in the wars of the 1990's.

It is ironical that Iran, which played a major role of inciting Islamic fundamentalism in Afghanistan in 1979, and which ultimately compelled Russian intervention there, sought Russian cooperation against the Taliban in Afghanistan in 1996. Islam was no longer a battle cry; the battle was now between Shia Iran and Sunni Afghan Taliban.

US analysts at the Pentagon observe that given the history of animosities and wars in the 19th century between Russia and Iran, Russian support of Iraq in the Iraq-Iran war, and Russia's earlier lukewarm support for Iran's nuclear policy, the ongoing amity could falter. The analysts must be aware that political equations are based not on memories of strife but the imperatives of survival.

Afghanistan

This land of formidable mountains, fast-flowing rivers and reckless people has been the fulcrum of empires. It was also the graveyard of empires. The dynasty of Ahmed Shah Durrani ruled a country that was a conglomerate of Pathans, Uzbeks, Tajiks, Kyrgyz, Turkmen, and Hazaras – descendants of the races that had tried to subdue this land of wild grandeur. They were as unruly as they were antagonistic to each other.

Romance for empires made Britain compete against Russia for pre-eminence in Afghanistan. This was known as the Great Game. The British waged two disastrous Afghan Wars until Prime Minister William Gladstone called a halt to bloodshed. Later into the 19th century mutual fear of German militarism in Central Asia compelled Britain and Russia to enter into the Pamir Convention of 1895 whereby Russia came into possession of three fourths of the territory known as the Pamir, and extended its control to the banks of the Oxus. Throughout the 19th century British politicians debated on the benefits of either the Forward Policy or the Regressive Policy.

End of British rule in India and the disastrous Partition that followed in 1947 also affected Afghanistan. Afghans declared null and void the treaty that established a border line, a partition agreed upon by King Abdur Rahman Khan and Mortimer Durand after whom the border was named. This cut across ethnic and tribal divisions; the arbitrary division of territory enacted by the British government to weaken Afghanistan now brought the governments of Afghanistan and Pakistan into bitter conflict. Pakistan demanded the continuation of the Durand Line. The Soviet Union condemned the Durand Line as yet another wicked act of British Imperialism.

King Zahir Shah felt that friendship with the Soviet Union would benefit Afghanistan; the Soviet Union responded by assisting Afghans to build roads between Kabul, Herat and Kandahar along the Hindu Kush, constructed strategic mountain tunnels and invested in small-scale industries and infrastructure. The Soviet Union concluded a $25 million arms deal with Afghanistan and gave an economic aid package worth $550 million. Russia's Aeroflot had daily flights from Kabul to Moscow and gave technical aid to Afghanistan's Ariana Airlines. Since the US supported the territorial claims of its ally Pakistan against Afghanistan, it declined to give Afghanistan economic, technical or military assistance. Even a few US-sponsored projects such as Helmand Valley Project ran into difficulties over terms and conditions. Deprived of American assistance, Afghanistan turned to the Soviet Union which readily offered economic and military aid. Afghanistan's defence personnel were trained in Russia, military equipments were supplied by Russia, 40 per cent of Afghan exports went to Russia. Young Afghans received medical and technical education in Soviet universities, and the Russian language was widely used. As the United States' allies – Iran and Turkey – encircled Russia's southern frontier, it invested in a stable and friendly Afghanistan.

The first signs of turmoil began when the benevolent King Zahir Shah was deposed by his cousin, Prince Muhammad Daoud. He did not know that the communist or Khalq party was gaining support and influence among the poorer people. He was assassinated and his government was overthrown in a violent coup by the People's Democratic Party of Afghanistan (PDPA) of which the Khalq was a constituent. Had this regime fulfilled their promise of social justice, the country would have benefitted. Encountering opposition from Muslim clerics and warlords, PDPA used violence to pursue its aims. Soviet leaders watched the turmoil with growing anxiety. While they gave economic assistance they did not wish to get involved militarily – until Hafizullah Amin not only alienated the Afghan people but began secret negotiations with the United States, which wanted bases on the Soviet-Afghan border. Pakistan was ready to broker the deal.

The Cold War was a "white man's war." Western agents penetrated Soviet intelligence circles. This was not possible in Afghanistan. So the United States poured millions of dollars to arm and instigate jihadists to instigate violence and subvert the government.

Russia was the first state to grasp the consequences of Islamic fundamentalism. The Central Asian Republics of the Soviet Union were peopled by Muslims who had been Russified and were secular. Soviet rule brought these republics material benefits and modernized medieval societies. A call to Islamic fundamentalism would dismember the Soviet Union. Robert

Gates, director of the United States' Central Intelligence Agency, persuaded President Carter that an uprising against the pro-Soviet government in Afghanistan would benefit the United States. Americans vowed to make Soviet intervention in Afghanistan "their Vietnam".

Soviet leaders realized that their ally Afghanistan was the target of Islamic propaganda. If theocratic Iran overran secular Afghanistan there would be serious repercussions on the Central Asian Republics. Apart from ethno-religious unrest, there were other dangers. Soviet nuclear stations and arsenals were located in the Central Asian Republics. The consequences of these falling into the hands of fanatic adversaries would be catastrophic. Soviet Union was caught between the imperative to protect its borders and was acutely aware that no foreign power had succeeded in Afghanistan. The Soviet Union reluctantly sent its army of intervention on 25 December 1979. From then on the events moved inexorably to a Sophoclean tragedy.

The United States intensified its military and financial aid to Pakistan's Inter-Services Intelligence (ISI) which in turn gave C4 plastic explosives, long-range sniper rifles, wire-guided anti-tank missiles, Stryir anti-aircraft missiles as well as external satellites, reconnaissance data on the location of Soviet targets. Some 90,000 Afghan guerrillas and another 100,000 reserve were trained in Pakistan and equipped with 122 mm howitzers, AGS-17, grenade launchers, M-4L 82 mm mortars, SA-7 surface to air missiles.

The incitement to Islamic fundamentalism came at a high price for the people of Pakistan. Future Pakistani terrorists siphoned off weapons and used these for killing their own people, not sparing even school children writing examinations. Army and navy personnel openly sold Western weapons to mujahideen who gave them heroin in return. The heroin trade route ran from Kandahar to Karachi. Pakistan's military government diverted development funds for warfare. Pakistan remained one of the poorest nations in the world while its bête noire India went on to become an economic and regional power.

Russian Foreign Minister Yevgeny Primakov wrote: "Weaponizing of militant Islam in order to bleed Moscow in Afghanistan in the 1980's was a reckless policy that continues to reverberate and may foretell ongoing disasters now and in the future."

China collaborated with Pakistan by setting up training camps for Afghan terrorists in Xinxiang to fight against Russia, the nation that had been their only benefactor and ally in the days of their isolation. China wanted to be the paramount power in Asia; it could not be that as long as Central Asia formed part of the Soviet Union. China and Pakistan aided Afghan terrorists to make a bridgehead for a war against Afghanistan.

Had Russia's relations with America been more amicable, the two powers could have ironed out their differences and arrived at a consensus regarding Iran and Afghanistan. Had the United States seen the real danger of Islamic fundamentalism in West Asia the events there would have been different. President Carter's backtracking on arms reduction and fortifying NATO's presence all around the Soviet Union intensified the Cold War.

Soviet leader Yury Andropov called the Soviet intervention in Afghanistan "a bleeding wound". He realized that the combined fight against USA-China-Pakistan on the one hand and Afghan rebels on the other was a losing battle. Before his untimely death he advised withdrawal from Afghanistan. But the United States wanted the bleeding to continue; 'Operation Cyclone' and the ill-conceived and fatal Reagan Doctrine inundated the mujahideen with arms and funds. The US Central Intelligence Agency funded Osama bin Laden and other Arab volunteers to assist the mujahideen against the 'infidel' Russians.

Thus al-Qaeda was born.

A decade later bin Laden turned his implacable wrath on 'infidel' Americans.

Military historians have been baffled by the reverses sustained by the Soviet Army in the war against Afghan mujahideen. The Soviet Army had defeated the formidable German Army in World War II. The nature of warfare in Afghanistan was different. Two professional armies of Russia and Germany fought each other during World War II on familiar European soil. Both armies were trained in conventional and large-scale warfare. But Soviet forces could not outwit the mujahideen in the formidable Afghan terrain and in guerrilla warfare. The mujahideen retreated into their hideouts; the heavy Soviet tanks and columns announced their presence with perilous consequences. Soviet soldiers were conscripts, and not always well-trained. The elite teams deployed such as Spetsnaz and VDV were inadequate in numbers and thinly spread across hazardous terrain. Success in guerrilla warfare requires effective counter-intelligence. Soviet forces relied on radio interceptions rather than infiltration into mujahideen ranks that would facilitate information gathering. The mujahideen were inspired not only by religious fervour but by the enormous funds provided by the United States, Pakistan and China. Further, the dangerous heroin trade had Pakistani blessings.

Finally all would-be conquerors of Afghanistan have been defeated not so much by the valour of its natives but by the unforgiving terrain that defeats open warfare because Afghans know the intricacies of their mountain fastness.

Had the United States not decided to "make Afghanistan Soviet Union's Vietnam", the displacement of Afghan people, destruction of the nation's infrastructure, the immense misery of the Afghan people would have been avoided. And there would have been no mujahideen, al-Qaeda, Jabhat al-Nusra and Taliban who are soaking the good earth in the blood of the innocent all over the world. Like Attila and his Huns, these groups are the scourge of God. Like the Huns, these assassins will also disappear. And hopefully civilization will reclaim humanity.

West Asia

As World War I raged in 1916 and Germany seemed triumphant, Turkey was making an attempt to stay alive. It was evident that smouldering Arab nationalism would shortly explode and dismantle the Ottoman Empire. For a century and half Britain and France had bolstered the Ottoman Empire to keep Russia away from this oil-rich region where "huge waves of oil" had been discovered in 1908 by the infamous duo William Knox D'Arcy and George Reynolds. In 1916 Britain and France sent two diplomats – Mark Sykes and François Georges-Picot – to redraw the map of West Asia. The two nations devised a secret plan to carve out "spheres of influence" which would protect the interests of these two nations. Arab and Persian nationalism had to be smothered. When the war ended Britain received mandates over Palestine and Iraq while France got suzerainty over present-day Syria. To end Ottoman rule, TE Lawrence incited an Arab revolt which was opposed by Britain. Kingdoms were carved out by Britain and France without any regard for ethnic or political considerations. Puppets were installed on uneasy thrones; the Saudis of Riyadh and Hashemites of Baghdad and Amman were expected to favour their patrons.

But Arab people were furious with the secret terms of the Sykes-Picot Pact which came to be revealed a few years later by Soviet Intelligence operatives. In its own interest Russia had opposed the Ottoman Empire which blocked its entry to the Mediterranean. It is this historical legacy which made most Arab states turn to the Soviet Union for assistance.

Iraq

This was the cradle of ancient civilizations – Sumerian, Assyrian, Babylonian, Akkadian – which had made immense contributions to the progress of humanity. The Greeks came here in the 3rd century, then the Romans, then the Persian Sassanid rulers. The first Christian church is said to have been built on the banks of the Euphrates in the 2nd century AD. The Abbasid dynasty made Baghdad a cosmopolitan city where Charlemagne sent his knights, where Hindu scholars and Chinese traders came to see the great city of Haroun al-Rashid whose contributions to civilization are immense. As in the case of all rich empires, the army grew lax and soon the vigorous Seljuk Turks of Central Asia conquered the land. They were followed by the devastating invasion by Genghiz Khan in the 13th century when thousands were put to the sword and Iraq's wealth taken back to the Mongol homeland. Other invaders followed until the 16th century, when the Ottoman Turks occupied modern-day Iraq.

The victors of World War I carved up slices of the Turkish Empire. This country was called the Mandatory Iraq in 1921. It comprised of lower Mesopotamia which was ancient Babylon, Upper Mesopotamia and the Syrian Desert. In 1933 the Kingdom of Iraq was placed under a Hashemite family. Like other Arab nations it had acute social and economic inequalities. The oil-rich land was drawn into the US-led Baghdad Pact in 1955, ostensibly to guard the country from Soviet rule. Iraq had to sever all connections with the Soviet Union. Young King Faisal had no idea of the groundswell of discontent in his kingdom. The Ba'thist party overthrew the monarchy in a bloody coup and established a secular republic.

When the Ba'athist regime of Abd al-Karim Qasim replaced the monarchy in 1958, Iraq resumed relations with the Soviet Union. The Soviet Arabist, intelligence officer and journalist Yevgeny Primakov assisted in facilitating a treaty between Russia and Socialist Baathist leader Abd al-Karim Qasim of Iraq and later with Hafez al-Assad of Syria. Iraq received military aid from the Soviet Union.

The republic was ruled by Saddam Hussein from 1979 to 2003. Able and astute, he maintained cordial relations with both the United States and Soviet Union. The people were well-fed, children went to school, and young people attended universities in Iraq and in the West. He put down the slightest sign of Islamic fundamentalism with a heavy hand. Iraq's war against Ayatollah Khomeni's Iran was motivated by the need to keep Islamic fundamentalism from disrupting the secular fabric of Iraq. The United States supported Iraq in this war because it opposed Iran, the 'axis of evil' according to the thespian-president Ronald Reagan. Saddam Hussein miscalculated in the Gulf War, incurring the wrath of the United States and Britain. Sanctions were imposed on Iraq but Saddam Hussein remained defiant. President George W Bush of the United States and British Prime Minister Tony Blair felt it was a time to teach Saddam Hussein a lesson. Bush's acolytes Dick Cheney and Donald Rumsfeld had oil interests, whose commercial and strategic interests would be best served by invasion and subsequent occupation of Iraq.

But a fig leaf was required for this illegal invasion of a sovereign state which had not carried out any aggression against the US and Britain. It was ostensibly "to disarm Iraq of weapons of mass destruction and to curtail Saddam Hussein's support of terrorism and to free the Iraqi people from oppression".

Blair, named 'B.Liar' by an infuriated British public, accused Saddam Hussein's refusal to take a "final opportunity" to disarm itself of alleged nuclear, chemical, and biological weapons that US and British officials called an immediate and intolerable threat to world peace.

Sir John Chilcott's report of 2016 reveals that both American and British Intelligence repeatedly warned their governments that overthrow of Saddam Hussein's government would bring chaos to the country and unleash on Iraq and West Asia the full blast of Islamic fundamentalism that waited impatiently on its secular frontiers. They warned that the threat of terrorism would spread from Iraq to the West. Their advice was ignored and suppressed.

The invasion of Iraq was vigorously opposed by US allies, especially the governments of France, Germany, and New Zealand. Their leaders argued that there was no evidence of weapons of mass destruction in Iraq and that invading that country was not justified under any provision of international law and was illegal under the Charter of the United Nations.

A month before the invasion there were mammoth anti-war rallies in European capitals, the largest being in London and Rome. Asian cities saw similar protests. An estimated thirty-six million people across the world participated in these mammoth rallies to protest against the war against Iraq. Until the eleventh hour member-states of the United Nations spoke angrily against the proposed US-UK invasion. In the UN Security Council the

French and German foreign ministers pleaded against such a war.

The invasion began on the morning of 19 March 2003. The bombardment of the capital was ferocious. Standing against the backdrop of explosions, a young BBC reporter, Rageh Omaar, said: "Even this city which has witnessed terrible invasions in the past by Mongol and other hordes has not seen such a ferocious attack on hapless civilians." The reporter was never again seen on BBC television. On 20 March the coalition forces launched an attack on Basra Province. The Bush-Blair plan became obvious next day when the Special Forces made an amphibious attack from the Persian Gulf to secure Basra and the surrounding petroleum fields. Battle after battle followed. The Iraqi forces could not combat the military might of the combined US-UK forces. Finding their land ruined, their people killed, their soldiers tortured, members of Saddam Hussein's disbanded army began their own war of resistance against the invading forces. As warned and predicted by US and British Intelligence reports, Islamic fundamentalists moved in. Together, the once secular army of Saddam Hussein and the jihadists opposed the US-UK forces. Members of the Iraqi government went into hiding but were found.

Saddam Hussein who maintained stability and secularism in Iraq was hanged for the alleged crime of having weapons of mass destruction which have not been found even after fifteen years. The invasion was intended to free Iraqi people from oppression, and according to Bush, bring them the benefit of democracy. Far from making the world safe for democracy as 'Bushy' George and Tony 'B.Liar' declared, the Islamic State formed out of the chaos is spreading its tentacles all over the world.

Iraq now lies in ruins, its once prosperous economy shattered, its citizens fleeing from one city to another for shelter and food.

The cradle land of civilization is now the cradle land of violence and terror.

Syria

Syria is a land of ancient civilizations. The ports of Tartus and Latakia were built during Roman rule. Damascus became the splendid capital of the first Muslim empire under the Umayyad dynasty in the 7th century. It produced a cosmopolitan culture that went westwards to North Africa and established Muslim kingdoms in Spain where grew an unique Iberian-Muslim culture. Two centuries later the power of the Arab world shifted from Umayyad Damascus to Abbasid Baghdad. Syria was occupied by the Seljuk Turks and witnessed a revival under Salah ud-Din known to the West as Saladin who is said to have observed rules of warfare while fighting the unscrupulous Crusaders under Richard I of England. The *entente cordiale* between local people and Crusaders can be seen in the grey-blue eyes and tawny hair of their descendants. Syria was part of the Ottoman Empire until Britain and France carved out new states from it.

Syria became a sovereign democratic republic in 1946. A military coup ended with a popular uprising in 1954. A civilian government came to power and later united with Egypt to form United Arab Republic. Then the Syrian Ba'athist party under Michel Aflaq and Salah al-Din al-Bitar staged a coup in 1963, their government to be overthrown in a second coup in 1966 engineered by General Hafez al-Assad, also of the Ba'ath Party. He became Prime Minister and then President in 1971, and ruled until his death in 2000.

While Sunni Muslims form the majority group in Syria, the Assad family belongs to the minority Alawite Shia sect of Islam.

The Kurds are another minority group. The minorities are generally protected in Syria. The secular Arab Socialist Ba'ath Party has governed since 1963, but without an Opposition.

Hafez al-Assad, continued the pro-Soviet policy of his predecessors and signed a peace and security pact with the Soviet Union. A Soviet naval base was established at Tartus. In return Syria received Soviet arms worth $135 million with the Soviet Union agreeing to send troops to Syria in the event of an Israeli attack. Syria was Soviet Union's staunchest ally in this region. By mid-1984, there were about 13,000 Soviet and Eastern European advisers in Syria.

There was a change of mood soon after Bashar al-Assad took charge; the Damascus Spring of 2000-2001 produced demands for democratic governance. New political parties were formed; programs for reform were discussed by liberal activists. This ended in August 2001 when the leaders called for civil disobedience. They were imprisoned but protests were not silenced. The Syrian parliament became the theatre for criticism of the regime whose chief critics are the Sunnis, who are also the poorest. As in other developing countries, globalization and free market deepened inequalities of wealth and opportunity between the commercial and political elite on one hand and the masses on the other. The severe and continuing drought between 2007 and 2010 produced a steep decline in food production which led to high prices and migration to urban areas. Refugees fleeing violence from Iraq swelled discontent. The classical ingredients of revolt presented themselves.

It came in mid-January 2011 when protest marches were held in Damascus. Police fired on them. In retaliation, protesters burned government buildings. President Bashar al-Assad accused foreign agents for fomenting trouble. Initially protesters wanted reforms, end to corruption, more freedom, and release of political prisoners. Clamour for the end of the Assad regime came in April 2011. As protests spread to other cities the regime's well equipped army retaliated with force. The towns of Jisr al-Shughur and Idlib broke into armed rebellion. Some security personnel defected to the growing ranks of protesters. These defectors formed the Free Syrian Army, funded now by the United States who wanted the end of Assad, and by Turkey's President Erdogan, supporter of the Muslim Brotherhood, and opponent of Assad's secular regime. Turkey's claim to non-interference in the Syrian civil war was belied when the Free Syrian Army moved its headquarters to southern Turkey.

In August the Syrian National Council comprising of various political groups and members of the Free Syrian Army was formed in Turkey. They were a disparate group with no unified agenda but received funds from President Recep Tayyip Erdogan to continue the struggle. The port town of Latakia, Rastan, Homs, Aleppo, Idlib, Jabal al-Zawiya, Binnish, and Marrat al-Numaan became scenes of terrible destruction as each side used its weaponry aimed at the other. Innocent, hapless civilians were the tragic victims of these reciprocal brutalities. The civil war intensified well into 2012. As the government forces reclaimed rebel-held cities and the rebels began a retreat, the United States intervened. A CIA operative, Philip Giraldi, declared that NATO warplanes, weaponry from Libya, French and British trainers in warfare were bolstering the flagging rebels. This led to intensified violence between the two combatants. In February 2012, Assad ordered the Syrian Army to reclaim Homs, Idlib and other rebel held towns and districts.

That same year Martti Ahtisaari, former Finnish President and winner of Nobel Peace Prize in 2008, held dialogues with both sides. President Vladimir Putin proposed a three-point agenda that included President Assad's resignation. The United States, UK and France rejected the proposal because they expected the regime to collapse during the civil war. When this did not actualize, Turkey and Saudi Arabia urged the United States to bomb Damascus which President Barack Obama refused to do. He had seen how the removal of Saddam Hussein in 2003 and Muammar Qaddafi in 2012 had plunged those two nations into chaos and bloodshed. Further, Assad's Russian advisers asked him to destroy all chemical weapons so that the United States had no excuse to invade Syria as it had invaded Iraq on the false allegation that Saddam Hussein had weapons of mass destruction.

Kofi Annan's mediation attempts failed miserably; neither side heeded him but the United Nations mediated a ceasefire in April which collapsed soon after. Renewed violence commenced; the battles for Damascus and Aleppo in late 2012 intensified. The Central Intelligence Agency channelled funds and arms through Saudi Arabia to assist the Syrian rebels. The Syrian Free Army (which was fighting for democracy) and Islamic State (which was massacring infidels) now made common cause.

In late 2013 the Jabhat al-Nusra, an affiliate of al-Qaeda took control of keys cities. They also seized Tabqa Dam, the largest dam in Syria and main source of hydroelectric power. Shia Iran saw the formidable onslaught of the Sunni Islamists which posed a threat to its security. So in 2013 Iran sent its Revolutionary Guards and Hezbollah troops to assist the Syrian army in their fights against the Islamic State.

Declaring itself the Islamic State of Iraq and Levant (ISIL) or Daesh in Arabic, these black-clad terrorists seized substantial territories in Iraq and weaponry from the Iraqi army. Both the governments of Iraq and Syria retaliated and bombed ISIL bases and other ISIL-held towns. ISIL concentrated on oilfields – Mosul, Shaar and Hajjar – and captured government-held lands. The ISIL seemed like an irresistible force of a new dark age as they ploughed their way through Syrian territory and detonated bombs outside a mosque that killed hundreds of Muslim worshippers – in the name of Allah.

The West looked on. British and American journalists were beheaded by ISIL. The Committee to Protect Journalists reported that seventy Western journalists covering the Syrian War were killed and more than eighty kidnapped. Scenes of beheading, executions, and mutilations were shown in videos and posted on YouTube. Behind the public outrage the United States continued to support ISIL. Turkey allowed ISIL to use its territory as a bridgehead to Iraq and Syria. Turkey purchased crude oil from ISIL which had stolen the oil from a battered Syria and Iraq.

The United States and its partners – Bahrain, Saudi Arabia, United Arab Emirates, Qatar and Jordan – began air strikes against ISIL in September 2014. These proved to be ineffective. The Syrian Air Force carried out over 200 air strikes on rebel-held areas in Syria. In January 2015 the Kurdish YPG forced the ISIL army to retreat. Aided by Turkey, Saudi Arabia, Qatar and Jordan who opposed the Syrian government ISIL extended control over strategic towns of Iraq and Syria.

Since non-Islamic heritage is considered heresy, these apocalyptic figures began the destruction of ancient cities – Nineveh, Nimrud, Palmyra – and demolished sculptures and edifices that had withstood depredations of nature and invasions of seven millennia.

Near defeat, Syrian President Bashar al-Assad sought Russian assistance in September 2015. The Russian Federation entered the road to Damascus.

Syria was the first conflict zone where both Russia and America were militarily opposed since the end of the Cold War. In a replay of past events a new proxy war began.

Syria has strategic importance for Russia. Outside former Soviet territories, Russia's only naval base is in the port city of Tartus which was developed and maintained by Soviet Union for keeping supplies – since 1971. Russia also has a base in Latakia. Russian intervention has re-established its former influence in West Asia which diminished after the dissolution of the Soviet Union. The Ba'athist government of Syria is important to Russia, which lost an ally in Ba'athist Iraq when Saddam Hussein was overthrown.

Russia initiated a new policy in Syria by making a three-pronged attack against ISIL. Russian Navy ships sailed to the Mediterranean coast of Syria from where they launched air cruise missiles and the Russian Aerospace Forces made some 5,240 air strikes against ISIL. These actions enabled Syrian government troops to advance against ISIL strongholds.

This combined action destroyed numerous strongholds, ammunition stores and logistic infrastructure of the Islamic State. Russia began intensive air campaigns in Syria in September 2015. Some three thousand militants of Jabhat al-Nusra and Jaish al-Yarmouk retreated to Jordan to escape the Russian air strikes, vowing retaliation. There is no cohesion among the fundamentalists; Saudis encourage the Jaish al-Islam, a coalition of Islamist and Salafist groups, Turkey and Qatar support Ahrar al-Sham who is an ally of the Jabhat al-Nusra.

Alarmed by Russian presence and change in the mediation of war the President of the United States stepped up support to anti-Syrian government forces. The lines between anti-government "moderate opposition" and ISIL became blurred.

The Russian military operation in Syria elevated the US-Russia conflict into a geopolitical confrontation.

In November 2015 France joined Russia in coordinated serial assaults on ISIL targets. By early November 2015 the Syrian army broke the two-year-old ISIL blockade of the Kweyris air base in Aleppo.

The West's growing anxiety about Russia's incursion into the Levant caused a conference at Vienna in October 2015. Syria, Iran and Russia refused to have the terrorist groups – Jaish al-Islam, a coalition of Islamist and Salafist groups and Ahrar al-Sham who are allies of the al-Nusra – at the negotiating table. Further, Russia refused to discuss the removal of Bashar al-Assad as a pre-condition of peace negotiations. Russian Foreign Minister Sergey Lavrov observed: "It is not for foreigners to decide who should govern Syria. This regime change doctrine has disrupted the Middle East. Removal of Saddam Hussein has brought chaos to Iraq. Killing Qaddafi has brought chaos to Libya and this chaos has led to the rise of the al-Qaeda and ISIL."

The conference yielded no result.

Turkey's growing fear of Russian intervention and the exposure of its relations with ISIL, made it retaliate. In late November 2015, Turkish forces shot down a Russian warplane on the ground that it had violated Turkish air space. Russia claimed that no such violations had taken place nor had the pilot been warned as is customary for incursion into foreign airspace. Russia intensified air strikes on ISIL targets causing collateral civilian damage.

Wiser after Afghanistan, Russia realised that the war against ISIL in Syria required an ally to fight on the ground. Iran's National Defence Forces and Lebanon's Hezbollah stepped into the fray. Joining them were armed opposition groups of Iraq which became allies of Iran after the US led invasion of Iraq in 2003. They have a common platform and common strategy – curtailing Israeli expansion and curbing US influence in the Middle East.

Russia provided the Syrian army with tanks, modern artillery systems, counter-battery radars, night vision gear. The Syrian National Army began to liberate towns of strategic importance and advanced towards the Turkish border and northern Aleppo where ISIL was holed up with their supply routes cut.

In violation of international law, President Erdogan of Turkey reacted by threatening to invade Syria. This adventurism was not without reason; Erdogan wanted restoration of oil supply lines and ammunition to the ISIL. Notwithstanding such postures, Turkey and Saudi Arabia and ISIL were aware that they were fighting a losing battle. There were suicide bombings in the Syrian capital and the city of Homs, killing hundreds and wounding many more. As a long-standing NATO ally, Turkey hoped to receive NATO intervention by claiming that Russian air strikes on the vital Incirlik airbase were acts of aggression. US President Obama and NATO refused to retaliate.

By the 'Law of Unintended Consequences' Russian air power and the Syrian Army defeated ISIL forces in some of their strongholds. The battle hardened Kurds and Syrians fought back fiercely. This halted Turkish invasion of Syria.

After two and half decades of being a spectator on the international scene, Russia's success in Syria announced its entry into the international scene as a global power.

Syria's regime agreed on a cease fire on 16 February 2016, an arrangement accepted by Russia and the United States. The cease fire soon ended with renewed hostilities. Throughout 2016 the battle waged between Russia-Iranian-Syrian forces on the one side and the US-led coalition forces on the other with another twist in which the US supported the anti-ISIL Kurdish YPG group. By March 2016 the Syrian army assisted by Russia and Iran recaptured the ancient heritage city of Palmyra from ISIL.

When it seemed as if the tide of the war had turned, Islamist rebels marched towards Syria's ancient city of Aleppo in July 2016. The battle of al-Hasakah began in August and the city was captured by Syrian forces. The relentless combined Russian and Syrian air strikes on IS strongholds in eastern Aleppo caused widespread havoc on the city. The besieged city ran out of food supplies, drinking water and medicines. As the Syrian forces closed in and the fighting intensified, the inhabitants began fleeing from the war-ravaged city.

UN humanitarian adviser Jan Egeland pleaded for a pause in the violence to enable UN to send medical workers, medical supplies and food into East Aleppo and enable the evacuation of the sick and wounded. Various European leaders condemned Russian military action which caused displacement of people, exodus of refugees to other areas, bombing of hospitals, schools and civilian enclaves.

On 12 December 2016 Russian Foreign Minister Sergey Lavrov stated that most of Aleppo was under Syrian government control. Large-scale evacuation of the citizens of Eastern Aleppo began on that day.

Sir Antony Brenton, former British Ambassador to Russia, observed in a BBC interview that Russia's success in Syria has implications beyond Syria. He said that the choice before President Putin was a secular and authoritarian Assad regime or the turmoil of a fundamentalist Islamist state which would destabilize an already volatile region. Sir Antony stated that there was no distinction or difference between "the moderate opposition" and ISIL. Many of the moderates defected to ISIL after being trained and armed by the United States. Sir Antony Brenton concluded by saying that Western interventions had brought disruption and terrible violence to West Asia. The people of West Asia have to solve their own problems of governance and progress.

Russian intervention in Syria was a watershed in geopolitics. For the first time since 1991, Russia played a major role in international politics. It is now a global power. For the first time since 1905, the United States was excluded from resolution of an international crisis. Decades of interventions by the United States and its allies to effect 'regime change' have been halted. But the havoc created will take decades to repair. Depredations of ISIL in Syria have been curtailed though not yet defeated.

In the unprecedented and nightmarish violence that followed, millions of refugees from Syria and Iraq began dangerous and desperate journeys across the Mediterranean Sea to seek refuge in Europe. This exodus from West Asia is unparalleled in history; thousands were drowned, thousands stranded, and millions rendered homeless. At first Europe gave them refuge, especially Germany, where the compassionate Chancellor Angela Merkel welcomed them.

Descendants of people who created great civilizations sailed on dangerous rafts over uncharted waters to encounter hostility and humiliation in alien lands. Cities that were once imperishable heritage of mankind lie in rubble. Millions are dead, millions are homeless, and hundreds of thousands of children have been orphaned.

Seeing the horrific scenes of devastation in Syria, one remembers words of the victorious Duke of Wellington after the carnage in the battle of Waterloo. "The saddest thing after a battle lost is a battle won."

Wars have no winners.

Egypt

The modern Arab Spring really began on the banks of the River Nile and under an Egyptian who was venerated as a Pharaoh by the Arab world. Had his dreams of political reform, social justice and a secular Arab world fructified, the scene in West Asia would have been very different.

The history of post-World War II Egypt begins with Gamal Abdel Nasser who remains an iconic figure in the Arab world. Continuing the tradition of Mustafa Kemal or Atatürk whom the young Nasser admired, he strove for social and economic justice, modernization of his ancient land, and Arab unity. He was especially influenced by Egyptian writer Tawfiq al-Hakim's novel *Return of the Spirit*, in which al-Hakim wrote that the Egyptian people were only in need of a "man in whom all their feelings and desires will be represented, and who will be for them a symbol of their objective".

During an unexceptional boyhood in Alexandria, except for the loss of his beloved mother, young Gamal spent many hours in libraries reading the works of great men. Biographies of national liberators inspired him enough to make him embark on a military career but his anti-government background prevented his entry into the Royal Military Academy for army officer training whereupon he joined the law school at King Fuad University. Eventually he gained admission to the Military Academy and was posted to Khartoum during World War II. Seeing the power Britain exerted on Egyptian affairs, Nasser formed a group of young military officers with nationalist sentiments who wanted a revolution and democratic government.

Nasser tasted war in Palestine during the Arab-Israeli War of 1948 where he served as a volunteer. In May 1948, following British withdrawal, King Farouk sent the Egyptian army into Palestine, where Nasser served in the 6th Infantry Battalion. He was horrified by the inexperience of the army. His Brigade was surrounded at Faluja but he refused to surrender. According to the famous journalist Eric Margolis, the "defenders of Faluja, including young army officer Gamal Abdel Nasser, became national heroes for enduring Israeli bombardment while isolated from their command".

After the war, Nasser returned to teach at the Royal Military Academy. He attempted an alliance with the Muslim Brotherhood but soon realized that their religious fundamentalism would impede development of a modern secular society.

In 1952 Colonel Nasser led the coup that deposed King Farouk. He introduced land reforms, free elementary education, free school meals, and strove for a secular society where women would have equal status. For this reason he cracked down on the Muslim Brotherhood, deposed President Naguib and eventually became President of Egypt in 1956.

He drew up plans for industrialization. To facilitate agriculture and food production in his country he promoted a huge irrigation project with the Aswan High Dam. The United States and Britain refused aid upon which he nationalized the Suez Canal. This provoked Britain and France along with Israel attacked Egypt. It was the height of the Cold War, but the United States and Russia jointly called for the removal of the invading forces. It was a victory which made Nasser one of the charismatic leaders of the non-aligned world. His pan-Arab sentiments led him to the

Arab-Israel War of 1967 which cost the Arab world dear and adversely affected the Palestinian cause. To regain lost territories he launched the War of Attrition, de-politicized the defence forces, and initiated political liberalization.

His untimely death in September 1970 was a catastrophic loss for the unity and progress of the Arab world. Aware of this, millions expressed their grief at his funeral.

Nasser's successor and friend, Anwar Sadat, wanted peace with Israel at any cost. He moved away from Nasser's non-alignment and became an ally of the United States, thus losing valuable Soviet military and technical aid. Under pressure from the United States, Sadat agreed to the terms set by the Camp David meeting in September 1978. The terms angered Egyptian and Arab nationalists who felt that Sadat had surrendered to Israeli demands. He was assassinated on 6 October 1981 while watching an annual Victory Parade in Cairo.

Another military man, Hosni Mubarak became the leader of Egypt. He more or less nullified many of the social and economic reforms initiated by Gamal Abdel Nasser and continued by Sadat. The de-politicization of the military sought by Nasser was put on the backburner. Indeed Mubarak enhanced the power of the military and curbed civil liberties.

Taking cue from the protests in Tunis in 2011, Egyptians staged massive rallies in Cairo's Tahrir or Freedom Square. Begun as peaceful demonstrations, these soon turned violent due to police brutality on one side and fury of the protesters on the other. Some nine hundred people were killed by the police. But the protests continued for almost three weeks at the end of which Hosni Mubarak resigned. He had ruled for three decades but had little to show by way of economic or social progress. He was arrested and convicted for the atrocities inflicted on his people.

Thereafter the Supreme Council of the Armed Forces (SCAF) assumed presidential powers. Parliamentary elections in 2011–12 brought the Islamist Muslim Brotherhood's Freedom and Justice Party and Salafist al-Nour party to power. Mohammed Morsi, leader of the Islamic Brotherhood was elected President in June 2012. He revoked a SCAF decree that limited his powers, dissolved the House of Representatives and changed the military's leadership, and named General Abdel Fattah al-Sisi as chief of staff and defence minister.

Morsi's subsequent actions deeply disappointed Egyptians. Public opinion began to turn against him because it became apparent that he was trying to assume arbitrary power and was encouraging Islamic fundamentalism. Once more there were protests and demonstrations; Morsi was deposed by the military in June 2013. An interim government took charge in June 2013. The military hunted down members of the Muslim Brotherhood who were arrested and killed. Soon after, the new regime drafted a fresh Constitution. The situation showed signs of erupting into a civil war; the country was divided between the supporters of the government and adherents of the Muslim Brotherhood.

Egypt is a populous country with a young population where cheap labour is available due to widespread unemployment. Egypt's industrial sector is largely based on energy extraction and production, which employs relatively few people and whose profits fluctuates with oil prices. Due to Egypt's ancient heritage and monuments, tourism accounts for one-tenth of the national income. But with West Asia descending into bloodshed and chaos, tourism too has suffered. A quarter of the government budget is allotted for salaries to government officials. The remaining pays for subsidies and interest payments. The Egyptian economy depends heavily on aid from other Sunni Muslim nations. A government pre-occupied with rivalry between the military and police and efforts to stamp out the Islamist threat, does not seem to have time to concentrate on economic development. For General Sisi, the priority is stability and cohesion of the country. How far he succeeds remain to be seen.

General Abdel Fattah al-Sisi is a far cry from Gamal Abdel Nasser.

Palestine

One of the grave injustices of the League of Nations was the case of Palestine. In November 1917 AJ Balfour, British Foreign Secretary, made a declaration that a national homeland would be established in Palestine for the Jewish people. This intention was conveyed to Baron LW Rothschild, an important member of the Jewish community. The intention contradicted the later terms of the Sykes-Picot Pact as well as the Husayn-McMahon exchanges. Two leading Jews, Chaim Weizmann and Nahum Sokolow, were its fervent supporters.

In the confusion and bitterness that followed the end of World War I and later the emotional charge created by the Holocaust, it has seldom been pointed out that when Palestine province became a British mandate under the League of Nations in 1922, it contained about *700,000 people*, of whom *only 58,000 were Jews*.

The Balfour Declaration also emphasized clearly that Mr Balfour's document was in no way detrimental to the longtime residents of the land. The Declaration specifically stated that *"nothing shall be done which may prejudice the civil and religious rights of existing non-Jewish communities in Palestine"*. Unfortunately it did not enunciate the political or national rights of these communities nor did it gave their names. But it was enough to enthuse the World Zionist Organization to press for a homeland in a region that they had abandoned two millennia back for a more prosperous life in Europe.

Two millennia ago, present-day Afghanistan was part of the Indian Maurya empire. The University of Takshashila as well as Gandhara art, a fusion of Greco-Indian style, are reflections of this heritage. The people were Hindus and then Buddhists. Later, after Islamic invasions the people became Muslims. A separate identity grew. No sane person in India would want to reclaim Afghanistan because of past links. Jews coming from Europe have done just that by claiming a land inhabited by Arabs for two millennia, and then displacing them. The history of Palestine is briefly narrated to indicate the predicaments and tragedy of the Palestinian people.

After suppression of Jewish revolts by Roman legions, Jews left their land and migrated to Europe where they led precarious lives as traders, pawn-brokers and money-lenders on the fringes of European-Christian society. Isabella of Spain's 'Edict of Faith' in March 1492 banished Jews and Muslims from Spain if they refused conversion. Those who refused left their homes and settled in the more tolerant terrains of England, France, Italy, Germany, North Africa and India's south-west coast. Periodic pogroms in Europe forced them to migrate from one city to another. Anti-Semitism was particularly strong in Eastern Europe where the Jewish community dominated commercial and financial sectors. Those who commanded respect were powerful bankers and entrepreneurs like the Rothschild family.

There was a cynical motive for proclaiming a Jewish homeland. Just before the outbreak of World War I, the British government hoped to garner support of the powerful Jewish lobby in the United States and urge the US government to join the Britain–France cause against Germany-Austria. Further, with a grateful

Jewish community in Palestine, Britain hoped to get their support for administering and enhancing the security of the Suez Canal, so crucial as a trade route to India. The Balfour Declaration was approved by the Allied Powers and then endorsed by the League of Nations in 1922.

There was however an afterthought when the British Foreign office realized the full implications of the Declaration. The British government limited the number of Jewish immigrants to 75,000 persons and an end to immigration by 1944 – unless the resident Palestinian Arabs of the region consented to further immigration. Zionists were furious and accused Britain of favouring the Arabs.

The Mandate not only reneged on an earlier promise made to protect Arab interests in 1914 but it ignored, and later obliterated, the crucial clause – **nothing shall be done which may prejudice the civil and religious rights of existing non-Jewish communities in Palestine**.

Later, Europe looked on while the Nazis slaughtered Jews. The Papacy's silence was deafening.

But a tall, blue-eyed, presumably Aryan Count Folke Bernadotte, a nephew of the King of Sweden, paid for the release of thousands of Jewish prisoners from Nazi concentration camps. Then he organized 'White Buses' to take them to safer places.

Britain left Palestine when the Mandate ended there in 1945. Ben Gurion immediately declared formation of a Jewish state and began occupying Arab lands. Holocaust survivors went to Palestine to establish a Jewish state. The Zionist organization Haganah began their work in right earnest. Faced with a fait accompli the newly formed United Nations approved the creation of Israel by its Resolution 181. Palestine was partitioned between

Arabs and Jews. Land disputes between Arabs and Jews led to violence between the Jews and Arabs in Palestine. A terrorist organization, Irgun, bombed Arab homes and shops, declaring that Arabs were greater enemies than the Nazis!! Lehi, a Zionist terrorist group, recruited retired Nazis to fight Palestine Arabs who retaliated.

In 1948 the United Nations sent Count Bernadotte to Palestine to negotiate peace between European Jews and Asian Arabs. The hero of 'White Buses' was able to negotiate a fragile truce; his peace plan would allow Arabs to return to their homeland. He proposed that Jerusalem would be administered by the United Nations. Jews rejected these terms. When Count Bernadotte arrived in Jerusalem in September 1948 for talks, he was assassinated at the gates of the holy city by the Zionist terrorist organization Lehi. One of the leaders of this Stern Gang, as the Lehi was pejoratively known, was Yitzhak Shamir who became Prime Minister of Israel in 1983.

This noble Swedish peacemakers' bullet-ridden body was taken on his white plane to his native Stockholm. He had fought for Jews who killed him and then consigned homeless Palestinians to *hafrada* or segregation, in tents. Palestinians retaliated with *intifada* or revolt.

Egypt, Iraq, and Syria established a common Federation in April 1953 to offer a united front against Israel's growing power. US Secretary of State, John Foster Dulles viewed these developments with unease. He believed nationalism would undermine US power. He was particularly distrustful of President Nasser. In 1955, Egypt signed an arms agreement with Czechoslovakia. This was actually a pact between Egypt and Soviet Union, which provided arms. President Nasser of Egypt was not keen to ally with the Soviet Union but he signed the agreement to send a message to the United States that he could look to Russia for aid if the United States did not oblige. The Soviet Union wanted to establish friendly relations with Arab nations and initiated its West Asian policy with this arms agreement.

President Nasser called for a meeting of the Arab League in Cairo in 1964. Arab nations agreed that steps should be taken for the establishment of the Palestine Liberation Organization (PLO) to represent the interests and aspirations of the Palestinian people. The Soviet Union recognized the PLO and gave all aid. This strained Soviet relations with Israel.

In the meantime Arab nationalism gained momentum under the charismatic leadership of President Nasser who supported Palestine. Supported by Egypt and Syria, dispossessed Palestinian guerrilla troops mounted attacks on the Israeli border. When Israel retaliated, Arab military forces were stationed around Israel's borders. American and British antagonism to Egypt and Syria had brought in the Soviet Union, which supported these two countries. Added to the territorial dispute was the anger provoked by Israel's action to channel waters of the River Jordan and the Sea of Galilee to irrigate the Negev desert. Syria implored the United States to restrain Israel's provocative acts and encroachment on demilitarized zones. Nevertheless Israel continued provocations along Arab frontiers. Egypt warned Israel against these manoeuvres. When these continued there was mobilization of the joint armies of the Arab states. The fierce response of Israel was not anticipated. Despite the massive mobilization of men and ammunition by Arab states, Israel inflicted crushing blows on the Egyptian and Syrian air force.

In March 1968, Yasser Arafat and his militant organization Fatah drew international attention when it attacked an Israeli force in the city of Karameh in Jordan. The Fatah joined the PLO and Arafat was appointed Chairman of the organization. The Soviet Union gave full support to Arafat and the Palestinian cause by supplying arms and training its soldiers. In an attempt to unite the divided Arabs, President Nasser formed an alliance with Jordan. After the debacle of the Six Day War, he realized that a policy of reconciliation with Israel might yield more results than aggression. He and King Hussein initiated peace moves with Israel. They negotiated for peace in return for restoration of the Sinai Peninsula and formation of a Palestinian State in the Gaza strip of the West Bank of River Jordan.

Though the Soviet Union supported the PLO cause, it also tried to influence a settlement between the Arab states and Israel through a Security Council resolution. The Camp David Accords nullified these plans. In response Leonid Brezhnev, President of the Soviet Union, urged nations to "respect the lawful rights of the Arab people of Palestine, including the right to create their own independent state". After Arafat went to Moscow in November 1978, Soviet Union recognized the PLO as the "sole legitimate representative of the Palestinian people".

After the death of President Nasser of Egypt, his successor Anwar Sadat turned to the United States for assisting in Egypt's development. The United States responded by inviting Sadat to Camp David and brokered peace between Egypt and Israel. According to the terms of the Camp David Accords, Israel agreed to leave the Sinai Peninsula in exchange for making the area a demilitarized zone. The United States offered economic assistance if Egypt renounced claims to a Palestinian state in the Gaza Strip and West Bank.

Today, the West Bank is nominally controlled by the Palestinian Authority but is under Israeli occupation. This comes in the form of Israeli troops, who enforce Israeli security restrictions on Palestinian movement and activities, and Israeli 'settlers' – Jews who build ever-expanding communities in the West Bank that effectively deny the land to Palestinians. Gaza is controlled by Hamas, an Islamist fundamentalist party, and is under Israeli blockade but not ground troop occupation.

The primary approach to solving the conflict today is a so-called 'two-state solution' that would establish Palestine as an independent state in Gaza and most of the West Bank, leaving the rest of the land to Israel. Though the two-state plan is clear in theory, the two sides are still deeply divided over its implementation.

The alternative to a two-state solution is a 'one-state solution', wherein all of the land becomes either one large Israel or one large Palestine. Most observers think this would cause more problems than it would solve, but this outcome is becoming more likely to be accepted due to political and demographic reasons.

The dispute between the Jews and Arabs has led to violence, mainly perpetrated by the heavily armed Israeli military and police. Watching the scenes of the bombing of Gaza, the arbitrary imprisonment of Palestinian youths, the shootings and killings, one wonders if these people – the Jews – were the same people who had suffered under Nazi rule, and whether they have forgotten the values of justice and humanity.

Yemen Arab Republic

It became free from British rule in 1962. The Soviet Union was one of the first nations to recognize the republic. In December 1962 the two nations signed two treaties on economic collaboration and in the following year diplomatic relations were established between the Soviet Union and Yemen. Soviet engineers were sent to explore possibilities of using soil and groundwater between the two countries. That same year Russians completed construction of Arrahaba International Airport. In a gesture of amity President Abdullah Assalal visited Moscow in 1964 during which visit a friendship treaty for economic and military relations was signed between the two nations.

It is a sad commentary on liberation movements that sometimes, a people fighting for national self-determination, after the departure of a colonial overlordship can so readily descend into the chaos of internecine strife. This has happened in the Yemen Arab Republic where a vicious and bloody war is being fought by two sides with total disregard for their own people. The United States and Saudi Arabia are backing one side, that of the former President, while the other is backed by Iran. The victims as always, in such civil wars, are innocent people who are not interested which government rules them so long as they are governed with a semblance of decency.

While the disasters in Iraq and Syria have grabbed headlines and television images, the plight of the ordinary people of Yemen goes somewhat un-noticed though that poor land is the scene of the greatest humanitarian disaster. Famine, pestilence, carnage – are all present like the dark horsemen of the Apocalypse.

Libya

The history of modern Libya is linked to the life of Muammar Qaddafi. He belonged to a poor Bedouin family in a Libya ruled by the Senussi monarchy of King Idris. While studying at the Royal Military Academy at Benghazi he established a revolutionary cell that planned to overthrow the monarchy.

King Idris, like other Arab monarchs, believed that power and privilege was theirs alone and the masses were there to serve them. Moreover, the unwise king, believing in the Roman dictum of divide and rule, deepened tribal and regional antagonism. He had total control over Libya's huge oil supply. Officials of this industry were immensely corrupt. During the Israeli-Arab War of 1967 the king's government was perceived as pro-Western and pro-Israeli. Riots erupted in the capital Tripoli and Benghazi; Libyan workers closed oil terminals to express solidarity with fellow Arabs.

As would happen in Afghanistan four years later, King Idris went for medical treatment and holiday to Greece and Turkey in the summer of 1969. During his absence Qaddafi's Free Officers seized the opportunity to overthrow the monarchy in what they called 'Operation Jerusalem'. Airports, police depots, radio stations, army barracks and government offices in Tripoli and Benghazi were taken over. The crown prince was arrested but he readily renounced the throne. The coup was therefore bloodless and there was no violence against the monarchists.

Soon after, Qaddafi announced establishment of the Libyan Arab Republic. He told Libyans that the "reactionary and corrupt regime" had ended and "the stench of which has sickened and horrified us all is over". The people were told that the coup was in the nature of a revolution which would usher in widespread change in the socio-economic and political nature of Libya. He proclaimed that the revolution meant "freedom, socialism, and unity" and over the coming years implemented measures to achieve this. The Revolutionary Command Council (RCC), as Qaddafi's group named themselves, had both civilians and military officials who were assigned appropriate tasks. They declared that their aim was to modernize the country and bring equality among the people. An amendment united secular and religious law codes, introducing shariah into the legal system. Land reforms were formulated along with the launch of a green revolution that would increase agricultural production. It was the Council's intention to reduce dependency on food imports. Qaddafi believed in aiding these sectors with government subsidies.

As crude oil was Libya's chief export, Qaddafi wanted to improve Libya's oil sector. In October 1969, he proclaimed that the prevailing trade terms were unfair as these benefitted foreign corporations more than the Libyan state. Accordingly he raised the price. In 1970 other OPEC states followed and enhanced prices which in turn led to increase of crude oil prices all over the world. The RCC pursued their agenda by securing taxes and arrears as well as followed with the Tripoli Agreement, in which they secured income tax, arrears and pricing from the oil corporations which brought additional revenues to the tune of one billion dollars. By 1979, profits from crude oil rose to twenty-five billion dollars. This dramatically raised the standard of living of Libyans along with income per capita. These were compatible to those of developed nations.

Unlike other Muslim nations whose elite only benefitted from oil profits, Qaddafi introduced many welfare schemes for his country in the sectors of housing, medical care, and compulsory primary education. The RCC passed laws doubling the minimum wage, statuary price controls, reduction of house rents. Qaddafi also wanted to remove seclusion and restriction of women's activities that had prevailed under the monarchy. Laws were passed prohibiting early marriage for women. Further legislation was passed whereby women had to consent to marriages arranged by their parents.

These reforms and welfare measures brought immense popular support to Qaddafi. Simultaneously, Islamic traditions were observed such as banning of alcohol consumption, night clubs. Churches were closed, the Arabic language was more in use, and dress code was Arabic. To remove tribal divisions, Qaddafi promoted the idea of a pan-Libyan identity to bring about national unity. To this end, modern-minded men were offered positions of importance, replacing the tribal leaders.

Qaddafi realized the necessity for Arab unity and mooted the idea of a pan-Arab mega state stretching from North Africa to West Asia. He persuaded other Arab leaders to pursue this plan. Libya signed the Tripoli Charter alongside Egypt and Sudan. This established the Arab Revolutionary Front, a pan-national union designed as a step towards the eventual political unification of the three North African nations. In 1970 Syria also decided to join this alliance. Qaddafi gave financial assistance to Egypt, Syria and other Arab states to implement this project. The idea of a pan-Arab state or a political federation suffered a setback after President Nasser's sudden death in September 1970. Thereafter Qaddafi pursued the idea of a pan-Africa movement. Qaddafi initiated measures to remove Western influence in Libya. One of these was by asking the United States not to use Malta as a NATO base. He supported the Popular Front for the Liberation of Palestine as well as other militant groups across the world. With the abundant financial resources from oil exports, he began arming Libya with modern weapons purchased from France and the Soviet Union.

In 1973 Qaddafi announced a Popular Revolution intended to remove foreign influence by introducing some draconian measures in the country's political life. He also initiated moves to involve the masses to participate in local governance whereby he hoped to weaken the sway of the old bureaucracy and enhance his power.

Qaddafi was anti-US and incurred the wrath of America which bombed the country after the crash of a passenger plane in Lockerbie in 1988. The United States and Britain urged the United Nations to impose sanctions on Libya. He changed course in 1999, veering away both from pan-Arab policies and socialism. Qaddafi recognized the need for stability in a region aflame with religious and sectarian violence. He kept fundamentalists under control and maintained the secular nature of the country – sometimes with the ruthless use of power.

When the so-called Arab Spring erupted in 2011 resulting in civil war, as in other Arab nations, NATO nations invaded the country, purportedly to bring in democracy to the Libyan people but really to garner the oil industry as they had done in Iraq. The rebels captured Qaddafi and killed him. The situation resembled Iraq where a strong, stable, if authoritarian leader ruled the country. And as in Iraq, the rebels were often men of the Islamic State.

Regime change, a favourite pastime of the United States, has taken place but Libya has descended into chaos and violence.

27

THE BYZANTINE COMMONWEALTH

The Balkans is a beautiful region crisscrossed by swift flowing rivers and fields framed against the rugged Dinaric mountains. Their people have lived on the path of invaders from various directions and have seen the rise and fall of numerous empires. The Greek Empire encompassed these territories and produced one of the greatest invaders of the world – Alexander of Macedon and introduced Greek culture here. Later Eastern Europe came under Rome; many of its emperors were natives of this land. The great historian and first frontline journalist Thucydides was a Thracian (present-day Bulgaria) prince who wrote the celebrated *History of the Peloponnesian War*. Later Slovanic tribes settled here and the population is now of Slav race and speak Slovanic languages.

The Roman Emperor Constantine drew Eastern Europe into the Byzantine Commonwealth. The Greek Orthodox religion and customs of this region date from the thousand years of Byzantine rule. Within the Byzantine Empire there were powerful kingdoms – Bulgaria under King Boris, Serbia under King Stefan Dusan whose alliance and friendship was sought by both Constantinople and Muscovy.

The Ottoman conquest of the Byzantine world was a disaster. A section of the population converted to Islam, either from fear of persecution or for profit. The Greco-Roman-Christian civilization was preserved in the hilltop monasteries of Rila and Athos. The legacy of five centuries of Ottoman rule may be seen in the racial strains, religion, architecture and cuisine of Eastern Europe. The ethno-religious antagonisms that have darkened the Balkan states today are also a legacy of the Ottoman past. They did not experience the effulgence of the European renaissance, the Reformation or the Enlightenment that shaped Western Europe.

But neither did they participate in the African slave trade carried on by Western European nations. Nor did they have imperial ambitions in Asia and Africa. It is possible they had neither the opportunity nor temperament for these because hemmed in between Slavic Russia and Teutonic Austria–Germany the Balkan people have seen their homes turned into battlegrounds between the Romanovs, Hapsburgs and Ottomans – a rivalry that ignited World War I in June 1914. They wanted stability – which always eluded them.

From the 19th century to World War I both Russia and Austria battled for the soul and soil of Eastern Europe. In 1918 both states were in shambles. The Treaty of Versailles gave the states of Eastern Europe independence but could not guarantee their freedom as the chess game of power politics unfolded during the inter-war years.

Yugoslavia

After military victory over Austria-Hungary during World War I, the Kingdom of Serbia was restored and joined with other South Slavic lands into the newly formed Kingdom of Serbs, Croats and Slovenes which was renamed Yugoslavia (land of Southern Slavs) in 1929. The Axis powers invaded Yugoslavia in 1941 and installed a puppet government. In 1944, the Soviet Army and Yugoslav Partisans evicted Axis troops and Yugoslavia was restored as a federation of six equal republics.

After the breakup of the Socialist Federal Republic of Yugoslavia in 1991–1992, Serbia and Montenegro formed a new federation of the two republics called the Federal Republic of Yugoslavia. When Kosovo ceded from Yugoslavia and the Serbian army fought them, NATO bombed Yugoslavia in 1999. The Federal Republic of Yugoslavia became the Union of Serbia and Montenegro.

Bulgaria

The country was inhabited by the Thracian tribe in the first millennium BC, until the Roman conquest, when it was made a Roman province with the capital at Serdica, present-day Sofia. Slavonic tribes settled here followed by Bulgars from Central Asia who founded the state of Bulgaria. King Boris I accepted Greek Orthodox Christianity in the 9th century when Kievan Russia also became Christian. Bulgaria became a powerful European state under Simeon the Great in the 10th century and then became part of the Byzantine Empire in the 11th century. The Ottoman Turks conquered Bulgaria in 1345 CE. Christians had either to convert to Islam or bear heavy taxes. They had to give their sons to the Ottomans to become an elite fighting group called Janissaries. These young men were taken as hostages to ensure loyalty to the Ottoman Empire. The Turkish tutelage lasted for five centuries.

Bulgaria attained independence by the Treaty of Berlin in 1878. Germany persuaded Bulgaria to join the Central Powers in October 1915; it was defeated and signed an armistice in 1918.

Bulgaria lost territories by the terms of the Treaty of Versailles. Attempts at democracy failed and a military coup took place. During World War II Bulgaria joined Germany and allowed German troops to pass through the country on their march to Greece. Russia declared war on Bulgaria in 1944 and entered the country. After the war Bulgaria became a communist nation and was a member of the Warsaw Pact. After the dissolution of the Soviet Union, Bulgaria became a member of NATO and the European Union. As this did not bring the promised benefits, Bulgaria has recently turned to Russia as a friend.

Baltic States – Finland, Estonia, Latvia, Lithuania

These did not form part of either the Byzantine or Ottoman empires. Their rulers were varied; some of them had their own dynasties. Hemmed in between two powerful nations – Germany to the west and Russia to the east – their independence was often challenged. On 18 December 1917 the Soviet government issued a decree, recognizing Finland's independence, and on 22 December it was approved by the highest Soviet executive body. After getting independence, Finland forged unity with other Scandinavian countries, and largely preserved economic and political stability. Without roots in democracy Estonia, Latvia, and Lithuania struggled and then succumbed to dictatorship. In September 1934, the three states signed a ten-year pact to cooperate in foreign affairs. After World War II these four nations became part of the Soviet Union and members of the Warsaw pact. After dissolution of the Soviet Union these states joined the European Union.

Poland

Freed from Russian rule in 1917, Poland established a democratic government in 1922, but economic and political turmoil compelled President Joseph Pilsudski to assume power as dictator in 1926. A new conservative constitution was drawn up in 1934 that accorded huge powers to the President. When Pilsudski died in 1935, powerful politicians in Poland consolidated power and established a 'non-party' system after the 1935 elections. The Camp of National Unity, an organization professing principles of nationalism and social justice, took over. With two powerful nations on its frontiers – Soviet Russia and Nazi Germany – Poland relied on Britain and France for protection but they were of no avail during World War II when Germany invaded Poland. After liberation by the Red Army in 1945, Poland became a Soviet satellite state and member of the Warsaw Pact with a communist government.

Hungary

Hungary enjoyed status as a major partner of the Hapsburg Austro-Hungarian monarchy. After the dissolution of the Hapsburg Empire, Hungary declared itself independent. It lost valuable agricultural lands to Romania, Yugoslavia, and Czechoslovakia as per the Versailles settlement. This had an adverse economic impact which deepened during the Great Depression in 1929. A liberal National Council took control over the government but was overthrown by its communist party under Bela Kun in 1919 which in turn was overthrown. A National Constituent Assembly was elected in January 1920 to determine the political future of Hungary. The old landed aristocracy ruled the country in an arbitrary fashion. As Prime Minister, General Gyula Gombos was a virtual dictator. Seeing the growing power of Nazi Germany he and his ministers cooperated with Hitler.

After World War II Hungary became a member of the Warsaw Pact with a communist government. In 1956 there was a revolt against Soviet authority led by Imre Nagy but the uprising was crushed; the fervent communist Janos Kader was installed as the head of state.

Czechoslovakia

The country declared its independence from Hungary and established the National Assembly in Prague in October 1918. The government dealt successfully with economic problems, especially agrarian ones by land reforms and redistribution. The political parties collaborated to preserve the unity and stability of the country during the 1920's. It was the only Central-Eastern European nation where democracy functioned under the able Antonin Svehla. The world depression impacted Czechoslovakia. This was accompanied by ethnic tensions, caused chiefly by ethnic Germans who lived in Sudetenland and who, instigated by Germany, demanded unification with Germany. Though an alliance had been signed by the Soviet Union, France and Czechoslovakia to protect it from German invasion they, including Britain, did nothing to prevent German annexation of Czechoslovakian Sudetenland in September 1938.

The reorganization of Europe after World War I was particularly significant in Eastern and Central Europe. The primary reason for turmoil was that the new nation states had little administrative experience in governance and because borders had been delineated without regard to racial and linguistic affinities. These nations made attempts to establish democracy but the power games of the major powers as well as lack of political leadership impeded both political and economic development. There was no strong professional middle class;

the peasantry was accustomed to arbitrary rule and the rich minority continued its irresponsible privileged existence. This was an ideal situation for usurping power. In the absence of strong national governments, foreign fascist groups usurped power – which is what happened in the early 1930's. But behind the scenes and encouraged by Soviet Russia, national communist parties began to organize resistance against the enemies at the gate.

It was with astonishment and dismay that these states saw the alliance of the Soviet Union and Nazi Germany through the Molotov-Ribbentrop Pact in 1939. It contained a secret protocol that divided Romania, Poland, Lithuania, Estonia and Finland into German and Soviet spheres of influence. Eastern Poland, Latvia, Estonia, Lithuania, Finland and Bessarabia in northern Romania were recognized as areas of Soviet influence. Soviet Union invaded parts of eastern Poland assigned to it by the Molotov-Ribbentrop Pact two weeks after the German invasion of western Poland. The Soviet Union occupied the Baltic States and named them Soviet Socialist Republics. Stalin justified this on the ground that Germany was likely to invade the Soviet Union from the frontiers of these nations. Germany invaded the Soviet Union in June 1941.

Several conferences were held in the middle of the war where the issue of Soviet sphere of influence was discussed between Roosevelt, Stalin and Churchill. The American President emphasized the need to secure Stalin's cooperation in the war against Germany and towards this, he stated, some concessions had to be made for the sake of world peace. The exact boundaries were discussed at the Tehran and Yalta Conferences.

The rift and serious differences between the Western Allies and the Soviet Union occurred almost as soon as the war ended.

In fact General Zhukov's race to plant the Soviet flag on the roof of the Reichstag before US General George S Patton could reach Berlin was symbolic of what lay ahead. Soviet victory, its military might and communist ideology caused anxiety in the West. It did not take long for the wartime allies to become peacetime adversaries.

The Soviet Union had demanded spheres of influence at the wartime conferences in Tehran and Yalta. This, Stalin declared, were vital for Soviet security because it was from Eastern Europe, particularly Poland and Finland, from where invasions were staged since the 12th century – except for the Mongol invasion which came from the east. In 1948 the Red Army rolled into Eastern Europe.

Fearing further Soviet incursions into Europe, the United States and its NATO allies admitted West Germany as a member-state of NATO. Russia considered this as direct provocation because the United States had agreed to Germany's neutrality after World War II.

Stalin died in 1953; Nikita Khrushchev assumed power in 1955 aided by Nikolai Bulganin. They decided that the Soviet Union must respond to formation of NATO by concluding the Warsaw Pact which drew in nations of Eastern Europe and the Baltic states. It was stated to be a mutual-defence organization constituted originally of the Soviet Union, Albania, Bulgaria, Czechoslovakia. The treaty provided for a unified military command and for the maintenance of Soviet military units in the territories of Warsaw Pact members. The Warsaw Pact was intended to strengthen Soviet hold over its allies, a program undertaken by the Soviet leaders. The treaty also provided leverage to the Soviet Union in international diplomacy. As a postscript it was added that the Warsaw agreement would lapse when and if a general East-West collective-security pact would come into force.

The Warsaw Pact nations were ruled by communist party members approved by and loyal to the Kremlin. Their economies were planned and regulated. Political restrictions resulted in uprisings as in Hungary in 1956 and Czechoslovakia in 1968. There was a revolt against Soviet authority led by Imre Nagy but the uprising was put down and Janos Kader was installed as the head of state. Anton Dubcek led the revolt against the Soviet Union in 1968. The Prague Spring was quelled. Albania under Enver Hoxha left the Warsaw Pact.

Paradoxically the power and unity of the Warsaw Pact was challenged not by Western neighbours but by the Communist Republic of China which was chafing in the role of the junior partner in the communist world where the Soviet Union was the star. China abused the Soviet Union saying its 'revisionist tendencies' would dilute the pristine nature of communism. But none of the Warsaw Pact members wanted to join hand with China except Albania.

One Eastern European nation which stood outside the Warsaw Pact was Yugoslavia. This was notwithstanding the fact that Josip Broz Tito was a communist and the government was a communist state. Marshal Tito had headed the Partisans and had fought Nazi Germany when it invaded Yugoslavia. At first a friend and ally of Stalin, Tito became a critic and was antagonistic towards Stalin after the war. Tito's Yugoslavia remained not only neutral but became one of the leaders of the Non-Aligned Movement in 1955.

Tito's death ushered in an era of ethnic tensions. Himself a Croat, Tito had kept the multi-racial union of Serbs, Croats,

Slovenes, Montenegrins and Macedonians in a stable and peaceful federation. The fragmentation of this federation, the wars in Kosovo and Bosnia, led by Muslim separatists, and instigated by NATO, shattered the multi-racial republic that Tito had built.

It was one of the tragedies of the 20th century.

28

RISE OF EAST ASIA

Japan

If Commodore Mathew Perry of the US Navy had foreseen how his bombardment of Shimoda port in 1854 would change the direction of American and Japanese history, he might have refrained from his high-handed action. The Japanese Shogunate which comprised of members of the Samurai or warrior class, gradually came to realize that medievalist isolation would be a disaster for a small nation and so they began building its military strength. The Meiji Restoration in 1867 accelerated modernization of Japan. By 1905 Japan was a world power and embarked on territorial expansion. It first challenged imperial Russia.

The Russian Tsar's government was unaware of the stunning transformation of Japan from a feudal Shogunate to a modern industrial power in two decades. Russia's Triple Entente allies, France and Britain, concealed the fact that they had given Japan technical assistance and training. Japan tried to negotiate with Russia on some island disputes but was rebuffed. Japan struck on sea and land. By the surprise attack Japan gained command of the sea; its destroyers, torpedoes and minefields dealt crushing blows to the imperial Russian navy. The flagship *Petropavlovsk,* was struck by a mine and sank with all seven hundred people on board. After gaining ascendency on sea, the Japanese forces marched into Korea and Manchuria. Finally, the Japanese army seized Port Arthur from Russia.

This Asian nation's military victory over a European one caused Britain and Germany grave anxiety; they belatedly rushed battleships and arms to Russia. In May 1905, the Russian imperial fleet sailed into the Straits of Tsushima. The waiting Japanese navy rained shells on Russian warships. The terrific destruction was concluded in an hour.

The battle of Tsushima shook the hauteur of the West because a small Asian nation had struck a blow on a mighty European empire. From 1498 European powers had commanded the high seas of Asia; they had annexed, colonized and imposed terms on Asian nations. Ironically it was the United States which negotiated peace between the two nations. Theodore Roosevelt, President of the United States and his fellow Americans were full of admiration for the "plucky little Japs". Peace was established by the Treaty of Portsmouth in 1905.

If Americans had noted the efficiency and secrecy with which the Japanese conducted military matters, they might not have experienced the disaster of Pearl Harbour perpetrated by the same "plucky little Japs". With the spirit of vengeance that is harboured in homo sapiens, the United States responded to the watery inferno of Pearl Harbour by the fiery inferno of Hiroshima and Nagasaki.

Japan cultivated Western allies; to please them it sent its soldiers to join the Army of Intervention that invaded Soviet Russia in 1919. The Russians kept a watchful eye on this unpredictable neighbour. As Japan's relation with China deteriorated, it was eager to mend fences with Soviet Russia over the Sakhalin Islands. In 1928 Japan and the Soviet Union reached an agreement which allowed Japanese fisheries on the Soviet-Pacific coast. Three years later Japan invaded Manchuria and established a puppet state there. The Soviet Union feared that its Far Eastern territories would soon become a target for Japanese expansion. To oppose international communism Japan signed the Anti-Comintern Pact with Nazi Germany in 1936. The brief interlude of peace between Japan and Russia ended. Just before Germany invaded Russia, Imperial Japan and the Soviet Union signed a non-aggression pact; this pact remained in force throughout World War II even though Japan was an ally of Germany. In April 1945 the Soviet Union ended the Pact with Japan and a month later moved Soviet forces across Siberia and invaded Manchuria. Shortly after, the United States atom-bombed Hiroshima and Nagasaki.

Just as the American Marshall Plan rebuilt a shattered Europe, so the United States began the revival of Japan by financial and technical aid even when the US Army of occupation remained on Japanese soil. Japan gained from this. Without having to spend immense sums on defence, Japan could build its industrial power. Until China's emergence in the last decade, Japan was the strongest economic power in Asia.

Russia did not wage war on Japan nor did it incinerate two Japanese cities during World War II, but fear of Soviet expansion kept Japan on America's side. In return the United States increased its defence forces in Japan and the western Pacific. The Soviet Union responded by substantial increase of naval and military presence in the Pacific Ocean, especially at the southern end of the Kuril Islands.

Today Japan remains a steadfast ally of the United States. They have common fears about China and North Korea which prompted President Obama to formulate his 'Pivot to East Asia' policy. Whether Prime Minister Shinzo Abe adheres to playing second fiddle to the United States remains to be seen.

Korea

Ancient Korea comprised of three kingdoms until the Silla dynasty united Korea and ruled for three centuries. Society was divided between landowners and their serfs. Chinese expansionist policy troubled the new kingdom. In the 4th century CE missionaries from India introduced Lord Buddha's teachings. The rulers eagerly embraced the new faith and built temples for their worship. Buddhism countered doctrines of Confucius. Chinese incursions were followed by Mongol invasions but they could not conquer Korea whose material and intellectual civilization flowered amidst tempests. The military and the civil service was a hereditary class. Korean society resembled Hindu society in its hereditary privileges.

Advent of European missionaries and merchants aroused Korean suspicions. At first foreign ships were unwelcome, until the pragmatic rulers realized that contact with the West would facilitate development. Emulating the Meiji policy in Japan, the Korean King Gojong advocated "eastern ethics and western technology". As in Japan, the reformists met resistance. Japan, a growing power, forced Koreans to open their ports to Japanese merchants and ships. Not be left behind, the United States, Britain, France and Germany followed suit.

Russia entered the Korean scene in the mid-19th century. The Treaties of Aigun in 1858 and Peking in 1860 accorded Russia rights on the northern bank of the Amur River, and six hundred miles of sea coast along the Maritime Province which included the important port of Vladivostok. This served imperial Russia's need to have a naval base on the Pacific and to participate in the growing lucrative trade with China and Japan. In 1884 Russia signed trade treaties with Korea. The Russians invited Koreans to settle in Russian villages across the border.

Japan eyed Russian expansion with alarm and sought to keep Korea as a buffer state while contending with China for control of East Asia. In 1898 Russia's presence was established in Korea when it acquired mining and forestry concessions near the Yalu and Tumen rivers. Sadly, the main depredations were by Japan, the closest Asian neighbour. A thwarted China looked on unable to challenge a rising Japan which dominated every sphere of Korean life. Japan annexed Korea in 1910 and made it a colony. Resembling Chinese policy in Tibet today, Japanese administrators made every attempt to subsume Korean national and cultural identity. Korea supplied food and raw material, forced labour and became the base for Japanese industrial expansion. Three decades of colonization are remembered with resentment in Korea. They therefore looked to the West for support. Pyongyang became a centre of Christian culture.

During World War II, United States, Britain, and Chiang Kai-shek's China met at Cairo in 1943, where they decided that all Japanese colonies would be liberated. In 1945 it was decided that the Soviet Union would accept the surrender of Japanese troops in the Korean peninsula north of the 38th parallel, while the United States would receive the surrender south of that line. This decision resulted in the division and separation of many villages along the 38th parallel and families who had connections across this line were divided.

After World War II the two superpowers divided Korea in two zones under their jurisdiction. Russian troops entered northern Korea in August 1945 and established a communist government there under Kim Il-Sung while the United States moved into the southern part. The United States supported Syngman Rhee in southern Korea. In August 1948 Syngman Rhee declared the formation of the Republic of Korea in Seoul. A month later Kim Il-Sung declared the formation of the Democratic People's Republic of Korea in Pyongyang. He also claimed jurisdiction over entire Korea. Both men claimed to be the legitimate government of Korea. But they also wanted to reunify the country and hold elections to decide which party would head the government.

In June 1950 the North Korean army crossed the 38th parallel and occupied much of South Korea and then captured the capital Seoul. The United States immediately called a meeting of the United Nations Security Council. Taking advantage of the absence of the Soviet representative (who would have vetoed the resolution) the Security Council passed a resolution that the North Korean army should withdraw immediately. The United Nations sent troops from fifteen nations to the peninsula to stop the North Korean advance. Most of the troops were from the United States.

What began as a civil war soon became a wider war between the Soviet Union, China and the United States. Fearing that Communist China would enter the fray and attack Chiang Kai-shek's Taiwan, the United States sent its Seventh Fleet into the Taiwan Strait. The People's Republic of China reacted to "American interference in China's internal affairs". In the meantime UN forces drove back the North Korean army to the 38th parallel. Dismissing Chinese warnings, General Douglas MacArthur advocated invading North Korea. By October 1950 US-led UN forces reached the Yalu River on the 38th parallel. With Soviet support and military aid Communist China entered the war and forced the US–UN troops to retreat. The war continued for three years in which American troops sustained heavy casualties, the Koreans even more. In between advances and retreats both sides arrived at a stalemate. In July 1953 an armistice was signed between the combatants at Panmunjom. (The authors' father was present there.)

But the dream of unifying the two Koreas was stillborn. The intensification of the Cold War deepened hostilities between the two Koreas. The Korean War was not so much a war between the two fraternal states as a Pawn's War between the superpowers.

From the time of establishment of a communist government in North Korea in 1949, the Soviet Union stood unwaveringly beside that country. North Korea was Russia's ally of the Cold War and supported the North against South Korea. Relations between Russia and South Korea reflected the animosities of the Cold War. South Koreans resented Soviet support of North Korea. Soviet Union regarded American bases in South Korea as a threat.

But when Soviet power began to decline in the late 1980's the new ruler Gorbachev looked westward for support and assistance. Before making overtures to South Korea for assistance and collaboration, Gorbachev began drastically reducing food, arms and energy aid to North Korea. A happy South Korea responded by giving the Soviet Union aid of $1.5 billion. This pro-South Korean policy was continued by the first president of the Russian Federation, Boris Yeltsin. While Moscow's military aid to North Korea ceased and trade between the two states declined, economic relations with South Korea improved.

Even earlier when Russo-Chinese relations cooled, South Korea sent feelers of friendship to the Soviet Union. In early

1979, South Korea signed a trade agreement with the Soviet Union and its Warsaw Pact allies. In late 1980's as Russia encountered economic difficulties, Gorbachev sought South Korean investment in Russia. Soon after, South Korean President Roh Tae-woo and Gorbachev sealed a rapprochement to erase past hostilities. To counter-balance growing Chinese dominance in the Asia-Pacific region, the Soviet Union sought to establish political and commercial relations in that region.

South Korea responded warmly; it required the oil, metals, timber, and fish of the Soviet Far East. The South Korean investment among the Soviet allies in Eastern Europe caused anxiety in the United States, which feared the possibility of high technology transfers to the Soviet bloc. Symbolic of this new amity was the Olympic Games held in Seoul in 1988 when thousands of Soviet citizens attended and participated in the Games. By 1988, trade was brisk between the two countries, though channelled through Japan, Hong Kong and the Soviet Union's Eastern European allies. Gorbachev initiated the move to establishing trade offices of the two nations in Moscow and Seoul in 1989. South Korean companies such as Daewoo and Sunkyong commenced direct commercial ties with the Soviet Union. South Korea's prosperity enabled it to invest in Soviet Union and other Warsaw Pact countries. Commercial expansion and technological connections with Eurasian neighbours was South Korea's response to American stranglehold and the ever present fear of Chinese/Japanese hegemony in East Asia.

South Korean and Soviet leaders held a summit in June 1989. There it was agreed among other things to allow some 300,000 Soviet-Koreans who were interned in Soviet Sakhalin since 1945 to return home. When the Soviet Union was dismantled in 1991 South Korea and Russia established formal diplomatic ties and later they signed a protocol permitting exchange of visits between defence personnel of the two states. The Russian Foreign Minister, Yevgeny Primakov initiated a move to establish a hotline between Presidents of the two states. This paved the way for important collaborations in development of the energy and railway sectors in the Russian Far East adjoining Korea.

Russia has predicaments about North Korea whose labour force is employed in Russia's Far Eastern industries and projects. Further, North Korea is an essential corridor for transshipment of natural gas to South Korea, Asia and Europe. Tensions that could escalate into armed skirmishes would endanger these economic-commercial projects. The Russian Federation is caught in a predicament; the compulsion to support a loyal and useful ally who must also be checked in its reckless nuclear games. At the same time President Putin believes that threats and punitive sanctions can only goad a desperate government into desperate acts. A Russian general observed: "A cornered rat acts like a tiger."

North Korea's assertive nuclear policy has not found favour with the Russian Federation. This has the potential to create serious disturbances in an already troubled region where China is extending tentacles on land and sea and provides covert support to North Korea. Punitive sanctions imposed on North Korea by the United States have not deterred Kim Jong-un from pushing ahead with nuclear tests. Russia advocates negotiation involving all the concerned states; the two Koreas, the United States and the Russian Federation, which in its earlier avatar as the Soviet Union has dealt with the political, economic and defence problems of North Korea.

Economic collaboration and prospective prosperity have erased memories of past hostilities. Throughout human history when the debris of wars have been cleared other considerations enter relations between nations.

Now, the Korean peninsula is the focus of world attention because dramatic changes seem to be on the horizon. Whether these will fructify will depend on the two unpredictable leaders who will decide how to proceed with their own conflicting agendas. President Donald Trump insists on abandonment of North Korea's nuclear weapons and this process will be closely monitored. North Korea wants guarantee of its security and lifting of sanctions. Which action will come first is yet to be decided. But Kim Jong-un fears that after he has lost his formidable arsenal the United States may commence procedure for regime change as it did in Libya. China and Russia support North Korea. Japan is wary of North Korea and will follow American diktat. South Korea wants peace on the peninsula.

At the meeting between the two leaders at Singapore on 12 June 2018, President Trump bent backwards to praise Chairman Kim and was keen to establish rapport with the man he had earlier called "a sick puppy" and "the little rocket man". He further stunned the world, his allies and particularly his aides by announcing suspension of military drills in South Korea.

There are other issues involved. Will denuclearization of North Korea lead to withdrawal of American troops from South Korea? This would be the ultimate goal of both North and South Korea for a comprehensive peace settlement. Analysts believe that once North Korea reaches an agreement with the international community and begins the process of denuclearization the United States and its volatile president must realize that they will have no reason to impose sanctions. Peace in the Korean peninsula will materialize if the denuclearization and the withdrawal of US troops happen simultaneously. This would be ideally done with the support of the international community, especially of Russia, China, India and the European Union nations. Whether the United States would like losing its grip on South Korea and thereby its influence in the region is a matter of debate. President Trump's rejection of the Iran Nuclear Deal made by his able predecessor will make Kim Jong-un think twice about a deal with the United States. American threat of decimating North Korea "like we did to Libya" is not conducive to peace negotiations.

The meetings of the leaders of the two Koreas in Pyongyang in mid September 2018 holds out hope for a settlement.

China

Three millennia of Chinese history did not witness the dramatic changes that took place from 1911 to the present-day. The ramshackle Manchu Empire was falling apart in the 19th century when numerous European powers laid siege to its ports, conducted infamous opium wars, established protectorates which did everything but protect this vast country. It was perhaps the most humiliating century in Chinese history.

Hopes of regeneration came with Sun Yat-sen's revolution in 1911. But those hopes began to flounder when his brother-in-law, General Chiang Kai-shek took charge of the country. The Kuomintang regime was riddled with corruption and nefarious deals. While courting Soviet Russia, Chiang arranged the massacre of Chinese communists in Shanghai in 1927. Mikhail Borodin's mission was a disaster. Rumour has it that Stalin instructed Chiang to make it a disaster because he did not want a powerful Communist China to challenge Soviet influence in the communist world. Not daring to anger the Soviet Union, Mikhail Borodin's 'escape' to Russia was arranged by Chiang

Kai-shek. As the flight began, Borodin lamented: "The revolution extends to the Yangtse River. If a diver were sent down to the bottom of this yellow stream he would rise again with an armful of shattered hopes."

Borodin's desertion was seen as a betrayal of the Chinese communists by Russia and rankled in their hearts. Communist China never forgot this betrayal.

Young Mao Zedong watched with anger and caution. Betrayal was in the Chinese air. He knew he could not rely on Stalin's Russia, nor in Roosevelt's United States, and certainly not on the inept League of Nations that acquiesced before the might of militarist Japan. Mao's famous Long March from the Yunnan caves to victory of the People's Liberation Army against Kuomintang forces in 1949 attained the impossible – establishment of the Communist People's Republic of China. However Chiang Kai-shek, operating from Taiwan remained the representative of China in the United Nations Security Council.

Communist Russia and Communist China became allies when the Korean War began in 1950. Russia gave massive aid to the struggling Chinese economy, trained its scientists, doctors and defence personnel. China received arms from Russia. Premier Khrushchev staged melodramatic scenes at the United Nations, demanding that Communist China and not Taiwan should represent China. Despite these declarations of comradeship the relations began to fray in 1959. The conflict came when China suppressed an uprising in Tibet in 1959, bringing it into conflict with India, with which it had earlier forged bonds and stressed peaceful coexistence at the Bandung Conference in 1954. Further, Prime Minister Nehru had championed Communist China's membership in the United Nations and a place in the Security Council. Caught in this conflict between friendly India and Communist China, Soviet leaders said they could not take sides in a dispute "between a brother and a friend".

More serious disputes between the two communist countries began in 1968 over the borders of Tumen and Ussuri Rivers; the areas became militarized with heavy concentration of tactical nuclear-armed missiles. There was a border war in 1969 which came perilously close to a nuclear showdown. Seeing the military might mobilized there, Chinese forces retreated and did not contest the region claimed by the Soviet Union. Sporadic skirmishes continued throughout 1969 to 1971. The Soviet Union could no longer regard China as a brother.

The Cultural Revolution disrupted China's political and economic life. Moderates like Zhou En-lai looked on helplessly as the Gang of Four headed by Mao Zedong's young fourth wife plunged China into a maelstrom. The ideological dispute between the two countries over revisionism was a camouflage for China's growing ambition to be a superpower and replace the Soviet Union's place and prestige in the non-aligned world. The two countries competed to exert influence in other communist states. China saw in its onetime benefactor and protector the principal obstacle to its ambitions. China abandoned its fierce Marxist-Leninist ideology in order to be more acceptable to the West. The debate over revisionism lessened after Leonid Brezhnev replaced Nikita Khrushchev and after Mao Zedong died in 1976.

Brezhnev and his colleagues wanted to strengthen Soviet power and influence in the communist states of Eastern Europe and Asia. This required thwarting China's aggressive hegemony in these areas. Brezhnev sought to bring China back into the fold but Mao Zedong's opposition to Soviet policy which he termed revisionist offended Soviet foreign policy makers who were pragmatic about international relations. The antagonism grew.

A dramatic change occurred in Sino-US relations in 1971. Seeing the growing antagonism between the Soviet Union and the People's Republic of China, the United States made overtures to China. The new friendship was brokered by Pakistan. After two decades of bitter hostility the US President visited China. Henry Kissinger's role in this negotiation earned him the title 'Metternich' – forgetting that the Austrian Chancellor's policies crumbled in the revolutions of 1848. China and the United States now had a common adversary in the Soviet Union; Pakistan was the sworn enemy of India. China's amity with the United States strengthened its position in the international arena.

Vietnam was recovering from a ruinous war with the United States from which she emerged victorious. China invaded Vietnam in 1979. Vietnam was an ally of the Soviet Union, which watched, gave arms and assistance, but did not intervene in Vietnam. That same year, when the Soviet Union intervened in Afghanistan on the request of President Nur Muhammad Taraki's socialist government, China joined the United States and Pakistan in arming and financing Afghans terrorists or mujahideen, to fight the Soviet Army. China established bases in its Muslim dominated Xinjiang province for training Muslim terrorists. By arming and training Afghan mujahideen, both China and Pakistan played a decisive role in the reverses encountered by the Soviet Army in Afghanistan.

Nevertheless, the Soviet Union sought reconciliation with China in 1982. Brezhnev and Deng Xiaoping agreed to restore diplomatic relations. In 1985, Soviet President Gorbachev continued the policy of rapprochement with China. The strength of Soviet garrisons was reduced on the Sino-Soviet border and in Mongolia. The long standing border-demarcation dispute which had been the main source of conflict was shelved. Trade relations, which had flourished from the time of Moscow-Beijing caravans in the 16th century, were resumed. When Soviet forces withdrew from Afghanistan in 1989, China's acts of provocations also ceased. China now planned dominance of Asia. A war-weary Russia made peace with China, which was becoming a power to contend with. There is now a semblance of peace and amity between the two.

Now, both countries oppose the 'Pivot to East Asia' policy of the United States, especially in the Indian Ocean and South China Sea. A new realignment of nations is taking place with Russia and China on one side and the United States, Japan and East Asian countries on the other that fear and resent Chinese domination in this region. The impressive display of Russian military might in Siberia in September 2018 and China's participation in the joint military exercises has caused anxiety in the West.

The situation is complicated by China's friendship with Pakistan. Russian policy makers cannot be unaware of Pakistan's past nefarious role as the United States' cat's paw in Afghanistan in the 1980's when Pakistani soldiers killed Soviet soldiers with impunity, and its present status as a rogue state. Whether they will lend themselves to this unholy trinity remains to be seen.

The future of Sino-Soviet relations is difficult to predict. As the Russian Federation retrieves its former eminence in military might and gains affluence, it will pose a challenge to Chinese power. Conflicts may start once more. Friends and foes keep changing.

29

LATIN AMERICA LIBERATED

Borrowed from Tasso's classic *Liberated Jersualem*

The tragedy of South America commenced with the advent of Christopher Columbus in 1492 followed by arrival of Spanish-Portuguese conquistadores in the early 16th century.

The new Spanish colonies in South America expanded when Nicolas de Ovando, Knight Commander of Alcantra, took charge. Member of a religious order that enforced Christianity in the outposts of the Spanish realm, he arrived in Hispaniola (Haiti) with 200 settlers and the survivors of Columbus' expeditionary force. Harsh and efficient, Ovando ensured that Spaniards became landlords and were able to utilize indigenous labour for cattle ranches, sugar mills and gold streams. Esquivel in Jamaica, and Velasquez in Cuba followed the same pattern. Pinzon, Ojeda, and Vasco Nuenez de Balboa extended Spanish territories in Antilles, Venezuela, Guinea. Central America became a thriving centre for plantations; its wealth was derived from the ruthless exploitation of the native population.

When news of these activities reached the Royal Council of Spain, King Ferdinand dispatched decrees on the administration of the colonies which were ignored by the conquistadores. The monarchs sometimes recalled them, put them in prisons and even executed a few flagrant cases of disobedience, but they could not control the soldiers of fortune across a vast ocean. Surprisingly, the Catholic Church opposed these spreaders of Christianity. Cardinal Ximenes and Emperor Charles V of Spain passed legislation to improve the treatment of local people through the 'Laws of Burgos'.

The new Hispanic empire was unique in history. This continent was the home of ancient civilizations whose origins are wrapped in mystery. The Maya in Guatemala, the Oaxaca, Aztecs and Toltecs of Mexico, and Incas of Peru practiced advanced agriculture. They had made progress in architecture, sculpture, mathematics, astronomy, medicine. The Mayan script was also developed in this period. When a growing population of this region increased the demand for land it caused warfare among the tribes. The capital of the Aztec Empire was in Tenochtitlan which had massive temples, palaces, aqueducts and markets that sold a variety of products. The Incas of Peru were the most advanced as may be seen by the city of Machu Picchu high on the Andes mountains. The central authority of the empire was the Sapa Inca. It was both its strength and weakness. Without his direct control the centralized system collapsed.

The conquistadores were drawn from the dregs of Iberian society; they had no status in their own society. Renegades from justice, they came to South America to make fortunes; with cunning and brutality they carved out kingdoms from legitimate native rulers. Impecunious, they were dazzled by the material wealth of these civilizations. When they recovered from astonishment at the splendour of the cities and simplicity of the people, they realized that the monolithic structure of society was weak and the people were passive. They knew that with superior warfare the people could be conquered.

Hernan Cortes was the archetypal conquistador; vicious, avaricious, unscrupulous and totally without the Christian virtues that he claimed to spread. After arriving in Mexico, he gathered information on the rivalries between the tribes and proceeded on the ancient Roman dictum – *divide et impera*. Meanwhile, the Aztec emperor Montezuma heard of the arrival of "the children of the sun", whom the royal priests had prophesized would one day rule Mexico.

Foolishly, the Mexican Emperor Montezuma sent the ruthless adventurers gifts of gold and begged Cortes and gang to "return to the sun". Aztec gold only whetted their appetites. Seated on a palanquin of burnished gold, dressed in robes encrusted with pearls and emeralds, Montezuma went to meet Cortes. While the emperor was filled with dread of the prophesied doom, the adventurer planned plunder and pillage. The Spaniards took Montezuma as hostage, made him swear allegiance to the Spanish king. The people stoned to death their emperor for his folly. Cortes took Montezuma's gold, burnt the golden pyramids and palaces of Tenochtitlan, and erected a statue of the Madonna. Cortes forcibly imposed Christianity on the people. Mexico City was built on the ashes of Tenochtitlan and the Aztec civilization.

The most infamous conquistador was Francisco Pizarro. Like the horsemen of the Apocalypse he and his army plundered Peru. Pizarro invited Atahualpa, the Sapa Inca to dinner, killed the royal guest and the trusting retinue. The stunned Inca population did not know how to retaliate. Pizarro and his four brutal brothers then went to the city of Cuzco and plundered the gold reserves. Here again the new city Lima was built on the ruins of Cuzco. In twenty-five years, the ruthless conquistadores had acquired an empire for Spain. Brazil was later conquered by

Portuguese warriors. Ironically and with some poetic justice the metropolitan government of Spain, especially the sagacious Spanish-Habsburg Emperor Charles V, refused them all rewards and recognition, and imprisoned them.

The Spaniards grabbed lands of the unarmed population, reduced them as tenants and then exacted rent from them. They were coerced into hard labour. Landowners produced wine, wheat, olive oil which brought huge profits. When the Spanish settlers discovered silver and tin deposits they began mining activities in which the native people were forced to work.

The ruthless exploitation of these people caused deep concern to the Spanish government in Madrid. Many were the voices of protest against the practices of the settlers. A Dominican friar, Francisco de Vitoria and a churchman, Bartolome de las Casas questioned the moral right of Spaniards to occupy alien lands, impose Spanish customs and the Christian religion in a famous book *Historia Apologética*. Emperor Charles V introduced the *Juzgado General de Indios* or summary courts where the native people could seek justice. But justice was seldom delivered. The condition of the native people swiftly deteriorated. Within a decade the native population suffered a drastic reduction. Only one-tenth of the original population survived. Indignant Spanish missionaries ascribed this demographic catastrophe to the terrible treatment of the native people.

Since cheap plentiful labour was no longer available for their profitable enterprises, food production declined and rising prices led to inflation. The lucrative export of food ended. As necessity is the mother of invention sudden adjustments were made. The vast fields were converted to grazing lands for cattle and sheep. This was the origin of the ranches that thrived in later centuries on export of meat and hides.

Meanwhile the near extinction of native labour compelled settlers to start the African slave trade which was gaining momentum in the late 16th century. Spanish settlers hoped that the sturdier African races would better withstand the grim labour facing them. The unfairly maligned King Philip II of Spain condemned and tried to stop African slave trade but the royal writ did not run to South America. Indeed many Spaniards profiting from business in South America upheld the conduct of the colonists and desperados in the new world. As time went on the Spanish government chose expediency over ethics. They deemed it necessary to consolidate their conquests and approve ruthless policies, especially as the Portuguese, Dutch and English empires in the New World and Far East began burgeoning. Viceroys and governors sent by Metropolitan Spain became far more dictatorial than their counterparts at home. They were the progenitors of military juntas that misruled South America.

The native people lived in shabby *barrios* and dared not oppose such formidable forces. In silent misery they watched their physical heritage destroyed, their languages obliterated, their ancient faith derided, their opportunities curtailed, and their very existence endangered.

Paradoxically it was the lower clergy of the Catholic Church that provided support to the poor, the exploited and the oppressed. It was the compassion of the priests and lay brothers that made the Maya, Inca, and other tribes embrace Christianity. The Catholic Church and the Communist Party had the same agenda – salvation of the masses. Yet they met in headlong conflict in the early 20th century.

A charismatic figure rose in the early 19th century; he was the founder and leader of South America's independence movement. Simon Bolivar's family came to South America in the 16th century and became one of the leading families of Venezuela. A brilliant general and statesman, Simon Bolivar dedicated his life to liberate South America from Spanish rule and is venerated such. Unfortunately, beneficiaries of the liberation were the landed and military classes that governed with impunity. The indigenous people and those of African descent encountered terrible suffering.

After the declaration of the Monroe Doctrine by US President James Monroe in 1823, the United States spread its own hegemony on the continent, sometimes supported, sometimes opposed by the South American rulers.

This grim scenario made the doctrine of communism very attractive. The first communist conference was held in Argentina in June 1929. Thirty-eight delegates representing Argentina, Brazil, Bolivia, El Salvador, Guatemala, Cuba, Columbia, Ecuador, Mexico, Panama, Paraguay, Peru, Uruguay and Venezuela participated in the conference. Though Chile had the only established communist party in the region, members were not allowed to participate by the oppressive Ibanez government which was then in power. Participants declared their opposition to imperialism and resistance to capitalism. This resulted in reprisal against communist party members by South American governments.

Argentine's President Juan Perón made overtures of friendship between his country and the Soviet Union. This was not intended to be a communist alliance but rather a means of countering the dominance of the United States in South America. The Soviet Union sought to win the goodwill of governments and people through technical assistance and moral support in their struggle against imperialism. The native people as well as South Americans of Spanish descent – professional classes, intellectuals and students – resented the domination of the military and commercial elite. It is among these people that the Soviet Union made inroads of friendship. The dispossessed saw in the Soviet Union a technologically advanced modern state, one that offered equal opportunities and basic amenities of life.

The first challenge to American influence in Cuba came from the Soviet Union which had earlier established connections when Maxim Litvinov, a former Soviet Foreign Minister was appointed Ambassador to the United States during World War II. Seeing the opportunity for spreading Soviet influence, Litvinov established the first Soviet Embassy in Havana and made contacts with Cuban communists. After the war the Cuban governments under Ramon Grau and Carlos Prio banned the Cuban Communist Party. After the coup d'etat by Batista, relations with Soviet Union were severed.

When the communist Fidel Castro came to power in 1959, the Soviet Union was not certain if assistance should be given to him, especially after the KGB informed Kremlin that Castro was actually a CIA double agent! When Castro's conflict with the United States escalated in early 1960, after the embargo imposed by the United States, Soviet Foreign Minister Anastas Mikoyan went to Cuba to resolve matters. He informed Khrushchev that Fidel Castro was a potential ally and recommended urgent economic and commercial assistance. After the fiasco of the Bay of Pigs in 1961, when Cuban soldiers repulsed the US-aided force, Fidel Castro declared Cuba a Socialist Republic.

This heightened tension with the United States. The Soviets responded by sending sixty ships carrying military material to Cuba. President John F Kennedy stated that any nuclear missile attack from Cuba would be regarded as an attack by the Soviet Union and that there would be appropriate retaliation. Between

October and November 1962 the world stood on the brink of a nuclear conflict. The Soviet Union agreed to withdraw the missiles in return for a US guarantee not to invade Cuba or support any invasion and to remove all missiles set in southern Italy and in Turkey. This deal was accepted and the crisis ended.

Fidel Castro was furious for not being consulted during the negotiations. Withdrawal of missiles and other weapons diminished Castro's prestige. It was clear that the Soviet Union would not wage war for other countries, even if they professed socialist ideology. Nevertheless, the Soviet Union established a base near Havana for collecting intelligence and monitoring all US military and civilian geosynchronous communications satellites. Cuba's friendship with Russia remained intact until 1991. Cuba's friendship was not free; the Soviet Union provided military and economic assistance. In 1972, Cuba became a member of the Council of Mutual Aid which fostered cooperation in national economic planning.

In the late 1980s Gorbachev's hastily formulated perestroika and glasnost triggered an economic crisis in the Soviet Union. Unfazed by the economic turmoil in the Soviet Union, Castro hardened his stand on pristine socialism. He accused the Soviet Union of "imperialism, change and counter-revolution". The real reason for this socialist purity was that massive exports to the Soviet Union – 80 per cent of all Cuban sugar, 40 per cent of all Cuban citrus fruits – dropped. Oil imports by Cuba dropped from 13 million tons in 1989 to about 3 million tons in the 1990's. Castro began looking towards China.

While it seems that the Monroe Doctrine is there to stay for a while with the Trump administrations praise for it, the charisma of Fidel Castro will remain over Central and South America. His defiance of American power and his independent stand on issues will continue to inspire that continent even after his death.

Fidel Castro's life is the stuff of legends. And legends don't die.

***

Another charismatic figure who appeared on the South American canvas was Che Guevara. He was an ardent revolutionary who believed that South American nations should formulate the economic and political policies best suited to the needs of the people.

Chile was the scene of a proxy war in the 1970's when Salvador Allende became President of Chile. He did not begin a confrontation with the United States. Indeed his Popular Unity government also tried to maintain normal relations with the United States but so intense was the fear of another socialist government in the western hemisphere that the United States took secret action to prevent Allende from taking office after election. The CIA unit in Chile was instructed to prepare a coup to overthrow Allende. That effort did not fructify. Despite this Allende tried to maintain normal relations with the United States as he did not want to have continual attrition with the nearby superpower. When Chile nationalized its copper industry, the United States not only terminated financial support but began vigorous support of Allende's opponents. As with several other non-Western nations, this policy compelled a potential pro-US government to turn to the Soviet Union for commercial and financial support. The Soviets pledged to invest $400 million in Chile in the future.

Allende embarked on a policy of economic development coupled with welfare measures. His government reduced inflation and unemployment by providing employment in the new nationalized enterprises and public works projects. There was redistribution of income, and increase in consumption of goods. The government raised salaries and wages, reduced taxes, and introduced free distribution of essential commodities. Pensions for the aged, widows, invalids, and orphans were enhanced. But due to reliance on imports of food products, the country's fiscal deficit increased and prices rose. Increases in wages and salaries were neutralized by high inflation. Chile's mainstay – copper exports – was adversely affected when the price of copper fell from $66 per ton in 1970 to only $48–49 in 1971 and 1972. Despite these setbacks support of Allende's Popular Unity coalition was undiminished.

The Soviet Union was scheduled to send military weapons to the Chilean army in 1973; when they learned that a coup was afoot by the Chilean army to oust Allende, the shipment was stopped. Afraid of Allende's growing popularity, his ally, the Christian Democrats, now allied itself with the right-wing National Party against Allende's government. The United States joined this coalition.

The democratically elected Salvador Allende was assassinated and his popular socialist government was overthrown by a bloody CIA coup in 1973. The great poet Pablo Neruda wrote of his friend:

Allende was assassinated for nationalizing...the wealth of Chilean subsoil...From the saltpetre deserts, the underwater coal mines, and the terrible heights where copper is extracted through inhuman work by the hands of my people, a liberating movement of great magnitude arose... This movement led a man named Salvador Allende to the presidency of Chile, to undertake reforms and measures of justice that could not be postponed. USA feared Allende who was 'dangerously independent, irredeemably leftist, irresponsibly anti-business' and – perhaps worst of all – because he openly thumbed his nose at the United States. He challenged American business with his doctrine of excess profits, arguing that the wages in Chile were paltry compared with extravagant gains by big U.S. corporations. Latin America, the argument went, had been reduced to a mere colony of the United States.

In contrast to the brutal conquistadores who ravaged Latin America, the continent has produced fiery leaders both of Iberian descent and of indigenous ancestry. Apart from Fidel Castro, Che Guevara and Salvador Allende, there have been other figures such as Hugo Chavez and Evo Morales. They have tried, not always successfully, to grapple with problems of economic development with that of political equality. Until recently even these leaders did not address themselves to the plight of the indigenous people who are descendants of the races – Aztec, Inca, Maya – that produced advanced civilizations in the pre-Columbian times. Countries that had endured the oppression of the Spanish-Portuguese conquistadores and later the hegemony of the United States exemplified in the United Fruit Company that governed Latin American policies have sought a better and more equitable future.

Che Guevara, Fidel Castro of Cuba, Hugo Chavez of Venezuela, and Evo Morales of Bolivia have carried the mantle of that Utopia dreamt by Simon Bolivar.

30

THE WEST, THE EAST AND RUSSIA

The dissolution of the Soviet Union created a unipolar world under the leadership of the United States. With the end of communism in Russia it was believed that the ideological warfare of seven decades between the West and Russia had ended. The new world order was declared to be a triumph of capitalist and democratic values fortified by American military might. It also appeared as if the political system of the West guaranteed economic affluence – though in fact the two were not necessarily related as may be seen by the prosperity of the Gulf States and Saudi Arabia which have fragile democratic values.

The new millennium that was predicted to be based on Western political ideas commenced with startling developments. The Islamic radicals that the United States had spawned and nursed in the 1980's in Afghanistan to fight the Soviet Union now trained their guns on their former sponsors. This impelled the United States to invade states perceived to be inimical to it and effect 'regime change'. Osama bin Laden was not found in the caves of Bora-Bora but Afghanistan was ripped apart in this fool's errand. The Taliban have not been evicted from Afghanistan; indeed their violence and that of the IS have increased and the carnage continues with interminable and vicious ferocity.

Civilians are killed, hospitals are blasted, journalists are murdered and foreign missions are bombed with almost predictable regularity. Even worshippers in mosques are not spared.

Again, weapons of mass destruction were not found in Iraq. Violating every principle of the UN Charter, the Bush-Blair duo invaded a country where a stable if authoritarian order had prevailed under Saddam Hussein. Iraq has been bloodied and brought near obliteration. The recent election in Iraq is no guarantee of stability between Shias and Sunnis.

The 2016 report of British parliamentarian Sir John Chilcot reveals the cat's cradle of chicanery that presaged Britain's war against Iraq. Sir John has mentioned that there were no proofs of the presence of weapons of mass destruction in Iraq and that it was a blatantly false accusation. Former British Prime Minister Blair made a brazen statement that he "would do it again" for bringing democracy to a benighted land. They insist that Saddam Hussein was "taken out" for making the world a safer place.

Hearing this, a young Iraqi who had lost both arms in one of the brutal bombings by the 'Alliance of the Willing' said with a bitter smile before BBC TV: "Let Blair say this before Iraqis who have lost limbs, loved ones, and homes."

Ignoring all warnings from British intelligence that removal of Saddam Hussein would unleash chaos and empower the al-Qaeda, the Bush-Blair duo did just that. They are responsible for making West Asia a dark and dangerous place.

Outraged by Saddam Hussein's execution, loyal Iraqi army officers as well as opponents of Saddam Hussein, swelled the ranks of the Islamist fundamentalists. No matter, the abundant oilfields of Tikrit and Mosul fell into the pro-democracy hands of Cheney and Rumsfeld.

To install a pro-US regime in oil-rich Libya, another alliance of the United States, Britain and France invaded Libya against all tenets of international law. Muammar Qaddafi was not posing a threat to any nation; he had destroyed his arsenal much earlier. Nevertheless he was assassinated and the al-Qaeda was left free to perpetrate travesties of human rights. Erringly echoing Julius Caesar, Hilary Clinton exulted, "We went, we saw and he died!" With Qaddafi's elimination the stability of Libya also died. Experiencing all this people of West Asia paused in their pursuit of democracy.

Notwithstanding global condemnation and massive protest marches across major European, British and American cities, these interventions fortified the United States as the only superpower.

After the dissolution of the Soviet Union, NATO expanded its boundaries by nibbling into territories of former Soviet republics through various coloured revolutions – rose, orange and jasmine. The dispute over Kosovo, the American abandonment of the Anti-Ballistic Missile Treaty and the Russo-Georgian War were causes of tension between Russia and the West. The prospect of Ukraine joining the European Union (EU) posed a serious challenge to the Russian Federation. Russians felt that the promised freedom and trade and movement from Vladivostok to Lisbon was a chimera. They said when Russia was in disorder it was welcomed but as the country's power and prosperity grew, the unease intensified. Old fears of the Cold War have resurfaced.

James Carden, an analyst of Russian affairs in the American government, has observed:

> Over the course of the past decade and a half, U.S.-Russia relations have also been shaped—and not for the better—by

the disparate foreign policy approaches taken by American and Russian governments.

Less well known, however, is that America's growing animus towards all things Russia is also characterized by the hostility borne of a frustrated project of liberal cultural imperialism. In the years following the end of the Soviet Union, the idea that Russia was 'ours to lose' gained wide currency in American foreign policy circles. The Clinton administration sought to dismantle the remaining state apparatus of Soviet-era Russia and replace it with a new liberal civil society that took its cues from Washington. In that way, it was believed, Russia could never again pose a challenge to the West. Of course, such efforts did not succeed, but our 'culture war' approach to foreign policy has only intensified since then. The failure of this project has contributed significantly to the present animus towards Russia and continues to hinder more reasonable diplomatic relations.

James Carden also states that the United States had dreams of a post-Soviet Union Russia becoming its satellite.

The failure of this project to remake Russia in the 1990s rankled those American economic, media, and political elites who unwisely embarked upon it. In due course, this disappointment gave rise not to a newfound introspection about the wisdom of such efforts, but instead motivated a search for someone or something to blame.

At first, it was not immediately obvious that this misplaced frustration would find its target in the person of Russian president Vladimir Putin. Indeed, many western observers seemed hopeful that the intelligence operative turned politician was someone who, like his predecessor Boris Yeltsin, would acquiesce to Washington's prerogatives. In their rush to embrace Putin, prominent Clinton administration officials — such as Secretary of State Madeline Albright, now among Putin's most vociferous critics — at the time angrily dismissed "all this psychobabble about Putin and the KGB thing".

But in the years following, Putin's numerous affronts against the American-led 'postwar international order' — including his opposition to regime change in Iraq (2003), Libya (2011), and Syria (2011), as well as to the so-called 'color revolutions' that took place in Georgia (2003) and Ukraine (2004), and finally the Russian intervention in the Ukraine since 2014 — caused a rapid turnabout in the American establishment's opinion.

In a speech before the February 2007 Munich Security Conference, Putin castigated the United States for its repeated violations of international law. This may have been the point of no return. From then on, the American political establishment would, over the course of the succeeding decade, seek to isolate, undermine, and anathematize Putin. The reason for this is straightforward: the American establishment's 'unipolar fantasy' — spawned in the immediate afterglow of the end of the Cold War and taken to absurd lengths by the Bush administration after 9/11 — had no place for a Russian leader who would declare, as Putin did in Munich, that "Russia is a country with a history that spans more than a thousand years. It has always used the privilege to carry out an independent foreign policy. We are not going to change this tradition today."

After becoming President of the United States in 2008, Barack Obama tried 'reset' and sought cooperation with Russia on various issues. He believed that the real threat to peace came from Islamic fundamentalism and a formidable China. The American president abandoned the previous administration's plans to build a missile defence system in Eastern Europe; Russia opened its skies to US airplanes to carry supplies to Afghanistan. Russian intervention in Georgia in 2008 caused some alarm but the two nations went ahead to sign a New Strategic Arms Reduction Treaty in 2010. It seemed as if past antagonisms were being cast aside.

The Russian annexation of Crimea (which was Russian territory from 1778 to 1963) and support to rebels in Eastern Ukraine caused deep anxiety in the West. The United States and its allies imposed sanctions but were unwilling to have a military showdown with Russia. In September 2015 Russia stepped in to give military support to the Syrian President's failing attempts to evict Syrian rebels and ISIL.

As a counterpoise to the West after annexation of Crimea in 2014, President Putin drew former Soviet republics into the Eurasian Economic Union to begin their economic collaboration. The Presidents of Kazakhstan and Belarus signed the treaty. Many sceptics expressed their views that this may be a nominal union without solid economic foundations. However two other such formations – the Shanghai Cooperation Organization (SCO) and the BRICS (Brazil, Russia, India, China, South Africa) forum have acquired substance and significance.

These semi-alliances have a Cold War flavour about them; After many decades of bitter dispute and rivalry, Russia and China are forging an alliance with the common purpose of forming a block against the West. Both states have fears about the United States making an incursion in the resource rich and strategic region of Central Asia. A strong American presence in

Central Asia would be a perpetual threat to both Russia and China – though Asian nations might favour such a presence to stall the Dragon's juggernaut!

New considerations have arisen in Central Asia since 2001 – controlling Islamic terrorism and separatist movements and growing demand for more freedom. While these are shared anxieties both by SCO and BRICS members, there are subtler subterranean uneasiness that are not articulated or expressed – the possible rivalry between Russia and China in the Central Asian heartland. While President Putin declared that Kazakhstan was part of the wider Russian world, China is investing heavily there to draw it as an ally. Though India has become a member of SCO, it has not agreed to join China's One Belt, One Road project and has anxieties of China moving closer to its frontiers. Deliberately, these groups have been termed as associations rather than alliances. However changed circumstances have altered the original tenor of SCO as Russia and China participate in joint military exercises. To allay hints of a military alliance the SCO has expanded its reach by inviting important nations of Eurasia – India, Iran, Turkey – as members and dialogue partners. Chinese proposal for the revival of Silk Road exchanges is another move in this direction. Within Eurasia lie divergent interests and contests that can create conflicts and disturb the uneasy equilibrium.

Notwithstanding this the SCO and BRICS do not have the military might of NATO. Nor do these loose non-military associations have the military bond and amity that the United States and Japan share in the Pacific region. This amity made President Obama propound the 'Pivot to East Asia' policy for containing Chinese expansion. President Trump has fortified this policy – first with the trade war with China and by trying to draw

India into the alliance by calling it the Indo-Pacific region. How this association will shape depends on mutual interests.

NATO member-nations view Russian resurgence with concern. In April 2016 the first formal meeting of the NATO-Russian Council took place to discuss the current scene. Soon after the meeting NATO Secretary-General Jens Stoltenberg stated at a press conference in Brussels that the "two sides disagree on facts, the narrative and the responsibilities...Russia and NATO have profound and persistent differences...".

The Russian envoy to NATO, Alexander Grushko responded by criticizing NATO military exercises on the Baltic Sea. In June 2016, NATO equated the danger of Russian expansion with the peril of ISIL. General Stoltenberg and his advisers declared that the danger to the United States, Europe and NATO members comes equally from Russian aggression and ISIL. They reported that Russian attack submarines were "prowling the coastline of Scandinavia and Scotland", Mediterranean Sea and North Atlantic. General Stoltenberg and earlier Anders Fogh Rasmussen observed that increased Russian presence contests the United States' and NATO's undersea dominance. The head of the US Navy in Europe has stated that the Russian Navy chief Viktor Chirkov has affirmed that their submarine presence has risen by 50 per cent. It is reported that President Putin has ordered expenditure of billions of dollars for manufacturing quieter diesel and nuclear powered submarines as well as augmenting the country's nuclear missile arsenal. These were put on full display in March 2018.

The Pentagon responded by requesting a massive budget of $8 billion for the US Navy and development of sophisticated technology to monitor encrypted messages from Russian submarines and remotely controlled autonomous vessels. NATO states are planning to build new submarines that can repel

Russian aggression in the Baltic and Arctic Seas. There is also serious concern in the West on intelligence reports that Russian submarines and spy ships operate in the vicinity of vital undersea cables of all international internet connections. There are fears in American defence circles that these could be vulnerable and endangered in times of conflict.

Magnus Nordenman, Director of the Atlantic Council's Trans-Atlantic Security Initiative observed that "Russia has a visceral fear of NATO" and "Russia regards NATO as an existential threat".

After three decades, Russia is making incursions into the Arctic region. Nuclear-powered icebreakers are stationed at the Atomflot base in the Arctic port of Murmansk. The Russian government is resuscitating disused Soviet air and naval bases in the region for docking new icebreakers which will allow entry of civil and military ships in Arctic waters. It is poised to claim half a million square miles of the Arctic land. This northern expansion will give Russia access to the immense hydro-carbon reserves. It will strengthen Russian power in the "high north" where it will compete with existing powers – the United States, Canada and Norway as well as China. This has caused consternation among NATO countries which have sent its marines for military exercises there.

The US 6th Fleet in Naples has been deployed to monitor 'maritime choke points' which separate Greenland, Iceland and UK – crucial to the defence of Europe. US-NATO forces have performed numerous military exercises on Russia's borders – Poland, Czechoslovakia, Romania, and Hungary and now Ukraine. The United States has placed missiles in Eastern Europe and Georgia.

A retired Admiral of the US Navy and former Supreme Allied Commander of NATO said: "We aren't quite back to the Cold War but I sure can see one from where I am standing."

The unfolding new contest between Russia and the United States will not be contests in military might or clashing political ideologies. The 20th century slogans of free enterprise and democracy versus socialism have lost their contentious nature as most nations have adopted free market economies.

On the frontiers of the new cold war stands a unique buffer – the EU. After World War II, Europeans were wary of being drawn into another world war, this time not between themselves but between the superpowers. To prevent hostilities between themselves (which had triggered both world wars) and facilitate cooperation, European leaders mooted the concept of the EU. The Treaty of Rome in 1957 defined European unity – political cohesion, economic collaboration and collective security.

The EU facilitated Germany's re-emergence as a major economic power. As the idea of a federal Europe evolved, Germany acquired political eminence under its Chancellors Gerhard Schroeder and accelerated under Angela Merkel. Germany's stern economic dictums raised fears once more of German domination especially in the poorer European nations of Southern and Eastern Europe.

Though a major player in the EU, Germany is reluctant to participate in military campaigns of the NATO and the firm policy that Germany should not be involved in wars or campaigns of aggression. Chancellor Angela Merkel refused to allow Germany to be involved in Iraq, Libya and Syria. The reluctance against wars / campaigns of armed intervention springs from the experiences of World War II. Britain and France do not share Germany's reluctance. Despite President Obama's appeal to NATO and EU members to resist Russia's annexation of Ukraine these nations, especially Germany have displayed a reluctance to do so. Germany has enjoyed a privileged relationship with Russia, due to economic and trade interests. Germany gets more than 30 per cent of its energy from Russia. These economic ties led Germany to be wary about agreeing to pursue a sanctions policy against Russia. Chancellor Merkel has repeatedly advised to seek a diplomatic solution to the Ukraine crisis instead of resorting to an armed conflict or a showdown.

In this situation former US Secretary of State, John Kerry met his Russian counterpart, Sergey Lavrov to formulate a strategy of cooperation to fight Islamic terrorism. The endless bloodshed in Syria, the decimation of defenceless people, the obliteration of cities, bombardment of the pro-Assad strongholds by the United Sates and ISIL bastions by Russia, have been done in the name of restoring order and peace. The United Nations looks on helplessly, offering advice and homilies but with no viable solution to end the carnage and exodus of people from their homeland.

A new dimension in geopolitics came with a failed coup in Turkey in which thousands overtly and covertly participated. Some fifty thousand were arrested on charges of conspiracy to overthrow President Erdogan's government. The cooling of relations between Turkey and the West as a result of this aborted coup and the attending punishment of the participants has subdued Turkish hostility to Russia. Soon after the aborted coup President Erdogan rushed to Moscow to mend fences with President Putin.

Russia is caught in a predicament. Seventy years of the Soviet Union's vigorous secularism removed religious antagonisms but attacks by Muslim separatists have revived fears long forgotten. Russian support of the Syrian government against the Islamic State demonstrates the complex factors that determine its political stance.

Resurgence of Russia has produced new alignments. In the shifting sands of power politics, the United States and China had united to challenge Russia from 1971 to the early 1990's. The coincidence of objectives was accompanied by a common strategy – the containment of Russia. Nixon and Kissinger did not heed Napoleon's warning of the awakening of the "sleeping giant". The United States slumbered as Chinese commerce and finance spread tentacles in the American economy. At the turn of the millennium the United States woke up to the formidable growing power of China in the East-Pacific region. The United States' traditional Asian allies – Japan, South Korea, Philippines, Thailand, Australia, New Zealand – watched apprehensively as the Chinese juggernaut ploughed through international waters to claim and grab what it could. In pursuance of President Obama's 'Pivot to East Asia' doctrine, the United States moved its warships there for protection of its allies. In application of the Indian political thinker Chanakya's formula (enemy's enemy is one's friend) Russia and China united – a volte face not anticipated by the United States.

Assisted by Russia, China began building nuclear and conventional deterrents in 2015. In November 2016 the Russian Defence Minister met his Chinese counterpart in Beijing to conclude a massive arms deal to supply China with advanced weaponry. China intends to use its power to nullify any US or Japanese attempts to attack the artificial islands on the South China Sea. Growing maritime tension in the Pacific region has made China turn to Russia. President Trump has responded by advocating a close partnership in what he calls "Indo-Pacific region" that is sweet music to India as he insists that India should take a robust stand.

Now, despite prodigious trade relations there is tension between the United States and China. President Trump has begun a trade and tariff war with his 'America First' slogan. China has declared its intention to retaliate.

Defence agreements were augmented by energy deals in which China depends heavily on Russia's vast reserves of gas, an important source of Russia's export earnings. With Russo-Chinese amity established once more, China can revert to its old dream of dominating the heartland of Eurasia that commenced from Han dynasty times.

There is however an inherent tension in this. Most of Central Asia was part of the Soviet Union until 1991. Communist rule brought benefits in the fields of health, education, irrigation and agriculture. Russians have settled here. The Russian language as well as the Cyrillic script is in use in the former Soviet republics. China does not have the same links of amity. Its armies came to plunder and take back booty. Chinese incursion into Afghanistan is also viewed with distrust due to reports of persecution of Uighur Muslims in Xinjiang and fear of China grabbing Afghanistan's natural resources.

Stressing past cultural links with Buddhist Central Asia, India would like to enter the scene through Afghanistan but this requires Pakistan's cooperation.

There is a possibility of a new 'great game' with the United States and its allies on one side opposed by Russia, China and those Asian nations with interests in Eurasia.

The G7 meeting in Canada in June 2018 has altered the scenario. President Trump announced that the members of this elite economic group should share financial responsibilities which created some disturbance. But his suggestion that Russia should be readmitted to the club created a furore. Europe may no longer follow American diktat in international relations. It remains to be seen if the new President of the United States will change American policy towards Russia as he announced on his campaign trail.

Until then there is the uncertainty that regional wars in Ukraine, Syria, Iraq, Yemen, South China Sea, could erupt into global wars. In the absence of these 'hot wars' the new 'cold war' may take other forms; cyber wars, hacking of military and political information. The new 'information war' has already commenced as NATO and Russia deplore each other's methods.

A new dimension came to the EU when Britain voted to leave it. Seeing in a weakened EU, a diminishing of American influence and possible dissolution of NATO President Obama advised Britons against the 'Brexit' Plan. Britons ignored his plea because the United States no longer inspired fear or offered security from the grim situation in Europe due to sanctions and an unprecedented emigration crisis.

Andrew Hill, Managing Editor of *Financial Times*, stated at a lecture in Bangalore (where the authors were present) the reason for this is in "the deep-rooted historic failures of EU leadership" and the "failure of British leaders to exert influence on EU". Hill also spoke of British leaders' "failure of teamwork", "unguided confusion" and "failure of a succession plan". The Brexit scenario offers prospect of commercial autonomy, like "a free trading Venice", free markets, hiring of local talents rather than from across the English Channel.

Brexit signalled British disenchantment with the EU, and a desire to shape its own destiny. European elections in Italy have demonstrated that the people voted against mainstream establishments in what has been called 'resentment voting'. French, Dutch and German people are taking notice of Rightist politicians. Eastern European nations such as Bulgaria and Hungary which were happy to be in NATO are now trying to build better relations with a resurgent Russia. Southern and Eastern European nations feel that the EU has not brought them any benefits. Hungary is keen to mend fences with Russia and move away from the EU and NATO. Bulgaria is also veering that way. Both need Russian oil and gas. The former Soviet bloc may not oppose Russian presence in Ukraine while EU and the United States vehemently oppose it for this seems like the thin end of the wedge.

Other EU nations are meditating on the benefits of remaining in a union which has lost its raison d'etre – an economic and commercial bulwark against communism. They would prefer to formulate their own economic policies rather than obey diktats from Brussels and Washington. Many EU nations want sanctions on Russia to be lifted because these have affected their trade with Russia. Other EU nations like Poland would like the sanctions to continue. They would like to strengthen NATO. In pursuance of this a proposal has been made for organizing a European Union Army in addition to the army of the NATO.

This could be very different from the chess-board of the old Cold War days. After disruption in Ukraine and annexation of Crimea, the United States sought to create fear of a Russian threat in Europe which would compel Europe to depend on NATO that is the long arm of American military power. Western Europeans are now becoming wary of becoming involved in American tensions with Russia. Further the anti-Russian psychosis in Europe has been replaced by Islamophobia after attacks in European cities by Islamic terrorists.

President Trump however does not want a Cold War; he wants Russian collaboration to contain both China and Islamic fundamentalism. Verbal announcements have been followed by phone calls between the two presidents. Many explanations have been offered for this sudden amity, including conspiracy theories of espionage and blackmail – something even Ian Fleming's morbid imagination or Eric Ambler's brilliant skill could not have conjured.

The United States and its allies made a miscalculation when they supported Syrian 'rebels'. In his last press conference, President Obama admitted that his policy in Syria had failed while President Putin has declared that he will not allow the world to be ruled by terrorists and fundamentalists, and will wage war if necessary. Russia will now and once again have a say in shaping the world order. A multi-polar world will prevent arbitrary violations of the sovereignty of unoffending nations. Whether this will guarantee peace is to be seen.

President Trump appears to believe that together with President Putin they can defeat Islamic fundamentalism – whose genesis was the creation of the mujahideen in Afghanistan by President Carter in 1979. In fact President Trump has deplored US intervention in Afghanistan, Iraq, Libya and Syria. Sincere US-Russian cooperation may finally bury the jihadi spectre.

President Trump declares NATO is obsolete and must be dismantled – which must be great comfort to President Putin as NATO appeared like an existentialist threat to Russia and vice versa. If President Trump allows President Putin a free hand in Ukraine, peace between them is possible.

There may be hurdles in the strategic partnership between the two nations because there is a problem in "this putative partnership". Jonathan Eyal of the The Straits Times observes: "Although Mr Trump has never spelt out in detail what he wants from Moscow, it is clear that there are two tasks for which he deems Russia useful. The first is Russian cooperation to 'eradicate completely from the face of the earth radical Islamic terrorism'." This may unite the two rival powers.

The second purpose is more difficult – "eliciting potential Russian support in cornering China, the one power Mr Trump sees as presenting the US with the biggest and most sustained strategic challenge". Eyal states that while Russia may have rivalry with China in Central Asia, it will not assist the United States in containing China because Russia needs peace with China to maintain its presence in Central Asian affairs which adds to its status as a global power. Chinese Chequers is a devious game in which the Chinese are adept. It is known to the Russians (who play a superior chess game) but it is not known to the Americans.

Jonathan Eyal concludes on a gloomy note or perhaps wishful thinking:

> The Russia-US relationship is doomed from the start; the partners are not merely incompatible; they do not even understand each other's aspirations, and most certainly have no incentive to address each other's needs....The only remaining question is whether President Trump wants to pursue this dream or...like a good businessman he cuts his losses and moves to another project.

As Donald Trump's presidency unfolded the world was both bewildered and fascinated by his unpredictable leaps from one issue to another.

He threatened the North Korean ruler with "such fury as never seen before" and then sent his Secretary of State to parley with the ruler he had called "little rocket man". Kim agreed to meet Trump in Singapore. Kim Jong-un also made peace overtures to and met his South Korean counterpart on the Korean peninsula's demilitarized zone. The meeting of the two leaders – of democratic United States and totalitarian North Korea was an epochal event after sixty-eight years of attrition and tension since the Korean War. What fructifies after the meeting is yet to be seen.

The American president has however been consistent in one project – scrapping the Iran Nuclear Deal.

The world was satisfied when the Nuclear Deal with Iran was put in place in 2015 by an agreement between Iran and the United States, Russia, China, Britain, Germany and France. The deal would prevent Iran from becoming a nuclear power and in response the United States and EU would lift sanctions on Iran. This was greeted with enthusiasm by the people of Iran though the religious leaders were not pleased as they considered this as acquiescence before the West.

The Ayatollahs soon had an unexpected ally – the new American president who castigated his predecessor by calling the nuclear agreement as the dumbest deal. President Trump kept his campaign promise; the United States ended its connection with the deal. Further, he threatened Iran with dire consequences, even war, if Iran continued with its nuclear policy. The other guarantors criticized President Trump for his action.

Politicians in the United States were against scrapping the agreement. So the US House of Representatives stepped in to prevent President Trump from starting a war against Iran. They unanimously passed an amendment making clear Congress's position that no law exists which gives the President power to launch a military strike against Iran. An amendment was passed as part of the National Defence Authorization Act of 2019. A member of the House of Representatives stated:

The unanimous passage of this bipartisan amendment is a strong and timely counter to the Trump administration's withdrawal from the Iran deal and its increasingly hostile rhetoric. This amendment sends a powerful message that the American people and Members of Congress do not want a war with Iran. Today, Congress acted to reclaim its authority over the use of military force.

Another member stated,

Congress is sending a clear message that President Trump does not have the authority to go to war with Iran.

Representative McGovern said:

With President Trump's reckless violation of the Iran Deal and failure to get Congressional approval for military strikes on Syria, there's never been a more important time for Congress to reassert its authority. It's long past time to end the White House's blank check on war and the passage of this amendment is a strong start.

The status and durability of the Iran Nuclear Deal will depend on the support it receives from other signatories and nations which are prepared to resist US pressure on sanctions. Reneging on this agreement has far wider implications than President Trump or his advisers imagine. American politicians and statesmen in both the Democratic and Republican parties have criticized the decision. Statesmen and high-level negotiators of major states – the United States, Russia, China, Germany, Britain, France – laboured for nearly nine years to formulate the agreement with Iran. It was greeted with relief and applause by most of the world – except Israel whose Prime Minister Benjamin Netanyahu and the Saudi king vehemently opposed it since they consider Iran as their chief enemy.

Except for Israel and Saudi Arabia, other states have publicly and privately condemned the US presidential decision. Members of the EU and Britain sent their emissaries – President Emmanuel Macron, Chancellor Angela Merkel, Foreign Secretary Boris Johnson – to the White House to dissuade President Trump from cancelling the Nuclear Deal. President Putin held telephone conversations with his American counterpart to save the agreement but to no avail.

Accustomed to past European acquiescence in international matters, especially those of a contentious nature, President Trump did not anticipate the stubborn resistance to his decision. Headed by Federica Mogherini, High Representative of the EU, and followed by a majority of the members, American withdrawal from the Nuclear Deal was perceived as short-sighted and unwise. It is not friendship or concern for Iran that has produced this reaction; it is their own necessity.

The European Commission, which is the executive arm of the EU, met in Brussels on 18 May 2018 to "launch the formal process to activate the blocking statute by updating the list of US sanctions on Iran falling within its scope". The Commission hopes the statute will be in force by August 2018 when the first batch of reimposed sanctions takes effect. The statute which the 28 EU member-states and the European Parliament must endorse, is intended to reassure European firms that invested in Iran after the deal. The blocking statute is a 1996 regulation originally created to circumvent a US trade embargo on Cuba which prohibits EU companies and courts from complying with specific foreign sanction laws. During the talks in Brussels Iran's Foreign Minister said efforts to save the deal were on the right track. The Commission called for doing more to allow the European Investment Bank to finance activities in Iran. The Commission also called for more assistance to Iran's energy sector and medium- to small-scale industries as a confidence building measure. Russia and China have expressed support for this strategy, particularly Russia, which is a close ally of Iran in the Syrian conflict. As China has started investment in Iran it too wants stability there.

The support which President Trump expected from European states has not materialized. The EU wants to save the international agreement on Iran's nuclear policy because it is in their interest to do so. Support of American policy is waning with the imposition of heavy tariffs on European imports to the United States. Jean-Claude Juncker, Chairman of EU has stated his regrets at this development. It would appear that Europe's ties with the United States are weakening after a century of amity and interdependence.

New agreements, if not alignments, appear to be taking place in East Asia. The long hostility and rivalry between China and Japan is undergoing changes. Here again it is President Trump's trade war against China which has brought the two powerful economic powers together. Japanese Prime Minister Shinzo Abe signalled the thaw by attending the Chinese National Day reception in Tokyo. Japan has also sought the intervention of China to curb North Korea, a request which recognizes China's influence in the region.

China's escalating trade war with the US is drawing Beijing and Moscow together. China's decision to curb soya bean imports from the US as part of the tit for tat tariff spiral between US China is bringing Russia, especially its less developed but resource rich "far east" into the equation. New links are being forged between the neighbours who are facing US hostility. Enduring stinging sanctions from USA and EU countries since 2014, this development suits Russian President's "pivot to the east" policy. Vladivostok and Khabarovsk have been identified as hub for development due to their proximity to the Chinese frontier. Russia is offering millions of hectares of land for cultivating soya beans and other crops in demand in China. As Chinese companies have expressed interest in investing here the Russian Taiga region is open for this. Chinese appear to be delighted over the de facto alliance that they feel will curb EU miliatry and economic hegemony.

After the dissolution of Soviet Union the development of Russia's Far East has been lagging behind. Realizing the importance of this vast resource rich region President Putin wants development of these lands.

However with his customary astuteness the Russian President is not depending on China alone. The past has dark memories. The two powerful nations were once bitter adversaries from the late 1960s over ideological reasons, territorial and riparian disputes over the Ussuri River lands, China's arming Afghan mujahidin against Russia, not to mention China's cordial trade relations with USA until now. So President Putin has also invited Japanese and South Korean companies to help develop the Russian Far East. If Japanese and Korean investors accept the Russian offer there will be twin benefits; Japanese and South Korean will restrain possible Chinese dominance as well as weakening America's ties with its East Asian allies.

How these new amities will develop will depend on the power, interests and influence of the concerned nations.

A new factor on the global scene is the economic rise and political power of China and India. For further progress both these nations require regional stability and a free and open global market to sustain their economic development. US President Barak Obama announced the 'Pivot to East Asia' reset to contain Chinese expansionism while his successor Donald Trump has announced 'America First' doctrine, trade tariffs, rising protectionism and anti-globalization views. In this scenario India and China need to cooperate to safeguard their common interests in trade and security.

All through history a common adversary has made foes into friends. India developed amity with both Japan and Britain after joining the Commonwealth. In the last decade and a half, India has veered away from its stern non-alignment policy in establishing stronger ties with Western nations, especially the United States. This has had an adverse effect on its relations with Russia, a friend and non-military ally for seven decades since Indian independence. Russian friendship has helped India in its conflicts with China and more importantly with Pakistan. As for the Indo-Pacific strategy, India is uncomfortable with America's definition of the strategy and lack of financial support. India is equally uneasy about Chinese aims and strategy both in Central Asia and in the Indo-Pacific region. India has joined with the United States, Japan and Australia to curb Chinese expansionism in the region and the economic alliances it has forged with the Maldives, Sri Lanka, Nepal and Pakistan. However cooperation between India and China may be facilitated by American opposition to free trade and opposition to the existing global trade system. It would be in the interest of both India and China to promote globalization, free trade, facilitate collaboration within the framework of SCO.

Finally, the burgeoning wealth of the few all over the world amidst the struggles of the many is slowly and steadily creating the scenario of another epochal event that might transform human society.

31

A BRAVE NEW WORLD

Globalization has created growing and dangerous economic inequalities between people; the resentment generated by this even in an aggressive capitalist system such as the United States indicates a search for new value systems. Donald Trump won on the card of catering to the neglected rural poor. Rightist parties in Europe decry immigration that threatens their workforce. Paradoxically, globalization has triggered xenophobia.

Samuel Huntington's theory of 'clash of civilizations' was denounced and derided when first propounded by historians such as Francis Fukuyama. Three decades later the validity of this theory is gaining ground. For the first time in three centuries religious antagonisms have unleashed violence. Accompanying this is an unreasoning racism. Unnerved by Islamic terrorist attacks in France, Belgium, Germany and Britain, the Christian West is sliding into Islamophobia. Even Muslims born and bred in the West are radicalized and reciprocate the hostility.

The other and more fruitful scenario is a multi-polar world. This would be a welcome prospect because no one nation would be able to wage wars and create turmoil as occurred in the opening years of the 21st century. As the world moves from a hegemonic system based on the United States' superpower status, European, Asian and African nations have roles to play. They can be mediators in international conflict zones, organize aid in areas of humanitarian crises, keep reserves of their troops as peace-keeping forces.

Both the Covenant of the League of Nations and the Charter of the United Nations wanted to outlaw war. The United Nations Organization for Education, Science and Culture has always sought to "build barricades against war in the minds of men" since it is in the minds of men that wars begin. There have been many localized wars, many armed interventions in sovereign countries, many unprovoked bombings of many cities, many unwarranted regime changes to suit the interests of a superpower. Genocides in the Balkans have drawn severe criticism and the offenders have been taken to the Court of Criminal Justice at The Hague but perpetrators of savagery in Rwanda and Burundi have not been punished because violence in these poor states have no international implications and do not affect global geopolitics.

Is violence and thirst for domination inherent in the minds of men? Will the barricades for peace prevent war? Problems of international peace and security can be solved by change in the mentality and attitude to violence. If two devastating world wars have not dissuaded nations from waging wars what will? Explosion of the atom bomb have not only changed the nature of warfare but the very idea of humanism.

Yet, and once again paradoxically, it is the threat of a nuclear war and extinction of homo sapiens that acts as a deterrent against waging a global war.

In what Dr Arnold Toynbee, the great British historian, calls a "roundabout of civilizational traffic", it would be of immense benefit to the world if Western, Russian and non-Western nations formulated a modus vivendi to unite against terrorism, genocide, pestilence and poverty, and strive together for world peace.

This may be a search for a Holy Grail but homo sapiens never ceases to dream.

Aloka Moulik Chatterjee

The authors with their mother Leela Moulik

Achala M Moulik

ABOUT THE AUTHORS

Aloka Moulik Chatterjee and her sister **Achala M Moulik** had their school education in London, Washington, New York. Aloka's tactful and disciplined nature won her recognition in the schools in Washington and London where she very soon became Senior Prefect and represented her schools in inter-school debates.

Both sisters graduated with honours in Economics, History and International Law and Relations; Aloka at the London School of Economics and Achala at University College, London. Aloka was an active member of LSE's social and cultural life.

After graduating, Aloka returned to India and taught her honours subjects at Indraprastha College in Delhi.

After marriage she moved to West Bengal and taught at Loreto Convent. A few years later she went on to become co-founder and then Principal of the first nationally accredited school in the town. She was a gifted and dedicated teacher; her humane personality and excellent teaching methods inspired her students to do well while she taught and instilled in them values they hold dear. Aloka was widely read in economics and political science. While living in Rome with her parents she studied Renaissance art and history. She learned Rabindra Sangeet and liked Western classical music. She grew beautiful gardens at her homes in Shantiniketan, Burnpur and Calcutta.

Aloka translated into English a famous Bengali children's classic, *Tales of Tuntuni: The Wise Bird*, which was published by AuthorsUpFront in December 2017.

After graduating from London University, Achala Moulik entered the Indian Administrative Service. She served as Education Secretary, Government of India; during her tenure the national education program, Sarva Shiksha Abhiyan was approved. As Director General Archaeological Survey of India she initiated numerous restoration and cultural projects. A noted professor of history, Dr Barun Dey, once remarked in public that Achala had brought the ASI to its pristine old standards.

Achala has written numerous books on cultural history, physical heritage, acclaimed novels, biographies and a play *"Pushkin's Last Poem"* which was published and then performed to standing ovation in Moscow and Petersburg during the Year of India in Russia. The Government of Russia awarded her the prestigious Pushkin Medal and the Sergei Yesenin Prize for her books on Russian history and culture.

In December 2013, she was invited to deliver lectures on Rabindranath Tagore in Stockholm for the centenary of his receiving the Nobel Prize.

BOOKS BY AUTHORS

Aloka Moulik Chatterjee

1. *Tales of Tuntuni: The Wise Bird,* AuthorsUpFront, 2017.
2. Academic papers on problems of international peace and security.

Achala Moulik Moses

Literary and Cultural History

1. *Silhouettes of Russian Literature,* Mysore University, 1976.
2. *Kings, Queens and Lovers,* India Book House, 1978 and UBS Publisher's Distributors, 1996.
3. *Our Bengal,* Writers Workshop, 1979.
4. *El Dorado Revisited – A Cultural History of Spain,* India Book House, 1982 and Palgrave/Macmillan, 1983.
5. *Pageant of Karnataka,* Government of Karnataka, 1983.
6. *Immortals of Italian Literature,* Vikas Publishers, 1988.
7. *Literary Titans of the Millennium,* UBS Publishers, 1999.
8. *Dialogue of Civilizations – William Jones and the Orientalists,* Co-authored with husband Mohandas Moses, IAS (Retired), Aryan Books International, 2009.
9. *The Russian Revolution – Storms Across A Century – 1917 to 2017,* AuthorsUpFront, 2017.

Architectural Heritage

1. *World Heritage Monuments of India*, Archaeological Survey of India Publications, 1994.
2. Editor of *India's Contribution to Conservation of Angkor Vat*, Archaeological Survey of India Publications, 1995.
3. *India – Monuments and Sites*, ICOMOS-UNESCO Publication, 1996.
4. *Captors of Time: Monument of the Millennium*, UBS Publishers, 2000.
5. *Monuments of India*, Archaeological Survey of India Publications, 2008
6. *Script for Sound & Light Show of Hampi*, ITDC.

Biography

1. *Dream Journey (biography of my parents)*, UBS Publishers, 2003.
2. *A Stranger in Paradise – Story of an Extraordinary Civil Servant*, Har Anand Publications, 2008.
3. *A Hundred Years of Lev Tolstoy and the Indian Connection*, Har Anand Publications, 2010.
4. *Rabindranath Tagore – A Man For All Times*, Har Anand Publications, 2011.

Fiction

1. *Seasons in Paradise*, India Book House, 1980.
2. *Camellias For Caroline*, Harlequins UK, 1985. (Translations in French, Swedish and Finnish.)
3. *The Conquerors*, UBS Publishers, 1996.
4. *Earth Is But A Star*, UBS Publishers, 1997.
5. *Dangerous Dispatches*, National Book Trust, 2016.

Play

1. *Pushkin's Last Poem – A Play*, National Book Trust of India, 2008.

Poetry

1. *Once Upon a Time- Poems*, Writers Workshop, 2007.

Translation

1. *Company Limited,* Orient Longman, 1977. (Translated from the original in Bengali, *Seemabaddho.*)

BIBLIOGRAPHY

Beevor, Antony. *Stalingrad – The Fateful Siege 1942–1943*. New York: Penguin, 1998.

Bullock, Allan. *Hitler – A Study in Tyranny*. London: Odhams Press, 1952.

Crankshaw, Edward (Ed.). *Khrushchev Remembers*. Boston: Little Brown and Company, 1970.

Deutscher, Isaac. *Stalin – A Political Biography*. New York: Oxford University Press 1967

Djilas, Milovan. *The New Class*. New York: Harcourt Brace, 1957.

Durant, Will. *The Age of Faith*. New York: Simon & Schuster, 1980.

Fischer, Louis. *Life of Lenin*. New York: Harper & Row, 1964

Fitzgerald, CP. *China – A Short Cultural History*. London: Cresset Press, 1961.

Gorbachev, Mikhal. *Memoirs*. New York: Doubleday, 1993.

Graebner, Norman A, and Edward M Bennett. *The Versailles Treaty and Its Legacy: The Failure of the Wilsonian Vision*. New York: Cambridge University Press, 2011.

Griffiths, John C. *Afghanistan*. London: Andre Deutsch, 2009.

Grube, Ernest J. *The World of Islam*. London: Paul Hamlyn Publisher, 1967.

Hunter, Shireen. *Central Asia Since Independence*. Westport, Connecticut: Greenwood Press, 1996.

Kennan, George. *Russia and the West*. New York: Little Brown and Company, 1961

Kinzer, Stephen. *All the Shah's Men*. New York: John Wiley, 2008.

Lassus, Jean. *The Early Christian Byzantine World*. London: Paul Hamlyn Publisher, 1967.

Luong, Pauline Jones (Ed.). *The Transformation of Central Asia: States and Societies from Soviet Rule to Independence.* Ithaca, New York: Cornell University Press, 2003.

Manning, CAW. *The Nature of International Society.* London: London School of Economics, 1962.

Massie, Robert. *Nicholas and Alexandra.* New York: Simon & Schuster, 1970.

Mirsky, Dmitry S. *Russia – A Social History.* London: Cresset Press, 1931.

Moses, Mohandas. *Dialogues of Civilization.* New Delhi: Aryan Books International, 2009.

Moulik, Achala. *Eldorado Revisited – A Spanish Chronicle.* London: Palgrave Macmillan, 1983/1985

Moulik, Moni. *Italian Economy & Culture.* Calcutta: Chuckervertty, Chatterjee and Co., Ltd., Publication Year: Unknown.

Primakov, Yevgeny. *Russia and the Arabs.* New York: Basic Books, 2009.

Rawlinson, HG. *India – A Short Cultural History.* London: Cresset Press, 1954

Record, Jeffrey. *The Spectre of Munich: Reconsidering the Lessons of Appeasing Hitler.* Washington D.C.: Potomac Books, 2007.

Reed, John. *Ten Days That Shook the World.* New York: Boni & Liveright, 1919.

Roosevelt, Eleanor. *This I Remember.* New York: Harper & Brother Publishers, 1949.

Sansom, GB. *The Western World and Japan.* London: Cresset Press, 1950.

Schwarzenberger, Georg. *Power Politics – A Study of International Society,* Published under the auspices of the London Institute of World Affairs. London: Stevens & Sons, 1951.

Seaman, LCB. *From Vienna to Versailles.* New York, Harper & Row, 1963.

Shirer, William L. *The Rise and Fall of the Third Reich.* New York: Simon & Schuster, 1960.

Slavicek, Louise Chipley. *The Treaty of Versailles*. New York: Chelsea House Publishers, 2010.

Smith, Denis M. *Mussolini: A Biography*. London: Vintage, 1983.

Strange, Susan. *The Retreat of the State: Diffusion of Power in World Economy*. Cambridge: Cambridge University Press, 1996.

Tagore, Rabindranath. *Letters from Russia*. Shantiniketan: Vishwa Bharati Press, 1932.

Taylor, AJP. *Vienna to Versailles*

Trotsky, Leon. *History of the Russian Revolution*. London: Haymarket Books, 1934

Twining, David T. *The New Eurasia: A Guide to the Republics of the Former Soviet Union*. Westport, Connecticut: Praeger Press, 1993.

Zickel, RE (Ed.). *Soviet Union – A Country Study*. Washington, D.C.: Federal Research Division, Library of Congress, 1991.

* Factual data from Internet.

Manufactured by Amazon.ca
Bolton, ON

35928832R00166